MAGNA TERRA
SMOKY

Barbara Jagoda

Order this book online at www.trafford.com
or email orders@trafford.com

Most Trafford titles are also available at major online book retailers.

© Copyright 2018 Barbara Jagoda.

All rights reserved. No part of this publication may be reproduced, stored in a retrieval system, or transmitted, in any form or by any means, electronic, mechanical, photocopying, recording, or otherwise, without the written prior permission of the author.

Print information available on the last page.

ISBN: 978-1-4907-9184-5 (sc)
ISBN: 978-1-4907-9185-2 (hc)
ISBN: 978-1-4907-9186-9 (e)

Library of Congress Control Number: 2018912939

Because of the dynamic nature of the Internet, any web addresses or links contained in this book may have changed since publication and may no longer be valid. The views expressed in this work are solely those of the author and do not necessarily reflect the views of the publisher, and the publisher hereby disclaims any responsibility for them.

Any people depicted in stock imagery provided by Getty Images are models, and such images are being used for illustrative purposes only.
Certain stock imagery © Getty Images.

Trafford rev. 12/12/2018

 www.trafford.com

North America & international
toll-free: 1 888 232 4444 (USA & Canada)
fax: 812 355 4082

CONTENTS

Preface vii
Dedication ix
Chapter 1   The Winds of Destiny 1
Chapter 2   The Promise 11
Chapter 3   The First Four... 16
Chapter 4   A Rough Start.. 21
Chapter 5   First Ride 28
Chapter 6   Dashed Dreams 36
Chapter 7   On the Road Again 42
Chapter 8   Stonewall Springs.. 49
Chapter 9   Smoky's First Race 56
Chapter 10   Kit, Ninatchka, and Manteeya 63
Chapter 11   A Restless Wind.. 75
Chapter 12   The Heartland of Racing.. 79
Chapter 13   Returning Home... 90
Chapter 14   Aurzel — A Lesson in Determination 94
Chapter 15   On to Holly 102
Chapter 16   California, Here We Come....................................... 115
Chapter 17   Races to Win Before We Sleep 119
Chapter 18   The Derby 132
Chapter 19   A Bad Decision 139
Chapter 20   The Darley Awards... 154
Chapter 21   1991 and Rio Hondo 161
Chapter 22   Wind and Sand 179
Chapter 23   His Undaunted Spirit.. 196
Chapter 24   A Cold and Relentless Wind 209
Chapter 25   A "New" Year . . . A Gentler Wind? 220
Chapter 26   More Problems Than the Wind 237
Chapter 27   Things Are Good... 248
Chapter 28   Records Are There to Be Broken............................. 260
Chapter 29   Oh, Fickle Wind! 266
Chapter 30   Perhaps the Time Has Come 270
Chapter 31   A Decision, A Lesson 274
Chapter 32   The Director's Sprint.. 279
Chapter 33   The Marathon 285
Chapter 34   1996 — A Tough Year 293
Chapter 35   So Close... 299
Chapter 36   The Promise 304
Chapter 37   Retirement... 308
Chapter 38   Home at Last... 311
Index 317

PREFACE

Magna Terra Smoky's story has been a 'GREAT RIDE' ... a ride that has encompassed almost three decades of the past and the most treasured part of my life. Rightfully, it might read like a fairy tale to some. This is the incredible adventure of a timid, insecure colt who battled adversity from the day he was conceived. But for the impeccable timing of events, and the uncanny ability to overcome one daunting obstacle after another, Smoky would be just another name in the Arabian horse registry books. His insecurities were daunting to overcome, his trainer a novice herself. How could this timid ranch pony from the Pawnee Grasslands of NE Colorado overcome his own personal issues as well as debilitating injuries including the loss of an eye, to earn Racing's top awards?

This is a story of how love, patience and determination turned an insecure reject into a champion of champions. A champion who would go on to demolish record after record in the Arabian racing books leaving a legacy in his wake.

This, then, is Smoky's story. It begins with the day I first saw him.

Sharing a bucket of chopped carrots
Los Al Race Course -1995

DEDICATED TO

My maternal grandfather, William Saunders, who surely passed on his love and appreciation of horses, and perhaps even some of his amazing horsemanship skills, through those remarkable strands of DNA that determine so much of who and what we are.

Marilyn, my horse-crazy childhood best friend, who ignited in me my love and passion for horses.

Bryan, without whose constant encouragement and bottomless sense of humor, I never would have had the courage or opportunity to continue on to bigger and broader horizons. Thank you for being there for this amazing journey.

Cover Design:

My cover design incorporates a prairie background symbolizing Smoky's humble beginning on the Pawnee Grasslands of Colorado and a super imposed photo that was taken at Smoky's retirement party at Los Al Race Track honoring his outstanding racing accomplishments.

Photo credit: Los Alamitos Race Course Photography

1   The Winds of Destiny

1988

This day was one I would never forget. I was excited and anxious, and there was a deliberate purpose in my step. I knew that I was impatient. It was difficult not to constantly look behind me, hoping to encourage my new husband and our friend, Alice, to hurry up. It was a beautiful fall morning and so very quiet and peaceful. I breathed in the fresh air and tried not to be impolite. I knew that Dick and Alice did not have many occasions to visit and that our trip out here was not all about me and what I wanted. I was a guest here on Alice's ranch, so with control that I had mustered from somewhere, I managed to divert my attention to the countryside around me. This land really was beautiful. Every direction that I looked, there was a never-ending expanse of rolling hills with flag-like stalks of grama grass swaying back and forth in massive undulating waves. A few white wisps of clouds were beginning to form on the horizon of an otherwise cloudless sky. This kind of country never failed to fill me with a feeling of awe and contentment. I felt a belonging here, a belonging that seemed to come from within the core of me.

    The scene before us was perfect. Not a fence post could be seen; not a single power line cut though the land. Even the sun had not overlooked anything, for stretched out amid the golden-tipped grama grasses were the glistening bodies of three equines who were oblivious to anything but the warmth and peacefulness of the moment. On one hand, I regretted that we were about to interrupt such a peaceful sight, but on the other hand, I couldn't wait to see more. As we drew even closer, our noisy approach was detected, and a perturbed gray head emerged from among the blanket of grass. I could see that it took a moment for this sleepy head to process that humans were approaching, but once it did, the rest of the equine body rose, alerting his buddies of our presence. Slowly and reluctantly, two other bodies emerged, and then there were three.

"The gray one is Smoky," Alice said quietly.

I smiled at Alice and then gazed back at the three horses. Alice had already told me quite a bit about Smoky and also a little about her other two horses. One was her riding gelding, Kroug, and the other her older broodmare, Babe.

I knew that Smoky had spent most of the past year or so enjoying his life here, grazing, playing, racing, and, frankly, just being a horse. These grasslands seemed to stretch forever, but of course, they no longer did. The land that had once been home to huge herds of buffalo and the Pawnee Indians who hunted them had been broken up into ranches now, and the land that Smoky enjoyed was part of Alice's ranch.

Alice Pollock was her full name, and she was a very active and exceedingly good-looking woman with skin that was radiant. Everyone, including Dick and I, marveled at the freshness and youthfulness she exuded. How she kept her complexion so flawless was something that totally amazed me. All three of us spent a great deal of time outside in the sun; however, Dick and I paid for it.

Alice's husband had died several years ago, leaving her to care for the ranch on her own. It didn't seem to daunt her. She had been determined to keep the ranch going and continued to raise and breed a herd of Hereford cattle that had supported the ranch through the years. The herd was not large by many standards, but it was impressive, and it was her pride and joy. Even with all the work that she had to do, Alice somehow found the time and energy to nurture another deep passion of hers, and that was to raise a small number of very fine Arabian horses. Pursuing this goal, several years ago, she had shipped a newly acquired mare named Cyroga to a stallion standing in Scottsdale, Arizona. She had hoped the cross would produce the foal of her dreams. However, her well-thought-out plans had not unfolded the way that she had wanted, and her dream foal never came to be. Instead, she had this dark-gray colt that stood before us . . . and she neither liked or wanted him. It was the reason that I was here.

The small group of horses continued to watch us approach. It was a pretty sight. I really did love this land. Wherever I gazed, I could envision the past. I could imagine herds of buffalo rumbling across the rolling countryside with Pawnee Indians and their tough little ponies galloping in pursuit. How many memories this land must hold! How many Indians had traversed these very hillsides? How many ponies had grown fat and sleek, grazing on the tall grasses and drinking from the pristine waters? That every horse should be so lucky as to spend at least part of its life in such a haven was a dream that was impossible, I knew, but I wished it anyway.

All of a sudden, the three horses broke into a trot. I chuckled as I could tell they knew that Alice had brought them treats. As I watched them trot toward us, I found that I liked the way this young gray colt named Smoky moved; his stride was so effortless and fluid. He was like an Indian pony, covering the ground beneath him with long and easy strides. Just as the horses got to within a few strides of us, however, Smoky slowed to a standstill, ears pricked and nostrils quivering.

What's he so afraid of? I wondered. Kroug and Babe certainly didn't hold back. They were right in our faces, jostling each other for the treats that Alice laughingly offered. I watched the activity, all the while concerned about the standoffish behavior that Smoky was exhibiting.

The shy young colt that I had come out here to see was officially named and registered in the Arabian Horse Registry as Magna Terra Smoky. It was, I thought, such a beautiful name. Alice had taken the "Magna Terra" (meaning "big earth"), part of his name, from her ranch name and the "Smoky" part from his steel-gray coloration. It seemed so very appropriate and natural that his name linked him to this land. It implied that he belonged here. Alice had named him well.

I studied him even more closely now. He really was a nice colt, with a slender build and strong legs with good bone. The only fault I could find was with his rather plain and straight head. Most Arabian horses had a charming, endearing dish to their foreheads that melted the hearts of many a horse person. On the other hand, Smoky did have an exquisite neck and hip and a great set of withers. His legs were clean and straight, and all his body parts fit together like a perfect puzzle. *Yes,* I found myself thinking, *I do like the overall looks of him.*

Still on my mind, however, was the question "Why was he so timid and retiring? Why did he have such a marked distrust of humans?" It didn't seem to make sense. Alice certainly wasn't mean to her animals, and Arabian horses were bred to be friendly, loving horses. Throughout history, the Arabian horse had been bred to be a kind, noble steed that was a faithful friend and partner. Why then, at such a young age and in the company of two horses who were overly friendly, was Smoky so afraid? I turned to Alice for an answer.

"What's up with Smoky, Alice?"

The story Alice had to tell explained a lot.

"That's the way he's always been, Barb. Right from the beginning, I just could never develop a rapport with him. And to tell the truth, over the months, I have just spent less and less time with him."

Alice had a sadness in her voice. It was obvious that she had expected so much more from this new acquisition.

"Smoky has always had a tendency to be distant and difficult. He's not a people's horse, and because I didn't spend much time with him, he became more and more difficult to work with. It just kinda snowballed. He kept getting worse and worse. So because I didn't want to fight him, I put things off, and then one day I realized he was just too big and too strong for me to handle at all. He's really a lot like his dam, Cyroga. I bought her because she had such a gorgeous build and such lovely big bone. I felt sure she could produce the foal of my dreams. But I could never trust Cyroga, and she was always so darn difficult to catch. After having Smoky, she didn't want me coming near him either, so Smoky picked up her behaviors. She became too much of a handful for me. I finally had enough, and I gave up on her. I took her to the horse and cattle auction in Fort Collins. I never stayed to see who bought her. Even with Cyroga out of the picture, Smoky still wasn't a colt I could work with, so I gave him to Larry, my veterinarian. Larry's a big strong man, but even he couldn't deal with Smoky. He gave him back to me and just told me to get rid of him. Frankly, I've been contemplating sending Smoky to the auction as well. I don't know what else to do with him. I just don't have the time or patience he needs."

Alice's last comments were very disheartening. It left a hollow void in the pit of my stomach.

"If you're interested in Smoky and think he might work into your plans, that would be wonderful. I don't know if he'll work out or not. If you take him and he doesn't, maybe you could work with him and get him gentled enough that I could sell him and find him a decent home."

As I listened to Alice, I realized that Smoky had no reason to believe any of us wanted to be his friend. I wondered how hard it was going to be to bring Smoky around and gain his trust. How much of his dam's personality was ingrained in his mentality? Was it a task I could deal with? Smoky had such amazing conformation and such easy, fluid movement. He really could have great possibilities, and on top of that, I found myself really liking this little devil. If I didn't work with Smoky, what would become of him? Would he end up with the same fate as his dam?

I wondered who had bought Cyroga. Had she been one of the lucky ones and found a good home, or had she, like so many others, ended up at the killers? At a cattle and horse auction, horses like her did not bring many bids. It made me sick to think about it. I knew I had to take Smoky, not only to perhaps save him from going to auction but also because I found myself thinking that this tough gray pony might be a real diamond in the rough.

It's going to take a lot of time and patience, I thought, *but it might just be worth it.*

I looked back at Smoky. "You funny little horse, do you have any idea how perilous your life has become?" I wondered to myself, *What if I hadn't come along?*

Thinking about all the things that had happened lately, it really was a wonder that I was even here. I hadn't even really known Alice until recently. I certainly wouldn't have known about her or Smoky at all if I hadn't married Dick. She was, after all, Dick's friend. And I had come very, very close to not marrying Dick.

For many years, Dick and I had known of each other because of our involvement in competitive trail riding. Then about two years ago, we had started dating. When Dick became serious about marriage, I kept fluctuating back and forth. I had become quite independent and liked my lifestyle very much. I loved my science teaching job and was very proud of and happy with the home that I had bought and worked on in the Black Forest, north of Colorado Springs. I had three horses that I thoroughly enjoyed. Life was good.

Then it was almost as if fate had played its hand to develop the next chapter in my life. For the first and only time that I was aware of, my school district offered a one-time early-retirement cash incentive to any teacher having accumulated twenty-three or more years of teaching experience with the district. Unbelievably, I had exactly twenty-three years with the district. Was this coincidental, or was it a sign that I was meant to marry Dick and move to Fort Collins? Things just seemed to fall together perfectly. The cash bonus would give me some money to fall back on until I could decide what employment to pursue in Fort Collins. We decided to get married in Colorado Springs, and then we settled into Dick's home in Fort Collins.

Before long, I started to explore possible teaching jobs available, but I found myself doing this halfheartedly. As the summer months slipped away after our May wedding, I found myself a whole lot more interested in a job centered around our horses. However, if this was to work out, I had to come up with a way to make enough money to make it feasible. Right now, we definitely needed an additional income to supplement money brought in by Dick's nursery business.

At first, we pondered the possibility that I could train and sell some of the horses that Dick and I had bred and raised before we married. We both treasured the same type of Arabian horses, those that were levelheaded and pleasing to the eye and had good bone and conformation. Both of us had competed and done quite well in competitive trail riding before we were married, and we strongly supported the values and horsemanship skills that this sport encouraged and developed.

Competitive trail was a wonderful sport. Not only did a rider get to enjoy being in the beautiful country, but also, the rider and his/her horse got to compete as a team in a paced cross-country event that usually covered two days of riding, with each day having a marked trail of approximately twenty to forty miles. During the competition, a rider's horse was judged on soundness, condition, manners, etc., and the rider was judged on horsemanship. It was truly a test of the homework that one had done with his/her mount as you never knew just what obstacles might be encountered nor how taxing the course might be. Little could I have foreseen how valuable the horsemanship skills that I learned from this sport would serve me so well in the next chapter of my life.

Sadly, when Dick and I sat down to figure out the math of marketing our horses for competitive trail riding, we realized we couldn't hope to make much of a profit. We knew that people looking for a horse to compete in this sport generally wanted to purchase a four-to-five-year-old horse that was ready to go or at least well along in his training. For us to provide such a horse, we would have to breed the mare and then support her financially for the year that she carried the foal. When the mare foaled, there would be additional costs of feeding, vaccinating, worming, and trimming the foal for an additional four to five years. And it wouldn't end there as we would also need to train this horse to be a reliable trail mount. All this had to be done while we prayed that our prospect stayed sound and healthy. Any profit we were hoping for started to look more like a debit in the ledger books. So our problem was what could we do with our horses to turn a profit? We did not come up with an answer.

Call it fate, or call it destiny. Whatever it was, soon after this, events started lining up that would change my life's direction immensely. It all began when I had chanced to read an article in a magazine that talked about a horse-racing meet at Adams County Fairgrounds in nearby Brighton. That wasn't all. To my surprise and amazement, this meet was offering races for Arabians.

I couldn't believe it. I never realized that Arabians even raced on a flat track. When had that started? All I was aware of were the fifty- or hundred-mile endurance races that took place cross-country. Arabians were bred for distance. They definitely weren't sprinters like quarter horses or even thoroughbreds. Yet there it was, in black-and-white print.

As I read more, my eyes really lit up. The article went on to say that Arabians would be racing for purses or "real" money, not just trophies and/or awards, as was the practice with distance riding.

A wave of excitement literally rushed through me. This was unreal, too good to be true. I was beside myself with excitement. Could this be the ticket to making money with our horses? Would the athletic ability that we had bred into our foals be enough to allow them to compete with any success in an endeavor based entirely on speed? I knew that any athlete that hoped to excel in a speed event needed a good strong body and a good mind that could focus on the job at hand. Our horses sure had good bodies and minds bred into them. Could we change the direction we were going with our horses? If we pursued this, would they prove to be fast enough? I sure didn't know any Arabian racehorses, and just as surely, I definitely didn't know anyone who bred them. To tell the truth, I didn't know how fast they needed to run, and on top of all this, I certainly didn't know what was involved in the training of a racehorse. Could I learn the ropes and, in turn, teach our horses? Where would I start? Could we really do this? I was getting more and more excited just thinking about the possibility. I couldn't wait to tell Dick. I wondered what he would think about it.

Over the next few days, I was driven with a newly focused purpose. I pursued this new and exciting career option. In fact, I became totally obsessed with the idea. I lived this new dream day and night. I found myself running out of control with the excitement of this new venture. Dick was both amused and hesitant. He laughed at my excitement and enthusiasm but was a little more practical about the expense that might be involved. Horse racing was not called the "sport of kings" for nothing. His biggest concern was logistics. If we did delve into this, where would we have access to a racetrack? And if we were to actually race, how could I be there and at home also?

For me, this was too exciting to think of things like that. I was sure we could work it all out somehow. So I scavenged through old magazines and checked through telephone books, searching for any possible lead to an Arabian horse owner or breeder that might know something about this racing venture. Most of my phone calls turned up to be dead ends. It seemed everyone was involved in showing their horses either at halter or in Western classes.

Then I hit the jackpot. A phone call to an owner/breeder named Jane Teutsch, who lived just north of the Black Forest, confirmed that she was indeed involved in Arabian racing. Not only that, but also, she was the driving force behind Arabian racing in Colorado. How lucky was this? I was ecstatic! She invited me to visit her ranch. I would not have missed the opportunity for the world.

When I met Jane, I was enthralled with both her and her ranch. She and her husband, Ray, owned a huge piece of land located on the northern skirt of the Black Forest that was to die for. Although very well off, Jane was totally genuine, down to earth, and most gracious. We found we had a great deal in common, from the type of horse we liked to the way we liked to raise and train them. She introduced me to her trainer, Mary Clark, and soon afterward, I was galloping and exercising Jane's horses right along with Mary. And it was great fun. I was going to love this.

Later in the summer, Jane invited me to go with her and Mary to the very same race meet at Adams County Fairgrounds that I had read and fantasied about. I loved it there, doing whatever chores needed done, including cleaning stalls, grooming and walking horses, saddling horses for gallop boys, and even galloping some of the horses. As I worked, I learned. I met thoroughbred trainers, jockeys, other Arabian horse trainers, and racing officials. I loved every moment of this new venture—and the actual racing best of all. The excitement of a race and the tremendous thrill of watching Jane's horses win races became an addiction for me. I not only loved it but also came to realize that the horses loved it also. The more I saw and the more I learned, the more I was certain that this was what I wanted to do.

Dick's biggest fear was coming true. I was already away from home . . . a lot. It didn't seem right; we were newlyweds, after all. He tried to convince me that we could get by. We didn't really need the extra income, he would say.

I, in turn, used all the charm that I could muster. "It will only be for a few months each year," I pleaded. "The rest of the time, I will be home." I cooked special meals. I did little things that he especially liked. When he finished work, I tried to make sure he felt loved and special. But I was possessed. I was beginning to realize horse racing can do that to you.

I figured that we had maybe two horses of our own that would be possibilities for next year's race meet. I needed more horses. Then . . . fate again? Destiny? For out of the blue, on the last day of the race meet, ARA (Arabian Racing Adventures), who was one of Mary's other clients, approached me with an offer to train six horses that Mary couldn't accommodate for the following year. I couldn't believe my ears. Was this really happening? It was exactly what I needed, exactly what I wanted.

My emotions soared. It was unreal, too good to be true. This was an opportunity of a lifetime thrown into my arms. What could I say? I was ecstatic. I knew Dick would be dismayed, but I still couldn't wait to tell him the news. I wanted to share this with him. He really had been very patient and quite supportive so far, considering everything he had had to endure. I knew I was not being fair to him. I knew this, yet I could not stop. It was like an addiction. No, it wasn't *like* an addiction. It *was* an addiction. I was totally smitten.

I rationalized with Dick that this new endeavor could be a great venue for our breeding program, that we had to do it now or we might not have another chance. Dick was hesitant and more than a little reluctant. He had already seen how much of my time and energy was involved. However, in spite of the fact that I would be away from home a lot, both of us knew that this was something I absolutely had to do. The joy and thrill of this sport literally possessed me. I couldn't let go of it. Things had miraculously come together for inexplicable reasons, and I was eager and excited for whatever adventures lay ahead.

Was it destiny again? For it was shortly thereafter Alice stopped by to visit with us. It was a simple social visit, and the three of us sat down to chat over coffee and doughnuts. Eventually, our conversation turned to my new plans to race our Arabian horses. Almost immediately, Alice's eyes lit up and came to life as she listened to this new plan of ours.

"Barb, you've got to have a look at a two-year-old colt I have. He's sure built right, and he acts like he can run. He's too much for me, and I've run out of options for him. He might be worth looking at. Who knows? He might just fit into your new plans."

This was another unexpected surprise. I did need another horse, especially a two-year-old to complete my proposed stable of horses for next year. I looked over at Dick. This racing thing was coming at him from all sides. Even his friend, Alice, was in on it now!

I gave him my best smile. "What do you think, hon? Should we take a look?"

"Do you think I could stop the two of you, even if I wanted to?" He laughed. I loved him for his laugh, for I knew it was probably the last thing he had wanted to hear from Alice.

I was ecstatic. *Thank goodness Dick thought so much of Alice*, I silently reflected. Responding for the both of us, I almost blurted out, "We'd love to, Alice. When can we come out?"

So here we were, on the rolling hills of Alice's ranch, and as I stood gazing at Magna Terra Smoky, never in a million years could I have ever foreseen how this innocent meeting would change my life so drastically and so completely.

2 The Promise

It wouldn't be until almost fourteen months later that I would learn the full story behind this timid pony from the Pawnee grasslands. And when I did, it would turn out to be quite a tale.

For now, however, I simply knew that we had a scared horse on our hands, and we had to figure out how to catch him so that I could take him home. I definitely wanted to begin my rapport with Smoky with the same gentle but firm hands and words that I hoped would eventually win him over.

The pasture that Smoky and his buddies were in was adjacent to a large corral, so it was a simple task to lure the horses into this smaller enclosure. They were obviously used to being fed here. To reassure Smoky, I brought some armfuls of hay over from Alice's barn and spread it in the corral. Although hesitant, Smoky couldn't resist such a temptation, and he followed the others into our trap.

We closed the gate and let the horses settle and eat. Off to the right was a smaller pen. The next step would be to get Smoky into this smaller area. I enjoyed watching Smoky munch his hay while keeping an observant eye on us humans. I could tell he figured that something was up, that this was not going to be just a normal snack in the corral. Even so, he did follow the lead of the other two horses, and he dove into the hay with relish.

"I'm going to get my halter and lead, Alice. Do you think we will need to catch up Kroug also? I have some horse cookies also. Think I might bring them back with me. They might come in handy."

Alice acknowledged that it sounded like a good plan, so I swung by the barn and picked up the halter and lead she indicated was for Kroug and then picked up a halter and lead and the horse cookies from our rig.

We decided to catch up Kroug first and lead him into the smaller corral. Alice took the halter and lead I had brought over and walked over to Kroug. Smoky quickly moved off. I chuckled as it was exactly what I had anticipated.

As she buckled the halter on Kroug, she announced, "Okay, I'll lead Kroug over to the small corral. Think you can to get Smoky to follow us and keep Babe out?"

I angled my way around Smoky. "What's up, Smoky? Think I'm the Cookie Monster?"

Smoky didn't trust me at all. He looked at me and then at Kroug, who was moving away from him. He didn't like me going around him like that, and I could almost see the wheels turning inside that head of his. He stepped to the side and then trotted off after Kroug. Quietly, I simply walked behind him, keeping my distance so as not to frighten him. Before he knew what had happened, I shut the gate to the small corral behind him. It had gone remarkably smoothly, mainly because Smoky seemed quite bonded to Kroug and didn't want to be left behind. Smoky had unwittingly cooperated with the second part of our plan to trap him.

"At least we now have them separated out!" I happily exclaimed.

I knew the hardest part was yet to come, however. I knew Smoky would realize we wanted to catch him, and I wasn't sure how he would react. Alice still held Kroug. Smoky was upset. He wanted no part of our devious plan, and he was becoming agitated and upset just knowing we wanted to catch him up. He started running in circles.

He's really scared, I thought. What's more, he started to act as if he didn't even know what he was doing. *You poor little devil, why are you so scared of us?*

I turned to Alice once again. "Alice, we need to back off and rethink this." I looked compassionately at this young little horse that had little control over his fate. I wished I could tell him that he wouldn't be harmed in any way. I wished he could understand the reason I was here.

"Maybe we should use Kroug to help use catch Smoky. He's sensible, big, and stout, and he'll reassure Smoky," I offered. "I don't want to upset Smoky any more than need be, and if I want to get him home today, we need to get a move on."

We let Smoky relax and regain his composure. There wasn't any sense in continuing with him when his mind was all scattered. Unknown to me at the time, this display of nervousness would crop up at different times in Smoky's life as if it were some sort of security system that he regressed into. It often didn't take much to set it off, but I knew enough to stop and slow things down and reassure Smoky that I was his friend, not someone who would hit him or punish him when he didn't understand.

Slowly and quietly, we got Kroug and Smoky into the setup we wanted. I never stopped talking quietly and reassuringly to Smoky. I wanted him to learn my voice and have confidence in me, and all this had to begin now, right from the beginning.

As we sided Kroug up against Smoky, Smoky started to get worried again. He tried running over and then through Kroug. But Kroug was a big solid horse who had roped and dragged many cows and heifers. Smoky was nothing compared to all that. It even looked as if Kroug was warning Smoky to just settle down and be quiet.

Good old Kroug, I thought. *We sure need more horses like you around!*

Alice and I backed off once again and let Smoky relax once more. Eventually, Smoky quit his antics and just eyed us suspiciously.

"Why don't I see if I can just talk to him and work with him slowly? We have to get this halter on him somehow."

Smoky was still shaking a little, but amazingly, he stood quietly and just watched me. Eventually, he decided it was okay if I stroked his neck.

"You won't admit it, I'm sure, but I think you kind of like this, don't you, Smoky?"

Pretty soon, I was scratching in his mane, which I was certain he liked. Even he couldn't resist tilting his neck a little when I hit a particularly itchy spot. I would have loved to rub a special spot on his withers, but I figured that might be pushing my good luck. I could tell he was relaxing. The tenseness had gone out of his muscles, and his eye was soft and content, not wild with the whites showing.

"How about I put my arm around your neck, just a little, Smoky? Could you go for that?"

Smoky was really settling down. Other than turning his head a little, he was pretty relaxed about me having my arm around his neck. Slowly, I brought the end of the halter up under his neck to my right arm.

"See, Smoke? Nothing's even hurting you, is it? You're doing great. You're going to love it at your new home. You just wait and see. Just let me get this harmless little strap around your neck."

I continued talking to Smoky, not saying much of anything important, just trying to keep him as relaxed as possible. I knew I might get a reaction when I lowered the halter a little to get it over his nose, but Smoky surprised me. With just a slight rise of his head, I slipped the nose band over his nose and found myself excitedly buckling the halter.

"Smoky, we've done it. You little rascal, I can't believe it was so easy. You're not such a wild thing after all, are you? What a champ. I'm so proud of you! There's something about you, Smoky, that is quite special. I have a feeling that you may be the one I've been looking for. How would you like to be a racehorse, Smoky? It may take a while and a lot of miles down the trail, but we'll show 'em, won't we?"

Smoky just looked at me with an expression that told me he was wondering what was up next. I kept stroking Smoky's neck as I rambled on and dreamed of our future.

Once Smoky was caught, he almost became a different horse. He led easily. He had been taught to do that well enough. He sure wasn't stupid, and with the encouragement of some grain and odds of three to one, we had him loaded into Dick's stock trailer in no time. Smoky was just about on his way to his new home.

Dick and I thanked Alice and wished her well, and in return, she wished us luck with Smoky. Dick started up the truck, and as we drove down her long driveway to the county road that would take us home, I gazed at the grasslands Smoky was leaving behind. I felt tears welling up in my eyes, tears of gratitude that our task at hand had gone so well but also tears for the young horse that was unknowingly entrusting his future into my hands. Would the winds of destiny that brought us together endure and carry us to destinations beyond imagination, or would they peter out and die, leaving only a glimpse of what might have been? Could I dare to hope that this unexpected addition to my life could become a racehorse? Would I find that Smoky had the courage, ability, and love of running like the wind to succeed as a racehorse? Could I dare to believe that I was horsewoman enough to develop Smoky's athletic abilities and mental concentration that race training would take?

I found myself looking back at the horse trailer. Then turning to face Dick, I asked, "Hon, I think Smoky is probably my most promising prospect. Do you think we can learn this racing thing together? Do you think I'll be able to help him overcome his nervousness and his insecurities?"

Dick squeezed my hand. "If anyone can do it, you can."

I looked up at him and smiled. His confidence in me meant so much. I realized how patient and supportive he had been in spite of his reservations about what I was embarking upon.

"Thank you, hon. This means so much to me. I think we have a pretty nice horse in that trailer behind us. I am *so* excited. I just hope Smoky will learn to trust me. If I can get that accomplished, the rest will fall into place. I think he needs his own person, and I intend to be there for him. You know something else? I love this land, and I feel that Smoky really belongs here. I can't explain it, this feeling of closeness, of love for something so special, but if Smoky gets that far, I'm going to train him to be a racehorse, not on a racetrack but on land like this. He'll be one heck of a tough little Indian pony that can fly over any surface imaginable. A smooth and flat racetrack will be like flying for him."

Looking back at the horse trailer, I imagined that I could see Smoky within, and I found myself thinking about our possible future. I knew it was a huge improbable dream, but I was ready to tackle it with every ounce of energy, perseverance, knowledge, and skill that I possessed. I wanted this to work, and I wanted it very badly.

Silently, to just myself, but hoping that Smoky could feel the intensity of my dream, I sealed a special pact between us. It was spontaneous and so premature, but it came from within the very depths of my heart and soul. I really did want this to work. So I laid everything on the line.

Smoky, I promise you this, that if you just work with me, even a little, and we make it to that racetrack and fly like the wind, at the end of our journey, I'll get you your grassland, and it'll be yours to enjoy. You'll get to live there as you should, to run happy and free and live to bask in the warm afternoon sun as many Indian ponies before you.

3 The First Four

Later on that evening and after Smoky had settled into his new home, I had time to reflect on the day's events. I couldn't believe or begin to understand why I had made such an outlandish promise to a horse I hardly knew. What had possessed me to do such a thing? I really didn't know much about this horse, let alone what he could do. How could I know what the future would bring? I didn't even own Smoky, and there were so many things that could happen, any one of which could destroy the best-laid plans. Could I even dare to hope that I could honor this promise? Was I so taken with this racing business that I was trying to force things to happen? Or did I need this challenge? Maybe this promise would push me harder. Maybe it would give me the determination and perseverance to follow through with my goals. Is that why I made this promise? Or did I truly see some untapped potential, some hidden talents just waiting to be unveiled?

What I did know was that I was tremendously excited. Although I didn't tell Alice, with the addition of Smoky, I felt that my potential racing stable was complete. It would be made up of Smoky, two mares that I had purchased just the month before, and a homegrown colt. These four would be supplemented by the six horses that ARA would send me in the spring. Ten would be a good number of horses, I thought. I figured that I had put together my personal stable, but I didn't even own Smoky. Alice hadn't offered to sell him, and I hadn't asked. It seemed inappropriate; plus, I really wanted to have Alice involved in this fledgling racing adventure. So I had made a promise to a horse that I didn't even own. *What next?* I wondered.

When I thought about my race prospects, not one of them was really bred to race. LL Manteeya was my favorite of the other three horses. As with Smoky, I thought her name was very special and unique. She was a beautiful chestnut mare that I loved the moment I saw her. Although her breeding was mainly "show horse," up to that time, she was, by far, the best horse I had come across in my long search. She had a beautiful and delicately dished head with large liquid eyes. When she looked into the distance, you could see the envied look of eagles in her eyes. I could easily see a Bedouin welcoming her into his tent and treasuring the new addition to his family.

I know a beautiful head and soulful eyes don't make a racehorse, but she was also a good-sized mare, about 15.1 hands, and she had good clean legs and was very nicely put together. She traveled easily around the large arena, and she loved it when she was asked to extend her gallop. Her hoof angles were a little off, but her hooves were also a little long, and I thought that my horseshoer could take care of both those things. I wanted to buy her stablemate also, except that he had one major flaw. He was a gorgeous gray and correct in every way except for a short neck. If fact, his neck was awfully short, and I thought he would lack the balance and length that a good racehorse would need. Months later, I wondered if I should have bought him anyway as the filly, Spring Fling, that I bought instead turned out to be a total mistake and a waste of a lot of time and effort. Spring Fling was also out of show horse stock.

My fourth horse, Independence Dai, named after his birth date of July 4, was our only homebred. He was an attractive chestnut colt by Dick's stallion, Dosil, and he had inherited Dosil's terrific mind, great bone, and balanced conformation. Although both Indy's dam and sire were very athletic, neither had any racehorses in their pedigree. As Smoky and Spring Fling were both two years old and Indy and Manteeya were three-year-olds, it meant that I would have one colt and one filly who would race as three-year-olds next summer and one colt and one filly who would race as four-year-olds. Arabians, just like thoroughbreds, became a year older each January 1. A colt such as Independence Dai, who was born in July, would be at quite a disadvantage as he would be half a year behind many of the four-year-olds that he would compete against. A young horse can do a lot of maturing, both mentally and physically, in half a year.

When I started to look at Smoky's pedigree, I found that I didn't know very much about his sire except that his name was SW David and that he had been shown at halter in his earlier years. For a long time, I would pronounce this name as "David" until I learned that it was pronounced "Dawid" as *v* is pronounced as *w* in Arabic. I knew a little bit more about Smoky's dam. She was a Hyannis Cattle

Company (HCC) mare bred to be a using kind of mare that could round up cattle and do ranch chores. HCC was well known for breeding athletic good-boned Arabian horses, and their horses were popular among endurance and competitive trail riding circles. Three years ago, in the spring of 1985, I had actually made a trip to Phoenix to attend an auction of Hyannis Cattle Company horses. The ranch owners were selling off a lot of their stock, and I was hoping to find a good gelding for NATRC (North American Trail Ride Conference) competitions to replace my retired gelding, Brandy.

To my surprise and delight, Dick Evans was also at the auction. It would make the auction a lot more fun, having someone there whom I knew. Dick was there with two friends whom he introduced as Alice Pollock and his business partner, Pat. I sat down with Dick, Alice, and Pat as the auction started, and it ended up being rather fun as Alice bid on several mares and ended up buying a big bay mare with outstanding conformation. The mare's name was Cyroga. However, to my dismay and disappointment, there wasn't a gelding that I really took a liking to, and not being interested in a mare or a stallion, I didn't even submit a single bid. I returned home empty-handed and quickly forgot about the auction and the new acquaintances I had made. Little could I have realized at the time the major role that these three people would play in my future and the intricate web that they, along with this bay mare named Cyroga, would weave through my life. I thought little more about the auction than the fact that I was disappointed in it. I still had to concentrate on finding a new competitive trail riding horse.

Now here it was, three years later, and lo and behold, if I wasn't married to Dick Evans and standing in our corral, was a skittish gray colt out of the bay mare that Alice had bought at the auction we had all attended in 1985. I wondered what quirk of fate had brought us all together again and what the unexpected addition of Alice's two-year-old gelding to my fledgling racing adventure would mean. So much had happened and changed in three short years. Not only had I changed residences and gotten married, but also, I had changed my profession from the very stable and financially secure life of a schoolteacher to that of a very financially challenging and unstable life of a racehorse owner and trainer. My new husband as well as my parents and friends wondered and worried about the new direction my life was headed. But in the midst of all this, out of the blue, I had suddenly and unexpectedly obtained what I was sure was my dream racehorse. I dared not think about all the things I did not know, and I certainly didn't have time to think about all the things that could go wrong. I was completely smitten with the idea of racing and getting my new stable of horses started on a journey that would lead us I knew not where. I was living and breathing in a dream world, and I had no intention of waking up until my dream was fulfilled.

Smoky in one of our pastures in Fort Collins
December, 1988

Independence Dai with author in saddle
February, 1989

LLManteeya with author and Thunder in front of our hay barn
early spring, 1989

4   A Rough Start

Long before I reached the corral, I knew that something was wrong with Smoky. He wasn't standing quite right, and he wasn't watching me approach his pen. As I increased my pace and I got closer, I could tell that Smoky's whole demeanor was anxious and that he was in a great deal of pain. Something was definitely wrong. Smoky had only been here three days. What was the matter? Then as his symptoms registered in my mind, the dreaded thought crossed my mind—surely it couldn't be founder! His drawn-out stance, with front feet extended in front of him and the pain registering in his eyes, confirmed that my gut feeling might be right. My stomach turned over inside me, and I felt a siege of panic.

Founder, along with colic, were the two horse problems that I dreaded and feared the most. Each disease, in its own way, caused terrible pain to a horse, and each could develop serious consequences, even death, if not treated promptly. Founder usually affects the front feet of a horse and is a very painful condition. The vascular (blood supply) system within the hoof is upset, and this leads to an increase in the volume of blood in the hoof and therefore an increase in pressure. Pain occurs because pressure is exerted on the sensitive structures in the hoof. These structures are unable to expand because they are contained within an unyielding hoof wall. The suffering horse is loath to put any weight on his affected front feet and therefore rocks his weight back toward his hind end and thrusts his front feet forward. It causes a look of acute distress.

Smoky wasn't at that point yet. I wondered how long this had been going on. I knew that time was the enemy now, so I didn't even try to evaluate the situation any further. I knew Smoky needed expert help that I could not provide. He was already showing discomfort, with his front feet stretched out in front of him. I turned and raced back to the house to call Dr. Carr, our veterinarian. Thank goodness it was early. She might still be at the clinic. It was music to my ears when I found she hadn't left her office yet. She hardly listened to me describe the symptoms before she said she would leave right away. Thank goodness her clinic wasn't far away.

I swung by the nursery office and yelled to Dick that Smoky was in trouble and raced back down to the barn. I badly wanted to do something, but I didn't want to upset Smoky any further and cause any more stress on an already stressed horse. What had I done to cause this? He hadn't had enough grain to feed a sparrow, and surely, the small amount of green grass growing in his pen wasn't rich enough to cause him to react this way. I had only fed him a little alfalfa as I knew he wasn't used to having much of it. I didn't think the grass hay that I had been feeding him should have caused a problem. I was at a loss to figure out what had caused this sudden turn of events.

Dr. Carr was prompt. She arrived at about the same time that Dick made it down from his office next to our house. She looked over the situation quickly and agreed that we had a horse intent upon foundering. As she busily and efficiently set up her supplies, she queried me to try to determine the cause. As she questioned me, she checked Smoky's vital signs. It had been easy to catch Smoky; he was plainly in too much distress to resist. Dick stood off to the side. He wanted to help but realized Smoky would do much better without his involvement. Smoky's pulse and temperature were elevated, and his feet were warm. He was anxious and trembling slightly now. What a terrible start to his new life here . . . He was in a strange place, no old friends around—and now this awful pain. My heart ached for him.

"We'd best relieve a little of his pain and then get to work. We also need to control the heat in his feet. Do you have some ice up at the house?"

I confirmed that we did and looked over to Dick. "Could you run up and grab the ice trays in the freezer, hon? I also have some frozen bottles of water and ice packs in the freezer that I keep ready for days that I take long rides. Could you grab those also?"

As Dick hurried off, I returned my attention to Dr. Carr and Smoky.

"I'm going to tranquilize Smoky, Barb, so that we don't cause him any more undue stress. Being we're not sure what caused this, we'd better flush out any possible culprit that might be in his digestive tract." Dr. Carr administered two shots to Smoky. I could tell Smoky didn't like it, but he was feeling too bad to resist very much.

"You're doing great, Smoky. Just hang in there. We're just trying to help." It made me almost cry to see him so forlorn, and hurting so much, I thought to myself, *Please, dear Lord, help Smoky though this. He's just needs a chance.*

Dr. Carr went back to her vet truck to prepare a laxative of mineral oil while I stroked Smoky tenderly. When she returned, Smoky was subdued and much more relaxed. Smoky already didn't like what was happening. You could see it in his pained eyes and his tensed and trembling body. He attempted to move away, but his body had a hard time responding.

I tried to reassure him with in a soft voice, "Easy, son, everything's going to be okay."

Dr. Carr slowly approached with the stomach tube and the bucket of laxative. "Just keep talking to him, Barb. I've oiled the tube, and this should go fairly easily for him."

"Please, Smoky. I know you can't possibly understand what's going on, but we are trying to help you. It won't take long. Please help us help you." I just kept talking to Smoky, trying to reassure him and trying to keep my mind off the problem.

Then Dr. Carr was inserting the tube. As she predicted, it slid fairly easily up his nostril. He was letting us do it.

"Thank goodness for sedatives!" I exclaimed.

"I'm going to start pumping the oil now, Barb . . . If he stays still now, we've got it made."

I could tell by the look in Smoky's eye that he was thinking about pulling back, but then he seemed to have second thoughts. His body wasn't responding very well. He had a hard-enough time just trying to keep his balance. The tranquilizer was doing its job. We were going to get the job done! At least this part of the treatment hadn't been too hard on Smoky or on us. Then the tube was coming out.

Dick had returned with the ice and was filling a tub with both it and some water. He brought it over and placed it in front of Smoky. I hoped that Smoky would let me lift his front leg and put it in the tub. I would have liked to ice both legs at the same time but knew that would be an impossible task with a horse that was so afraid of human contact to start with.

I handed the lead rope to Dr. Carr and talked softly to Smoky as I stroked his shoulder and front leg. As the tranquilizer was still in effect and some of Smoky's pain had been abetted, I felt that I might have half a chance of putting one foot in the ice water if I took my time and did things slowly. Smoky clearly didn't want to lift a foot as it meant he had to put more weight on his right front foot. However, after several attempts, I had his foot up and in the tub. The surprise of the ice water registered with Smoky, but he didn't pull back. Again, I thanked the Lord for tranquilizers and pain medication. I had no idea if it felt good to Smoky; I was just glad that he was letting the ice water do its work. Both Dick and Dr. Carr expressed their delight at Smoky's cooperation. I hoped it would go as well when it came time to change feet.

"Well, that's about all we can do for now, Barb. I'm going to leave you this medicine to give Smoky for the next five days. Hopefully, Smoky will let you give it to him. Let me know if you can't get it into him, and I'll come back out tomorrow. Good luck with the icing. If you can't get his other foot into the tub, try hosing it down. The more of that you can do, the better Smoky will be. Give me a call tonight and let me know how he is doing. You should see a big change by this evening. I think we caught this in its initial stages. When he comes out of this sedative, you can offer him some water. I'd like you to not give him anything to eat for the rest of the day. Tomorrow, if he's improved, you can give him some grass hay. Give me a holler if you see any regression."

Dr. Carr had impressed me with her professionalism and her quiet and gentle way with Smoky. I thanked her, and we said our goodbyes.

Dick, bless his heart, said his landscaping work could wait and took Smoky's lead rope as I continued to stroke Smoky's leg and reassure him that we were trying to make his pain go away. I wondered if Smoky understood any of what was being done for him. It was going to be a long day, but Smoky was helping us help him. It was more than I thought possible.

Later on, after the initial icing, I sat down on the ground beside Smoky's corral. Beside me, Thunder, my loyal and much-loved German shepherd, lay down to keep me company. After the tranquilizer wore off, Smoky wasn't having any more to do with the buckets of ice water or the cold water from the garden hose. I wanted to watch over Smoky and make sure he seemed all right. I hoped and prayed that this was just a bump in the road for the both of us and not a dead end. I tried, for the life of me, to figure out what had caused this tragic turn of events. Even Dr. Carr had been at a loss for a cause. His diet had been deliberately lacking in anything that would really trigger foundering.

I wondered if Smoky could have been more stressed than I had thought. Was he internalizing all his worries and fears? How could he know what was going to happen to him here? Could this have helped trigger or added to some of his digestive turmoil? What was going through that head of his? There wasn't any scientific evidence that I knew of that claimed anxiety and nervousness could cause founder, but you could not have convinced me of that.

"Smoky, you poor little devil . . . You've lost all your security blankets, haven't you? Even dear old Kroug is gone. Are you so worried about what will happen to you that your whole body is in turmoil?"

I had no idea really if any of this was part of the problem, but I decided I'd better double my efforts to make him feel safe and secure. I decided to bring Indy in and put him in the pen next to Smoky. I hoped Smoky would feel a bond with Indy that might replace his loss of Kroug. Then I decided I would spend even more time just being visible and working with Smoky. Even if I was just cleaning his pen, stroking his neck, or just plain talking to him, I would be there, highly visible and always quiet, friendly and nonthreatening. And last of all, I would become a carrot lady. I would always have a carrot ready for the taking if Smoky just made one positive step to help himself or me.

Remarkably, Smoky ended up recovering from this bout of founder, and ever so fortunately, he never exhibited any of the complications that I was afraid might be displayed in his hooves. Today we would have called his problem "laminitis," which is really a mild form of founder. Whatever the name, it was the fact that it was caught in its very early stages that saved us from more serious problems. Founder is not to be taken lightly; it was, in fact, the culprit in the demise of the racing legend Secretariat.

For Smoky and me, this bout with laminitis actually ended up having some very positive consequences, for it allowed me to work with him in a way and at a time that a great rapport developed between the two of us. It established for him the beginning of a confidence in me that would last throughout the years. Smoky definitely wasn't a dumb horse. I could sense that he was beginning to understand that I was trying to and wanted to be his friend. I had no way of knowing, but I liked to think that he understood that I had reduced the pain for him—and of course, he loved those carrots!

What Smoky needed most of all, I was willing and able to provide. He needed a new friend. He needed security. He needed to feel safe. He needed me to lean on for the time being, but I also knew I had to teach him to trust himself, to do what he needed to do the way he needed to do it. He had to discover himself. All of Smoky's problems stemmed from his overwhelming lack of security. By being his security blanket, I intended to teach him to have confidence not only in me but also in himself. I wanted to be worthy of his trust, and in return, I wanted to be able to trust him. Only then could we progress into becoming the ultimate team. It is mutual trust that cements relationships together, whether the relationship be between humans or a human and an animal. It was an exciting possibility, but we also had a lot of work to do. I knew that what he would learn now, in his youth, he would remember for the rest of his life.

I spent many hours just grooming every part of Smoky's body, all the while telling him all the plans I had in store for us. And during this time, Smoky got to practice basic horse manners without even realizing it. There's nothing like spending the time that it takes to make something work.

Soon, we began taking walks together. We explored the entirety of Dick's farm and nursery. We walked down between the aisles of evergreens and cottonwoods and maples. I stood with him as we watched Dick's tractor lift trees from the ground to be transplanted. We walked around the greenhouses and Dick's office and the main house. We visited Manteeya and Spring Fling and the other horses out in the big irrigated pastures. We watched and listened to the noisy trains go by with their load of coal from the mines in Wyoming. Smoky got to know all the things that encompassed his new world.

Then we practiced walking over or past slickers and old tarps, puddles and bridges, trains and trucks. Whatever was there, we practiced getting used to and comfortable with it. I started putting a blanket and then a saddle upon his back, and our walks continued. And always, there were lots of positive strokes on the neck and shoulder, and of course, there were always carrots.

With Dick's encouragement from behind, I taught Smoky to run behind me and then, for safety reasons, to run beside me. I didn't want a spooked horse running over me before I even realized what was happening. As I loved running, it was an ideal way to get Smoky used to a bouncing saddle and stirrups. He didn't like it at first, which I more or less expected. He would fishtail and kick out his left hind leg. This habit would become ingrained, and he would repeat this display of jumping up and kicking out his left hind leg whenever he was upset and then eventually even when he was feeling extra good and happy. It may not have developed into such a habit, except that he made me laugh when he did it.

"Oh, you crazy horse, Smoky! What a character you are," I would say as I laughed at his antics. What I failed to realize was how quickly Smoky was picking up on my moods and actions. *If this makes her laugh*, he thought, *I'll do it all the time*. Thus, this new show of exuberance became a Smoky trademark.

Soon, I was putting weights over the saddle and tying them down with rope. We would continue our runs. Some things developed a reaction; others didn't. He did not at all like it when anything became unbalanced in the saddle, and although I worked and worked with him on this issue, he never really got over it. It was all part of his desperate need for security in his world. It was up to me to ensure that things were safe and without danger to him. And although I was teaching Smoky to learn to trust, I also realized that this little gray horse had a lot to teach me if I would just watch and listen to the things he was telling me.

5 First Ride

The day finally came when I felt it was time to get on Smoky. I was feeling good about the rapport that Smoky and I were developing. Smoky was placing a lot more confidence in me, and I was developing a deep pride in this young two-year-old colt. As I looked forward to this first ride, I found myself reminiscing about my grandpa, William Saunders, and my first really good childhood friend, Marilyn Buck. Of all the people in my life, I felt that it was these two individuals who either gave me or developed in me my deep love of horses.

Grandpa Saunders was my mom's dad. He had been the first one to set me upon the back of a horse. I was just two years old at the time. My father had been shot down before I was born while on a bombing mission over Germany (World War II) and was still a prisoner of war. Grandpa assumed the roles of both father and grandfather. He loved to take me for walks, and I loved being with him. Up the hill from their home in Leamington Spa, England, was a grassy field where several old milk-wagon horses lived. They must have been kind, gentle souls, for Grandpa sometimes put me aboard their backs, and Mom told me years later that I loved every minute of it. Grandpa had been quite the horseman in his younger days, and he had won numerous awards for his horsemanship skills while serving in the Royal Horse Artillery in India. Although he had died early in my life and we lived an ocean apart after Dad was freed, I always felt that his animal savvy and ability to work with horses was passed on to me. Whenever I encountered a rough spot with a horse or whenever I needed a helping hand or guidance, I would find myself silently talking and praying to Grandpa. For whatever reasons, it always seemed to help.

Marilyn was horse crazy when I met her. After the war ended, our family of three was shipped back to Canada. After numerous transfers across the country, the RCAF (Royal Canadian Air Force) saw fit to send Dad to Ottawa, Ontario. Mom and Dad bought a house for our family (now numbering five) on the outskirts of the city. Marilyn lived on the street just behind us. We soon became fast friends, and she quickly turned me into both a lover of horses and a renegade tomboy. The two of us collected huge arrays of horse statues and amassed stacks of horse comic books (some of which I have to this day). We hoarded horse pictures and photos and played with our toy horses that replaced the dolls that most girls our age focused on. We raced home in the afternoons to watch our favorite TV programs, starring "Trigger" with Roy Rogers and "Champion," Gene Autry's horse.

We were both ten years old and full of energy, so we also rode our bicycles around the countryside, looking for horses in pastures that we could admire and pet. One horse in particular was a favorite. He was a huge bay workhorse with gorgeous big brown eyes, a magnificent flowing mane, and a big white blaze down the center of his face. I eventually named him Twilight as it seemed appropriate to give him a romantic and somewhat different name.

Visiting Twilight soon became a daily occurrence, and he became as eager to see us as we him, mainly because we would bring him armfuls of alfalfa that we picked from a field across the road. He would come magnificently trotting up to the fence for his daily ration. We would fuss over him and slowly dole out the alfalfa as we, all the while, groomed our newfound friend with our hairbrushes. If ever our moms knew!

It wasn't long before I yearned for more. I could hardly control my desire to be upon Twilight's back. However, he towered above us, and I knew that I could never hope to climb up upon him. Then I had an idea.

"Marilyn, let's get some more alfalfa. We can use it to lure Twilight over to that section of fence under that big cottonwood tree. If we can get him to stand there and eat the alfalfa, I can climb up in the tree and get high enough to get on his back."

Marilyn was all for it, and off we went to collect the alfalfa. Twilight watched eagerly, and when we returned, he followed us right into our trap. I climbed up into the tree and instructed Marilyn as to where she needed to bring Twilight. It was a tricky maneuver as Twilight had to stand in just the right place. Finally, it was a go, and I dropped slowly onto his back. I must have felt less than a peanut to Twilight, but he reacted nonetheless and started off at a trot. I was on the ground in a flash. He might just as well have bucked up a storm for all I knew about riding a horse. But it was my first ride, and in spite of being dirty and a little bruised, I knew I wanted to do it again. Marilyn wasn't so sure. She thought for sure that I was going to get hurt.

Twilight didn't want any more of it that day, so we said goodbye and packed up our things. "We'll be back, Twilight. See you tomorrow! Thanks for the ride."

Tomorrow seemed to take forever to come, but it finally did, and off we rode on our bicycles to see our newfound friend. As we approached his pasture, I could see Twilight watching us. He knew by now that we always brought alfalfa treats, and he waited patiently for his scrumptious reward.

"I'll be more prepared this time, Marilyn. Let's get him set up."

So once again, I ventured down onto that mighty expanse of brown hide. I grabbed a huge handful of mane this time in anticipation of being "bucked off "again. Nothing! He did absolutely nothing. My hand was clenched around a fistful of mane still. Finally, I thought I should move a little, shift my weight or something. Still nothing. I decided I would sit and enjoy. I was staying on my mighty steed. I felt on top of the world. Marilyn kept feeding. Twilight was as happy as a clam.

"You should try this next, Marilyn. It is *so-o-o-o* neat!"

However, the real twilight was coming, and it was getting late.

"How should I get off, Marilyn?" It was a long way down to the ground. We eventually decided that Marilyn should continue to feed him while I leaned over his left shoulder to see if he did anything. With nary a response from him, I got braver and lifted my right leg over his back. Still holding onto a handful of mane, I decided that I would go for it.

"Get out of his way, Marilyn, in case he gets scared. I'm coming down!"

Then more because I was scared of what he might do than anything that he actually did, I fell clumsily to the ground. Twilight took a step and just looked at me. I did not land gracefully, but nonetheless, I was very surprised and impressed. Twilight was completely at ease. All my antics didn't even phase him. Once again, I could hardly wait for tomorrow when we could do this all again.

We both gave him great big pats and thanked him for a wonderful day. All the way home, we raved about our marvelous and exciting adventure.

It never had occurred to us to use a halter or a bridle because we didn't have one. Besides, we never could have reached high enough to put it on Twilight. So we continued happily on in our naivete with absolutely no way of controlling our mighty steed. It never registered either that we were both learning valuable lessons in horse psychology during those happy days, and that was to have patience and take things slowly. It would be a lesson repeated for me over and over through the years, and the patience learned would become one of my greatest assets when it came to working with my new gray colt.

In the days that followed, we repeated and then expanded our endeavors. We taught Twilight to walk with me on him, all the while Marilyn encouraging him with bunches of alfalfa. It amazed me that Marilyn was content in her role as feeder and walker as I was the one having all the fun, but she continually balked at getting on him. I hadn't fallen off again and began to want more. I wanted to go faster.

"Could you try running with the alfalfa, Marilyn? I'll try kicking him a little at the same time."

Marilyn started running, and I started kicking. Nothing.

"You know what? I think I need a whip. Not to hurt him—just to show him."

Marilyn broke a small sapling growing from the base of the cottonwood and passed it up to me. Then she took to running with the alfalfa while I waved the new whip. Almost immediately, Twilight was running.

"Wow, watch out, Marilyn . . . He's going to run over you."

We were both laughing in our excitement. Then just as quickly, he came to a stop. Twilight expected his alfalfa, and we happily gave it to him.

It didn't seem long before we had Twilight trained to trot with me on him. I fell off occasionally as I sometimes had a hard time calculating his moves and his rhythm, but I was never hurt, and Twilight just seemed to think that it was part of the game. We progressed so well that eventually, Twilight would make a short loop around the pasture without Marilyn running in front of him. He would return to the fence where Marilyn stood for his reward.

But then one day, which was to be our last day, I neglected to see a farmer's truck stop alongside the road. I could not have done much anyway. Twilight brought me right back to the fence where the farmer now stood next to a "caught red-handed" Marilyn.

"What in tarnation are you doing with my horse? He's no bloody riding horse. Get the hell out of here and don't come back. I'll have the cops after you."

He was angry, and we were terrified. I tried to mumble an apology, but he wouldn't hear any of it. We grabbed our bicycles and peddled away as fast as we could.

"Darn it, we should have been watching."

Marilyn agreed. "I tried to yell at you, but it was already too late."

We visited Twilight's pasture again, but the farmer had moved our newfound friend. We thought we saw him behind the farmhouse and barn that were a mile or so down the road, but we dared not go closer to find out.

"Thank you, Twilight, for all the good times. We already miss you!"

I thought Twilight might miss us too.

I remember those days vividly some sixty-plus years later. It had been my introduction to not only riding but also basic horsemanship, which involved patience, persistence, and teamwork. I never realized that at the time, I was learning far more than Twilight. Our newfound four-legged friend had done things willingly, and it had been fun for the both of us. It was the way I wanted it to be for Smoky and me.

"Yes, Smoky . . . It really is the way I want it to be between the two of us. I want you to be a willing and happy horse. I want us to both learn from each other, and I want it to be fun. What do you think? Are you game?"

Smoky just looked for his carrot.

For the past several days, I had been practicing putting my weight in the left stirrup, bouncing lightly up and down beside Smoky, and now I wasn't getting much of a reaction. I had even stood vertical in the left stirrup beside him. I had practiced some of the same on his right side, but he was not near as comfortable with that. Dick and I agreed that as a precaution, it might be best to have Dick hold on to Smoky the first time I tried to get on him.

Everything seemed to go fine when I did all the preliminaries with Dick holding him. I looked at Dick and said, "I'm going to do it this time, hon. Are you ready?"

"Are you ready, Smoky? I sure hope so."

Then very quietly and slowly, I put my foot in the stirrup and rose up beside Smoky, but instead of just leaning over him as I had done before, I passed my right leg over his back and settled easily into the saddle.

"Holy mackerel, hold on to him, Dick."

All hell had broken loose. Dick tried to hold him but couldn't. Smoky was all over the place. It wasn't any predictable pattern of bucking, and I was afraid I would soon go off. Then all of a sudden, he just came to a standstill. I was shaken but *so* glad I was still on his back. I wasn't really sure if he was finished.

"Man, that surprised me," I heard Dick say. "I'm sorry . . . I just couldn't hold him."

"Yeah, it surprised me too! Do you think he's finished?"

"Don't count on it." Dick laughed.

But Smoky still didn't do anything. I just let him stand and settle himself. Maybe he would process what had happened. I talked to him and petted him, and then slowly, without Dick holding him, I dismounted and petted him some more. I was so relieved he hadn't bucked me off. I sure didn't want him learning that little trick. Unlike Twilight, Smoky had bucked, and he was quite good at it!

I knew we had to do it all over again for both our sakes. For Smoky, it meant learning not to buck; for me, it meant not being afraid to go through it again. I walked him around and talked to him, all the while explaining what I needed him to do, telling him that things really were all right. "We've got to do this again, Smoky. I can't let it go on this bad note. Let's see if we can at least get it halfway right. Then we can call it quits. Deal?"

Smoky looked at me. He really did have an intelligent look about him. How much did he understand? Did he understand any of the words I said? He certainly understood tones of voice, and I knew the quieter and more relaxed I was, the quieter and more relaxed Smoky was. If I was going to be a role model here, I had to be careful in what I picked and chose for him to learn. It didn't seem much different from raising a kid.

I felt that Smoky may have been reacting to Dick as much as he was to me. This time, I asked Dick not to take such a short hold of him and to talk quietly to him. I just wanted Dick to be able to restrain him if he started to run away while he was bucking. We weren't in a round pen or anything, mainly because we didn't have one. It was my idea to be out in the open, away from any dangerous objects. So Dick's job was to keep me out in the open and away from those dangerous objects.

So we repeated the process. Dick and I were better prepared this time, but when I finally settled in the saddle, Smoky didn't do anything. I waited—and still nothing.

"Smoky, you little devil. You're amazing. How can you go from one extreme to the other so quickly? I'm not complaining, mind you. I'm just very surprised."

But then, why should I be so surprised? Didn't Twilight behave much the same way? I was running my hand up and down his neck now, delighted with the turn of events.

"I'm going to call it quits, Dick. This is all he needs to do today. He's done everything right this time, and I want to end on that good note. There's certainly no need to push our good fortune."

That day, Smoky didn't get alfalfa, but he did get extra carrots. In the days that followed, Smoky progressed nicely, just as Twilight had. I rode Smoky everywhere I could, around the nursery and across the road onto a series of trails along the Cache la Poudre River.

There is much to be said about riding a horse alone, even if at times, I missed the human companionship. I could almost see, on a daily basis, the trust and rapport that was developing between us. He had only me to rely on. There was no other horse to bond with or depend upon. Only me. I loved riding Smoky, and he really seemed to enjoy our rides also. We were beginning to feel comfortable and very happy with each other. We were having fun. Smoky had a friend, and so did I.

Then I began to notice a problem.

Smoky with author in the saddle. This was our first official ride although all we did was stand there. Fall, 1988

Smoky and author getting used to the activity in and around Dick's tree nursery winter, 1988

6 Dashed Dreams

It was happening again. I knew I couldn't keep ignoring the problem. Smoky had caught his left stifle just as we were returning home from a trot around an old alfalfa field next to our farm. For some time now, I had felt that something was definitely wrong with Smoky's hind end, and now I had to finally acknowledge that the problem wasn't going to go away. It felt as if Smoky had caught his hind leg on a branch or something, but of course, I knew he hadn't.

When I was competing in competitive trail riding, I had seen this problem occur twice on different rides. The second time I witnessed it happening, a horse had been stepping over a log obstacle that was being judged by the ride veterinarian. As the horse stepped over the log, his back leg had become momentarily paralyzed or locked, causing both the horse and rider to lose balance and lurch forward. The rider went off but luckily was unhurt. I really wanted to know what had happened. However, as this was a judged obstacle, I felt pressured to have my horse do the obstacle and clear the way for other competitors. I caught up with the rider that evening after the day's ride and learned that the veterinarian judge had told her that her horse had locked its stifle. I had never heard of that before. She pulled her horse from the ride, and I never knew what she did for her horse as follow-up.

Thanks to my experiences with NATRC, I realized what Smoky's problem was, but I still didn't have any expertise as to what was really happening or how to fix it. I also realized that if I let it keep happening, I was probably going to end up with damage and calcification in that joint. So when I got back home, I decided to call Dr. Carr. She listened to my account of Smoky's problem and said that she had an appointment out my way that afternoon and would swing by on her way back and take a look at him. Just before five, Dr. Carr drove up, and I brought Smoky out.

"My, has he ever changed since the last time I saw him, Barb. He's really come around for you, hasn't he? He looks so much better and acts like an entirely different horse. And no additional founder problems!"

I was delighted that she saw and acknowledged a big change in Smoky. He was at ease and looked happy and eager to see what was up. He didn't exhibit the "flight avoidance" behavior that had been his trademark. He had come a long way from that first visit.

"You know, Doc, I think Smoky must have realized that we helped him through that bout of founder. Anyway, he was much easier to work with after that, and I've really seen a bond develop between the two of us. He really trusts me now, and it's made all the difference in the world. I think I have a very special horse here. He has that something 'extra' about him."

Yes, I thought, *Magna Terra Smoky really has changed, and he definitely has grown on me.*

"You might have that right on, Barb. It's exactly what needed to happen. In the beginning, I was a little afraid that he might hurt you as he was so scared and unpredictable. I'm glad for the both of you that it worked out."

I really liked Dr. Carr. She understood the bond that Smoky and I had, and she genuinely liked working with animals. As she massaged and palpated Smoky's stifles, I explained again what had been happening while riding Smoky.

"I'm going to try some flexion tests on Smoky, Barb, and we'll see how he responds. I'll be holding up a hind leg for a bit and then letting it down. I want you to trot him out as soon as I let his hind leg down."

We did this for both hind legs with no real problems being observed. Dr. Carr then extended both hind legs forward and backward. As I watched Smoky being so cooperative, I couldn't help thinking, *Boy, I wish Alice and Larry could see this.*

"Well, Smoky appears to have a little fill and inflammation in both stifles, more so in his left stifle. I'd venture to say he'll outgrow this. He's only two and a half years old, and he's a good-sized horse. I don't know if time will solve your problem or not. Most veterinarians today would probably recommend letting his body parts catch up to each other."

"I know that time is often the best healer, Doc, but it seems to me that every time this happens, Smoky's stifle joints are suffering additional trauma. Isn't that friction and rubbing going to cause calcification and irreversible damage?"

We talked on and on and finally decided to wait a few days while we both thought more about it. We decided I should continue to ride Smoky as I wasn't doing anything strenuous with him and see what happened. In the meantime, we would both do a little research.

These days, I probably would have stopped all activity with Smoky and just let him rest. In those days, I didn't know a lot of the things that only time and experience bring. To tell the truth, I could not have pushed Smoky today like I did back then. Over the years, I have changed my philosophy about starting two-year-olds and racing them as three-year-olds. Now I feel that horses this young are just too immature both physically and mentally to hold up to all the stress that this level of training requires. Bones have not had time to strengthen enough, and joints have not had time to fully close. However, if I had not been so naive and such an amateur, I probably never would have done what I ended up doing to Smoky, *and* Smoky would probably *never* have even become a racehorse. I guess there are times when all the expertise and knowledge that one has cannot compare to the gut feelings that sometimes come with naivete.

There wasn't much information to be gleaned about the fixation of the stifle joint from any of the veterinary texts or magazines that I had. Apparently, this issue hadn't really garnered much interest or attention among veterinarians or horsemen. I decided to give Dr. Naugle a call. He had been my veterinarian for many years when I competed in competitive trail riding. He was always willing to help you with a problem and was very knowledgeable about lameness problems in horses.

When Dr. Naugle basically advised waiting the situation out because of Smoky's young age and because he felt surgery was too risky and didn't have a high success rate, I wondered if maybe I really should just have more patience. I really valued his opinion. It seemed that surgery didn't appear to be a very viable solution. I thanked him and told him I would let him know if I ever made it to the racetrack with any of my horses. Dr. Naugle had raced some thoroughbreds a few years back and did enjoy horse racing.

While Dr. Naugle's advice made sense and it seemed I should leave it at that, I kept having uncomfortable feelings about it. Earlier on, I had debated calling Larry, Alice's veterinarian, about Smoky's stifle. In a moment of bravery, I dialed his clinic and left a message. Larry didn't call back until the following morning. He seemed friendly enough on the phone and didn't mind my questions about Smoky. After hearing my explanation of the situation, he also advised against surgery, agreeing with Dr. Naugle that many young horses needed time to grow into themselves. Surgery appeared less and less of an option. Dr. Carr, in the meantime, had conferred with her colleagues. All conferred, "Give him time."

That night, I went to bed but couldn't sleep. Dick had been working hard on a landscape project and was sleeping soundly. I got up quietly, made a cup of decaf, and went to sit in my favorite rocker. Thunder had risen with me and now lay contentedly beside me.

I still wasn't convinced about Smoky's stifles. I couldn't figure how Smoky would outgrow this. I knew that the stifle joint was basically the same as the knee joint in humans; however, in horses, it was up in the horse's flank. It was the joint that enabled the whole hind leg to move forward or back. It seemed to me that the joint would become more and more irritated unless something was done to relieve the tension and friction.

By morning, I had convinced myself to explore the cost of the surgery option. I found out from Dr. Carr that it would about $150 for each stifle and that she could perform the surgery with just a local anesthetic. We talked about doing one stifle or both of them. The surgery involved making a small incision and severing a ligament near its attachment to the tibia. It seemed to be a relatively simple procedure. It was becoming obvious that I was not going to have any peace or rest just letting things remain status quo. I had to do something.

Alice and I had been in touch about Smoky's problem, and now I called her to tell her that I felt we should do the surgery. I explained what it entailed and what it would cost. Alice was not happy about the news, and her reaction shocked me.

"I'm not putting any more money into this horse, Barb. It seems we just get one thing fixed and something else pops up. He's not worth the money I'm having to put into him. All I see is a horse that appears to be one problem after another."

I had been afraid of Alice's reaction. She never had really liked this colt. I guess I should have expected this from her. I found myself asking, "What would it take to buy this colt from you, Alice?" Although I had been thinking about this, it surprised me how suddenly I had said it. I really had no idea if I was proposing to buy a horse that even would be sound to ride, let alone race. I had no idea if the surgery would help. But I really liked this colt. We were just starting to get somewhere together. I wasn't being practical, even very smart, but I sure didn't want to give up on Smoky now.

There was a pause on the other end of the line. I didn't know if it meant Alice didn't want to sell him now or if my question had surprised her. Then she responded, "Are you sure you want to do that? I hardly know what he'd be worth . . . and what if the surgery doesn't work?"

"It might not, Alice. I guess that's the chance I would be taking. Nobody seems to know much about his problem, let alone what will work. I'm probably not being very smart about this. Who knows?"

"Well, I would hate to see you get stuck with a lame or useless horse. How about making a trade?"

"What?"

"I mean how would you feel about trading some training for Smoky?"

"Well, sure, yeah . . . That would be great! What were you thinking?" I couldn't believe what I was hearing. Alice would actually let him go, even knowing that he had changed so much. "Who do you want trained?"

"I was thinking of Kroug. He has gotten so darn ornery. He hardly listens to me anymore. I used to enjoy riding him, but now it's no fun at all." Kroug was the big chestnut gelding we had used to trap Smoky. He was a gentle soul but big and smart enough to try to get away with anything he could. Alice really didn't ride him regularly enough or hard enough to keep him from being overly energetic. He'd kept pushing his limits until he was now quite spoiled.

By the time we had finished talking, it was decided that in addition to putting some retraining on Kroug, I'd also ride her old Orzel broodmare so that she would be a reliable horse for her grandkids to ride. Alice also had a long two-year-old Dunajec colt that she had bred for racing. He was small but correct and did have good racing bloodlines. I would start him to see if he had any racing potential.

Dick had been listening to this whole conversation. He had stayed at the kitchen table so he wouldn't miss anything. We had been grinning at each other throughout the whole conversation.

"So you got Smoky, did you? Congratulations, babe, I know it's what you really wanted. Hope you can fix those stifles."

His look melted me. I reached over and took his hand and kissed him. He pulled me into his arms and embraced me in a long, warm, and sensual hug. It felt wonderful. I didn't think any man could possibly hug as well as my new husband. My time, commitment, and involvement with the horses had been hard on him and, at times, very tedious for the both of us. It really meant a lot to me that he realized how important this was to me and to have his support and blessings right now. For now, the horses would have to wait. We had another matter to attend to. It was all that was on both our minds.

Later that morning, I was able to reflect upon this incredible turn of events. It had been so unexpected. Was it meant to be? Was it fate? Smoky had become mine, but would his stifle problem dash all the dreams that I had for us? Would Smoky end up as just one more statistic in the long list of race prospects that never even made it to the racetrack? Was I doing the right thing by listening to my gut feelings? Or was I being too premature in my decision? Would time prove me wrong? Would I regret this decision forever?

I breathed a sigh of both fear and hope as I dialed Dr. Carr's number to schedule the surgery.

7 On the Road Again

Smoky's stifle surgery was scheduled, of all places, at Dr. Larry's vet clinic. Dr. Carr didn't have the facilities to perform the surgery at the clinic where she worked, so she had an arrangement with Larry to perform her surgeries there. I wondered how Dr. Larry would react to seeing Smoky again.

Smoky entered the huge portion of clinic that was designed for large animals. He definitely was eyeballing everything and everyone, including Dr. Larry, whom I was happy to see had made a point of coming in to see his old outlaw. Smoky was impressive. This was our first trailer trip away from home, and although he was certainly looking around, he was not spooky or acting silly. He was being extremely cooperative and responsive. I could tell that Dr. Larry was impressed and surprised at how well Smoky was behaving. Needless to say, I was very proud of Smoky.

As Dr. Carr prepared for the surgery, she explained once again the incisions that she would need to make. We had decided to do both stifles as we both felt that was a good preventive measure. The surgery would be performed with local anesthesia. She had already administered the necessary tranquilizer and prepared the surgery area with a betadine scrub.

"Basically," she explained, as she pointed to the surgery site, "this procedure involves completely severing a stabilizing ligament right here at the stifle joint. It's really minimally invasive and won't even leave a scar."

I was amazed. It involved a much smaller incision than I thought possible, and as the surgery progressed, Dr. Carr made it look easy and painless. Everything went extremely smoothly and quickly, and Smoky never realized anything was happening to him. He was an oblivious and model patient.

I was able to take Smoky home the same day. The big thing now was time and rest. It would take two to three months for the healing to take place. I knew only too well from all my years of NATRC trail competition that time was a phenomenal healer, and I intended to give Smoky all the time he needed. As we carefully loaded Smoky into the horse trailer, I could have no way of knowing that the future would prove just how fortunate I had been to decide to do this surgery right now. Whether it was my naivete, uncanny good luck, God's intention, or honest-to-goodness destiny, the road that we had chosen to travel, although full of bumps and potholes, was looking as if it had some direction to it. We would find out several years later that I had indeed chosen the best possible fork in the road.

Smoky had to be fairly confined at first, but he seemed happy enough. Indy was there, in the pen next door, and I made a point of visiting Smoky frequently throughout the day to brush him, clean his stall, or just to pet him and offer him a carrot. Eventually, his confines were expanded. He was soon allowed to move around in a small pen.

Then I began the same ritual we had gone through when I first got him. We began our walks, slow, short walks at first, expanding into longer and slightly faster walks. I really didn't have any guidelines as to how much walking was good or bad, so we just did what we thought was appropriate. Smoky loved these walks as he had before. He loved to nibble along the way and mapped out favorite dining areas that he would literally drag me toward. It was another habit that would help him through another difficult recovery later in his life, and in so doing, he was establishing patterns and behaviors that would mold Smoky into the extra special and endearing character that he was becoming.

Smoky continued to heal well. He never showed any signs of lameness or discomfort. He never caught his stifle. He seemed happy, and that, in turn, made me happy.

When Smoky seemed well on his way to healing, he was turned out into a larger corral. In the meantime, Dick had been pressing to go on a vacation to New Mexico. We had never really had a honeymoon, so this would be our time to enjoy ourselves and our horses. There was some land there that he had seen and fallen in love with. He thought that it would be the ideal place for a "riding" vacation. It sounded wonderful to me.

"Let's do it," I excitedly responded. I loved the idea of being able to ride in a brand-new exciting area, and I was delighted at the idea of riding with Dick.

We decided to take four horses on our vacation; three of them would be Indy, Spring Fling, and Manteeya so that we could expose them to different situations and also build up their condition. The fourth would be one of Dick's favorite young colts that he had named Legs. The area that Dick chose for our vacation was north of Silver City, near the Gila Wilderness area in New Mexico. It turned out to be very beautiful country. The leaves were still turning, and the countryside was a vast expanse of rolling grassy hills backed up against the magnificent Gila Mountains. The weather was perfect.

After several dead ends and much backtracking, we found an area where we felt we would love to camp. It was open-range country, and we had no idea who to contact for permission to stay there. As it was late in the day, we decided to take our chances and unload the horses. The next day, we would take the truck and try to find the owners and perhaps get permission to stay. We tethered the horses to the horse trailer, leaving them with lots of hay and water. Indy and Spring were very used to being tied and adapted well to their new environment. I didn't even think about this being an unusual way for racehorses to be trained. We left Thunder to guard both the horses and our rigs. I knew things would be very safe with her there.

The next day, we were able to find the ranch headquarters, and we were delighted at how friendly the rancher and his wife were. They were happy to have us stay and ride on their land and even told us how to access the Gila Wilderness area.

We had a wonderful time until the day I decided to ride Indy with a cantle bag (a banana-shaped bag that tied onto the back of the saddle). We were planning on going a little farther than usual and decided to pack a lunch and carry extra water. All except the water went into the cantle bag. I never thought the cantle bag would be a problem as I had draped all sorts of things over Indy during his training. What a mistake! We had only gone a short way when Indy picked up a trot to catch up to Dick and Legs. Well, the cantle bag bounced slightly, and you'd have thought a mountain lion had leapt down upon him. He put his head down, and up went his back heels.

Off I went, right into a pile of rocks. I knew that I was hurt even before I tried to get up.

A trip to the doctor in Silver City revealed a broken collarbone and two fractured ribs. It was the end of our riding vacation. We returned home. It was to be one of several occasions when Smoky and I would be recovering from injuries at the same time.

It seemed like eons, but eventually, Smoky and I both healed. It was time to get Smoky back into training and get my other three horses in shape. ARA would soon be sending me their six horses to train, and I wanted to be ready. I knew that I would need help exercising and conditioning all these horses, so I decided to place an ad at the CSU (Colorado State University) vet school. The requirements I listed were the following: applicants should possess a genuine love of horses, should be able ride English style at a trot and canter (with the ownership of an English saddle very helpful), and have a three-to-four-hour block of time available several times a week. Pay would be $7 a ride. A ride included grooming, saddling, riding, and aftercare of the horse ridden. I was amazed to receive over fifty responses. Evidently, there were a lot of horse-crazy people out there who just wanted to ride a horse.

It was a time-consuming task, but I eventually whittled the number of applicants down to seven. From that list, I then decided on three prevet students (all girls) who seemed to genuinely want to do this. I kept the other four on a reserve list. The three girls I hired were so dependable and such good riders and horsemen that I never had to call on the other four. Eventually, time restraints narrowed it down to two girls, Lisa and Nancy. Lisa (Berg) turned out to be exceptional, and she would prove to be a tremendous asset in developing Smoky's racing skills.

Initially, we did all our riding around the nursery and on a very rough simulation of a racetrack that Dick had carved out for me in one of our unused alfalfa fields. I never let anyone else ride Smoky. I figured not only did he need the security, but also, I could best monitor how much riding and what he needed each day. I knew he was really extra special by this time, and I didn't want to take the chance of him having any kind of accident if I could help it. The three of us practiced walking, trotting, loping, stopping, turning, and going in front of and behind one another and side by side. Smoky mastered all but one of these things. When we added a little speed to our pace,

Smoky would not go up beside or pass another horse unless he had what seemed to be a football field between him and the other horse.

On one such day, I rode Smoky slowly back to the barn to find Dick waiting there. I dismounted and reached over to give him a kiss. He always had such a sexy look about him even when he was covered in dirt from working in the field. Lisa was riding Indy, so she took him over to the hitching rail and unbridled him. Dick had been watching us ride.

"You still can't get Smoky to pass Indy, can you?"

Indy had turned out to be an excellent horse to teach Smoky new things, but in spite of all this and all of my and Lisa's efforts, we hadn't been able to get Smoky to pass Indy or any other horse for that matter.

"No," I said. "I don't know what it's going to take to get him over that. He has so little confidence in himself. I wanted so badly for Smoky to be able to do this simple thing, but it had turned into a reoccurring nightmare for me. He loves our gallops around our makeshift racetrack and our trots and canters across the meadows, and he does everything else so nicely. He knows all the other horses and certainly isn't afraid of any of them, so it should be a piece of cake for him. Why is this passing thing such an ordeal for him?"

"I don't think you're ever going to make a racehorse out of Smoky. He's just too insecure. He doesn't have any confidence in himself. I've never known any athlete that's worth a darn that didn't have confidence in himself and think he was the best. I think you're wasting your time on Smoky."

Dick's comments surprised me, and they hurt. I had felt badly about the day's progress even before we began unsaddling. I had hoped for some words of encouragement. I thought back to the days when we had talked about making this racing venture work as a team. Now it seemed like this dream that I had envisioned and so excitedly embraced was dissipating right before my eyes.

"Sure wish you hadn't said that. You of all people know how important this is to me, to us, and how much work I've put into it."

I looked over at Lisa. She was trying to act busy, as if she hadn't heard any of this. Dick didn't say anything more. He just stared at me. Then he turned and headed up to the house. I felt like crying, but Lisa was still here. I straightened up and turned back to her.

"It's okay, Barb. I know that Smoky will make it. I see how far he's come."

I didn't know what to say. I patted Smoky, and as I did, a new plan came to mind.

"Lisa, you know what? This may be the time . . . I think we need to ride somewhere else, and . . . maybe we need to try something different with Smoky. What would you think about including Nancy and hauling the horses up to our ranch near Virginia Dale and riding cross-country in the foothills? We would have access to all kinds of ranch land, and there are miles and miles of rolling foothills to gallop across. With so much room, maybe we could trick Smoky into passing our other horses. It's worth a try, don't you think?"

"Wow. You bet! That sounds like a lot of fun! I'd love to. When do you want to start?"

Lisa was such a good sport. She was always game for anything. I knew I was very lucky to have her working for and with me.

"Great! Let me call Nancy and see what's on her agenda. Then I'll get back with you. Why don't you leave me your schedule and I'll try to work out some dates and times?"

We both were excited now. Forgotten were the sadness and hurt of the moments before. I could hardly wait to implement this new plan.

Unknown to me at the time, once again, as far as Smoky was concerned, this would prove to be another decision that was exactly the right one at exactly the right time.

Our vacation to the Gila Wilderness area..New Mexico
    photo 1: our rig, Dick is saddling Indy
    photo2: we often tied 2 horses to our rig and let the other two free roam and graze.
    Photo 3: Dick is teaching Indy not to buck with a cantle bag AFTER he bucked me off
    Photo 4: Spring Fling loved chasing the resident cattle away from our rig. I should have
        known then that perhaps I was training her for the wrong profession.

8   Stonewall Springs

1989

Stonewall Springs was the name given to Dick's ranch north of Fort Collins and near the very small and pretty town of Virginia Dale. It was a beautiful piece of land, and I thought the Indians must have treasured this place. Dick's ranch was comprised of 320 acres of rolling hills with a long narrow canyon the length of which meandered a happy, gurgling stream. Grass, water, and shelter were in abundance for the horses, and the varied terrain made for agile, sure-footed, and fit horses. Dick had tapped a spring in a pretty grove of cottonwoods and set up a small travel trailer to provide a self-sufficient, secluded hideaway from the pressures of the city and of work. He kept a small herd of horses here, and this was where Indy was born and raised. From this land, one had access to thousands of acres in which to ride. This was where we could condition and train Smoky and his companions.

Lisa, Nancy, and I were able to work out a schedule, and we would trailer three horses up to Stonewall Springs at a time. If just Lisa and I went, we would trailer four horses and ride twice. I generously upped the pay to $10 a ride. Everyone was happy. These girls just wanted to ride.

We had several loops that we used. At first, we just used the six-mile loop to leg our horses up and get them used to trotting uphill. We would always walk the down hills, and pretty soon, all the horses stopped on their own as soon as we reached the top of a hill. We would walk down, and then we were off again. Gradually, we increased the distance and the speed of the loops. The horses loved it, and we loved it. Many years later, when I would again come in contact with Lisa, she joked about how scared she had been at first, galloping across the uneven and sometimes challenging terrain. She said she hadn't wanted to appear a "woose" (our term for "chicken") and so gritted her teeth and stuck with it.

Eventually, the time came to address Smoky's pet peeve—passing. I already had him thinking this was a game and it was fun. So now he was ready to be tricked. On one of the loops, there was a nice sandy road used by the rancher who owned the land to check his cattle. It had a nice easy gradual climb to it and good grassy footing on either side. I asked Lisa and Nancy to trot on ahead a short ways and stay about ten to twelve feet apart. I was going to try to lope Smoky between them. I waited until Smoky got worried that his friends were leaving. Then I asked him to pick up a trot and then a lope. I started singing as I often did when I rode. We cantered right past his buddies. Smoky didn't even realize what he had done. I made a fuss over him anyway. We did it again, and this time, Lisa and Nancy were closer together. Again, he passed with flying colors.

I was ecstatic and feeling so full of it and brave that I decided to try it one more time, with Lisa and Nancy coming even closer together. But this time, if the passing worked, I wanted Lisa and Nancy to ask their horses to run after Smoky as soon as he had passed and try to catch him. Again, Smoky passed between them. As soon as we had passed, I asked Smoky for more speed. Smoky always liked going fast, so he delighted at this. Then when he realized Indy and Manteeya were coming after him, he kicked into a gear that blew me away. We were flying.

I remember thinking, *Man, do I have a racehorse under me!* Manteeya and Indy couldn't catch him, and he was having the time of his life. I knew that day that we had overcome Smoky's demon. It would only get better from this point on.

When we all finally pulled up, the three of us all wanted to talk at the same time. None of us ever guessed it would be so easy nor that it would be so successful. We were all very happy campers. I would remain on a high all the way home and into the next day and the next day!

After that, Smoky actually looked forward to his little races, with the passing included. He loved the fact that no other horse could catch him. He actually went from being a low horse on the totem pole to king of the hill in the pasture of horses he lived with. The change in his attitude and demeanor was absolutely amazing. He took over the pasture. He ate at the first tub of feed. Manteeya became his number-one girlfriend. Indy became his loyal little sidekick. The others rated lower. Smoky had arrived.

No one could have been happier over this change of events than I was. I wondered how many other potential racehorses could have benefited from a place like Stonewall Springs to overcome some problem in their psyche, how many other racehorses would have relished the opportunity to gallop across these open fields with their manes streaming back, their nostrils filled with the sweet fresh mountain air, and their muscled bodies rippling in the sun. I wondered how many racehorses had ever had this opportunity. Did their life simply involve the tedious routine of going from stall to walker to racetrack and back again? It was not the way I had wanted it to be for my horses. I hoped this new approach would reflect kindly when we arrived at the races.

Not long after this, ARA's six horses arrived. Heidi and Keith, two of my favorite ARA people, came with them. I had met all the horses in an earlier visit to ARA's ranch in California. My favorite of the bunch was Kit Chamanet. "Kit" was a sweetheart of a mare, very willing and eager to please. She was a very pretty bay with a nice eye and wonderful conformation.

Another mare, Ninatchka, was a different matter. She was a gorgeous chestnut mare, well-built and sturdier than Kit—but did she have an attitude! And she was terribly overweight, indicating that she had not been ridden or exercised much at the farm in California. She would bare her teeth at you and lay her ears flat back against her head. Although she never kicked me, she always seemed as if she were about to. I initially did not like her and was concerned that her attitude would prevent her from attaining her potential. However, as the weeks progressed, I found her coming around little by little. She lost some weight and began to look forward to her carrots and attention. She would even prick her ears forward on occasion. She seemed to realize that she didn't have to put on her defensive bluff quite so regularly. She started to express a more likable personality. She had evidently run up against somebody she didn't like or respect and had gotten away with this bluffing behavior for some time. It would take time and trust to overcome this. I hoped that we had enough time.

Of the others, SK Kaybabb was the prettiest and the easiest to ride. She was a delight to work with, and Lisa and Nancy always wanted to ride her. She had the disposition and the build to be the best of the bunch, but she would prove to be the worst. At the racetrack, the jockeys would actually fight over who would get to ride her in a race. She looked like a small thoroughbred. However, I was to learn that her pedigree favored Western pleasure and trail work and she did not have the competitive edge or the desire to win a race that a racehorse needs.

The race meet at Adams County was to begin the second week in May and run through the end of July. Before that, I needed to take my trainer's test. I was very apprehensive. I had studied hard and hoped that I would do well. The stewards administering the test were very pleasant. I remember Ed Hafeli the best as he personally congratulated me on making a very rare 100 percent on the first part of the test. He also informed me, however, that I made a number of errors in the second part, mainly involving claiming procedures. I did pass the trainer's test, however, and I was very proud of that.

Soon after, we hauled the horses up to the racetrack and set up our stalls. This did not go without a few problems. On the ramp off Highway 85 and going to the racetrack, I heard a terrible thud, and all forward motion of my vehicle and the horse trailer came to a stop. I think my heart must have skipped a beat or two. I was barely able to get my rig onto the shoulder of the road. It was one time that I was really appreciative of a good shoulder on the side of the road. Many parts of the state and of the country really didn't have much of a shoulder at all.

I was not much of an auto mechanic, and I had no idea what was wrong with our truck or what to do about it. After regaining some of my composure, I decided my best plan was to leave the rig and walk about three quarters of a mile to a country store I saw down the hill and on the road going east. I hated to leave the rig and the horses and all my tack, but at the time, I did not see any alternatives. Unfortunately, this all happened before cell phones were invented!

Thank goodness for the little country store. I actually ran most of the way to the store, where I found a pay phone and called Dick to the rescue. Fortunately, he was in the office and not out in the field on some landscaping project. I explained the situation, and he felt that the drive shaft had gone out. He told me that I would be able to continue onto the track if I put the vehicle in four-wheel drive and proceeded slowly. He would have the truck repaired later. When

I returned to the vehicle, I found another motorist had stopped to assist. He confirmed that the drive shaft was the culprit and waited to see that I got the rig moving. It was not to be the last time I would experience vehicle problems hauling horses, but it was the first with so many horses aboard, and it was quite stressful. I did arrive, if a little harried, safely at the racetrack.

ARA had provided a groom as promised. Her name was Louise, and she turned out to be a wonderful help. I would saddle and ride the horses, and she would clean the stalls and brush up the horses. It kept us both very busy, but we worked well as a team. It was hectic at first, getting used to a new setup and learning track rules and courtesies plus attempting to meet riders, jockeys, and other trainers. We did not even have access to a hot walker so had to spend time hand-walking the horses I rode. This all took up precious time, and as the track was only open from 6:00 a.m. to 10:00 a.m., I would end up exercising the rest of the horses in a field located behind the race barns.

Smoky was to prove to be the most difficult of all the horses. He was really hyped up, being at such an exciting place. He loved the racetrack. In fact, he loved it so much that it was difficult to pull him up at the end of his gallops. He always wanted more, and he always wanted to go faster. When I pulled him up at the end of his workout to backtrack him off the track, he would watch for horses that were working or two-minute clipping (that being essentially any horse that was going a little faster than a normal gallop). He would whirl on a dime and go racing after them, and many times, it would be without me as I would be on the ground, wondering how he had dumped me once again. Each time I had to backtrack him off the track, I swore I would be ready for his antics. As I galloped my horses in an English saddle, I would lock my legs around his girth and vow I would stay on. But he was extremely quick, and much of the time, he won.

Although I was forty-six at the time, I attributed my *youth* and good physical condition to the fact that I was never injured badly enough not to get up on my next horse. And thank goodness the gate crew and trainers at the track liked me enough to put up with all this. They would even bet on how many days in a row I could stay on Smoky. It was also good that they saw me ride so many other horses and stay on them. It gave me a little credibility. I never did cure Smoky of this habit, and it was something we had to deal with throughout his racing career.

With legs and feet to be taken care of after the horses had been exercised, Louise and I were working almost all day with scarcely a break. ARA thankfully sent another helper. Sometimes it was Heidi, sometimes Keith. Both were excellent workers, and I loved both of them. Eventually, I also ended up persuading a quarter-horse trainer to lend us an arm on his walker when he wasn't using it. I learned later that the $25 per month that I gave him paid for the rental of the whole walker (four arms), but it saved us immensely time wise, so we were grateful. Up the shed row from us, a quarter-horse trainer had two sons who were both jockeys. This is how I came to know John Hood, who would become Smoky's first jockey.

I also learned that I would need to lease my horses out to different individuals so that I could enter two or three horses in the same race if need be. Arabians were a small and an emerging breed, and all the Arabian trainers had to cooperate and enter as many horses as we could to fill the races offered to us. As a trainer could not enter another horse in a race if he/she was the owner of one, I had to put Smoky in Mom's name, Manteeya in the Stonewall Springs name, Indy in my sister's husband's name, etc.

Finally, the day arrived. On Wednesday, May 17, I got to enter Smoky in a maiden race to be run on Saturday, May 20, 1989. The term *maiden* refers to a horse that has never won a race. The distance of the race was six furlongs (a furlong being one-eighth of a mile). I also entered LL Manteeya and SK Kaybabb in the race. The favorite in the race would end up being Sahibers Diamond, a mare owned by Jane Teutsch. The racing program listed her odds at two to one. Smoky's was the long shot at nine to one. Since this was a small county meet, horses only had to have one official timed work to qualify them to enter a race, and Smoky had worked three furlongs in forty-seven seconds—not exactly an earth-shattering time.

We all worked hard and long hours seven days a week, but when I look back on those days, I realize that they were some of the most rewarding and cherished days of my life. I would not have traded them for anything.

Lisa posing Smoky for his Racing ID supplement
March, 1989

Lisa and Manteeya getting ready
for one of our many early morning
rides at Stonewall Springs February, 1989

Some of our young horses
enjoying life at Stonewall Spring

9 Smoky's First Race

1989

It was the night before Smoky's first race. It was what we had spent all these months preparing for. Was he ready? What more should I have done? I wished we had a couple more weeks to prepare. On the other hand, we had to jump in at some point and find out what Smoky could do, what he was made of. I had to find out if my training strategies were on target at all. Would I be made a fool of? Would Smoky fail to break from the gates? Would he even make it to the gates? Would he remember the things he had learned, or would he balk at passing other horses? Would I get the saddle on correctly? Would it be tight enough, too tight? Would the bridle reins break? Would Smoky get scared and get loose in the paddock and run back to the barn? Would he dump the jockey in the post parade like he had dumped me so many times?

My head was full of all these thoughts, and my stomach was in knots. I was a mess, but I was an excited mess! I knew I would get very little sleep this night. I hoped my concerns and fears hadn't rubbed off on Smoky. How would I make it through tonight and tomorrow? I got up and retrieved a novel I had been reading and tried to read. I found myself turning the pages but having no idea of what I had read. I turned to some note paper and started writing a list of things I needed to remember to do tomorrow. It might be a good idea to have a list to check off. That way, I would hopefully remember everything that needed to be done. Manteeya and SK Kaybabb were also in Smoky's race, so I had triple the items to organize.

Our race would be the last race of the day, going off at 6:14 p.m. I had already planned out the gallop schedule for the morning as the other horses still had to be taken care of. Smoky would also gallop that morning. I dared not leave him a day without some form of exercise, or he would be too much of a handful at race time. I made a note of bath times for the three horses racing today and then their feed times, when to remove hay and feed from the stalls, and who would be in charge of each horse. I had already set out bridles and equipment needed for the races as well as the red-and-purple outfit I would wear to match my racing colors. Dick had bought me the red jumpsuit that I intended to wear as a birthday present, and I added the accessories of a purple belt and a purple necklace and earrings. I would not own my own racing silks until 1990, the following year. I had special-ordered a red-and-purple bridle, halter, and lead rope and had saved these to be used on Smoky. I made a note to clean brushes, to check for tight and secure horseshoes, to braid manes and forelocks, to have water and a syringe for rinsing the horses' mouths, and to set out a nose cleaner. I even made a note to have buckets of carrots ready for the horses after the race. I wanted to reward a good performance, even if it wasn't a win. I made a time schedule for myself and Louise and Heidi. I redid the lists to make them neater and more organized. I hoped I had covered everything. I turned off the light and tried to get to sleep.

    I realized that I must have fallen asleep at some point, for I heard the alarm ringing, signaling that it was 4:30 a.m. I hopped out of bed, excited for the day ahead. My camper was parked just behind the stable area, so I was at the barn, ready to feed the horses before 5:00 a.m. I always liked greeting the horses in the morning. Their friendly and hungry nickers and whinnies made me feel so happy and content. As I doled out each horse's allotted amount of grain, I gave each horse a general look over to make sure no injury had occurred during the night and then checked and refilled their water buckets. Everyone looked fine and happy. Then I went for some coffee and waited for the others to arrive.

    The morning's program went without mishap. It was good to be busy, for it took my mind off the race to be held later in the day. At noon, however, when we had finished, I felt the jitters return. I reminded everyone when we would need to return to the barn and thanked them for a good morning. The race was getting closer.

    I decided to spend some time studying the program. There wasn't much to study as most of the horses didn't have past race performances. However, Sahibers Diamond, owned by Jane Teutsch and trained by my friend, Crystal Milewski, did. She had run a second in her last race and was the favorite at two to one. Smoky was listed as the long shot at nine to one. Smoky would break from post position four, Manteeya from two, and Kaybabb from post position six.

Preparation for the race went well. Then it was our call to walk over to the saddling paddock. The excitement in the barn was evident. The horses knew something different was up. I had already planned to lead Smoky over myself as I felt I could be the reassurance he might need, and I needed to be involved and busy with something. He had been walked over to the saddling paddock many times during practice sessions, so this was not anything new to him. Even so, he picked up that today was going to be different. I worked on keeping him quiet and made sure he walked next to Manteeya so that he knew she was going to the same place.

When we got to the saddling paddock, another trainer held Smoky for me as I saddled him. He was a quiet man, and he dealt with Smoky's excitement well. This was my first real saddle. Man, I hoped I would do it right. I concentrated on every aspect. It seemed to take forever as my hands were shaking, but we got it done. I quickly checked things over, and then I had Smoky circled around the paddock and took my place in the saddling ring, where John Hood would join me for riding instructions. John came toward me; we greeted each other and shook hands. We had already talked race strategy earlier that morning.

"Just make sure he knows Manteeya is there, John. We don't know how Smoky will break from the gates or what he will do. Just try to give him a good clean trip. You know him. Just see how things play out. Good luck, and have a safe trip."

Then it was "riders up." Smoky was jigging and hunched up a little for the mount, but John knew him well and, with a "not so good" boost from me, arrived in the saddle without any trouble. Smoky tried to get away and run off, but we were both ready and prevented any episode. A quick pat on the neck, and Smoky was in the post parade.

This was it. What a relief to have gotten this far. How fine Smoky looked! Manteeya too . . . and, of course, Kaybabb. Sahibers Diamond looked so confident. Would Smoky beat anyone in this field? I prayed to God to let this be a good trip for Smoky and the others. I prayed to my grandfather Saunders in heaven also. *Grandpa, please help this be a good race for Smoky, Manteeya, and Kaybabb. Please let them all come back sound.*

Then they were at the gates. I was beside myself with excitement and nervous energy. I prayed they all would be good in the gates. I strained to see. Someone was acting up. Was it Smoky? *Please don't touch his ears. Please be gentle with him in the gates.*

Then the bell rang, and the gates sprang open. The horses were out and running.

I looked for a gray horse. All the horses had broken about equally, and Smoky was in the middle of the group. Then Celes bolted for the lead, and I saw that Manteeya, bless her soul, was chasing him. Thank goodness the break had gone well. Another worry was over.

Then the unexpected happened. Manteeya was absolutely flying and overtaking Celes. Suddenly, she was in the lead. I could tell Smoky saw her, for he too raced by Celes. Shivers ran through me. My two horses were now in the lead. How awesome they looked! I prayed that they could maintain their run. Manteeya seemed to know Smoky was chasing her. She dug in and continued to lead. What a tough and determined mare she was! To my utter amazement and delight, Manteeya kept leading down the backside and into the clubhouse turn. Out of the turn, she was still leading.

"Go, Manteeya, you can do it! You can do it!" I yelled as if she could hear me.

Smoky was still chasing—and now the two of them were widening the gap between them and the rest of the field by leaps and bounds. Manteeya was awesome. What a mare! There had to be ten lengths between the two of them and the rest of the field. I felt immense pride flow through me. If nothing terrible happened in the last moments of the race, we would run first and second. What could be more exciting than that?

But wait—Smoky was moving up. He was flying! I started to wonder if he would pass Manteeya. Would she indeed let him? For a few precious moments, Smoky seemed to hang, content to be at Manteeya's shoulder. Then suddenly, he oh-so-easily kicked in a new gear and literally flew past Manteeya right at the finish line. It was Smoky by a head.

Oh my lord! He had done it. He had won. And Manteeya had shown more promise, more guts, and more determination than I could have ever hoped for. I wished she could have won too! What a dream of a race though, to run first and second and for both horses to beat the others so convincingly. I could hardly believe that Smoky seemed to know exactly where that finish line was. His first race, and he timed everything perfectly. His first race, and he had won it. He did everything right, including passing. I was absolutely and totally ecstatic. I flew to the winner's circle.

John rode up, grinning from ear to ear. I ran over and congratulated him profusely, all the while hugging and petting Smoky. Smoky was more excited now than before the race. He seemed to be saying he loved this game. I swore he now knew his purpose in life, and I knew I had one hell of a racehorse.

Although Dick had not come up for this race, Alice was there to enjoy Smoky's accomplishment. It was a wonderful feeling to be in the winner's circle. I hugged Smoky repeatedly and never stopped smiling. The photographer was so taken with the race that he later gave me an eagle-eye photo of the race showing the immense distance between Smoky and Manteeya and the rest of the field. I have cherished that photo to this day. Smoky paid $14.60 to win. The exacta (a bet on Smoky to win and Manteeya to run second) paid $139. I wished I'd have placed a bet on him and on his exacta with Manteeya. Just the same, Smoky would earn a whopping $389.75 for his victory, and I thought I was on my way to becoming a millionaire.

We had made it to the races, and even more amazingly, we had won. In spite of all the obstacles thrown at us, we had made it to the races, and we had come out a winner in every sense of the word. It made me really ponder how close it had come to us not even being here, not just once but on several occasions. I wondered where we would be if I had followed popular advice and not elected to have the stifle surgery done. What if the founder had been just a little worse? What if I hadn't thought to use Stonewall Springs and two great riders to help me teach Smoky to pass? Even more unbelievable, I marveled at how many circumstances had come together at exactly the right time to make all this happen. What if I hadn't married Dick, or what if Dick hadn't known Alice? What if I had taken a teaching job in Fort Collins? What if I hadn't seen that article about horse racing at Adams County? It made my head reel to think about how many things had worked out and come together at just the right time.

Smoky had definitely shown me how things can go wrong. I could not even begin to guess how many horses never made it to their first race when things went wrong. How many horsemen's dreams were shattered along the way? How many talented equines lay by the wayside? How many potentially great racehorses never even got the opportunity to prove it? Sometimes it seems easier to give up on a horse than to see things through. Maybe finances were an issue, or maybe time was a factor, or maybe those horses didn't have a "Stonewall Springs"!

The "EAGLE EYE VIEW" of Smoky and Manteeya battling for the "WIN" in their first race .... Adams County Fairgrounds, May 20th, 1989

Smoky in the Winner's Circle.. shown with Alice Pollock (left) and author, John Hood (Jockey) May 20th, 1989

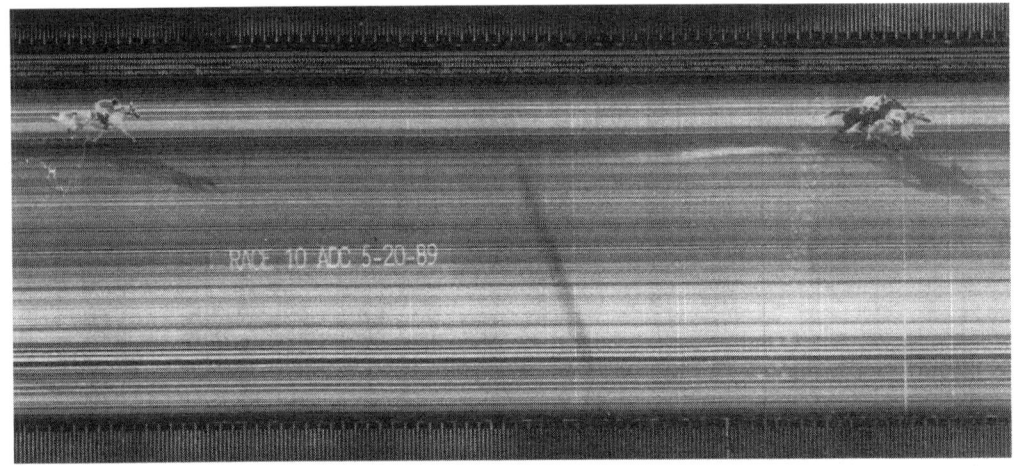

Photo Credits: Gene Wilson and Associates Photography

10   Kit, Ninatchka, and Manteeya

Amid all the excitement of Smoky and Manteeya's awesome race, I now had to concentrate on Kit and Ninatchka as they would race tomorrow. Smoky and I had gone to the test barn after his race as a requirement for winning. He had still been very excited, but a bath and thirty minutes of walking quieted him down enough that he was ready to give a urine sample when he was taken into the test stall. A blood sample was also taken, and now both he and Manteeya were back at our barn, bedded on a clean bed of golden straw, and each was happily munching on a treat of chopped carrots.

I was relieved that Smoky was so good in the test barn. Although he was always ravenous and was always looking for food, he did not take long to produce a urine sample. In the beginning, I had been afraid that he might not feel comfortable enough around strangers to give a sample. Many horses would not, and many grooms spent a long time in the test barn waiting for their horse to pee. When your horse would not urinate, it meant leaving the test stall and walking more circles in the area provided for just that.

Back at our barn, everyone was settled and happy. Even Kaybabb was munching on carrots, for although she had finished next to last, she had done everything else correctly. It was to be the first of several disappointing races that she would run. This was really an experimental year for both ARA and myself. I was brand-new to this sport of horse racing, and we were both racing bloodlines that were basically unproven, although Smoky did have one half brother (out of the same sire) that was racing back east named Ibn Bint Hilyuri. Most horse people only call horses half brothers if they are out of the same mare. I always felt horses should also be called half brothers if they were out of the same daddy (just like people are), and so I considered Smoky and Ibn Bint Hilyuri half brothers.

The following day, Kit Chamanet and Ninatchka both ran huge races, with Kit not only winning but also setting a new track record for six furlongs by a full one and one-fifth seconds. Ninatchka ran second, eight lengths behind. I, who hadn't come down from my high the day before, was completely and totally above the clouds. If I hadn't been hooked on horse racing before, I certainly was now.

Smoky's next race had him facing the champion and older horse named Silver sp Carter. Kevin and Mona Hussein had brought Carter and several other good racehorses down from their ranch in Wyoming to participate in this race meet. They had done very well the previous year, with Silver sp Carter carving out a name for himself as the best Arabian racehorse around. Smoky faced his first defeat while running his heart out the entire length of the stretch. It pained me to watch him try so hard and yet lose the race. However, it was a sign of things to come as he had run remarkably well against the toughest racehorse around. Smoky, at three, was just a baby, with only one race under his belt. He had given Silver sp Carter fair warning indeed.

Up next, on June 10, was the Korbel Performance Arabian Cup Stakes Race for three- and four-year-old horses. Silver sp Carter did not qualify for this stakes race as he was an older horse. However, both Smoky and Manteeya did. Mom and Dad came up from Colorado Springs to watch the race. Mom was listed as Smoky's owner as a trainer was not permitted to have more than one horse in a race if he/she also owned horses. Manteeya was listed under Dick's mom's name. The race turned out to be one that brought fans in the stands to their feet and all of us yelling and cheering with all our might. Smoky and Manteeya completely electrified the crowd, this time battling furiously the entire length of the stretch, with Smoky once again drawing away right before the wire. I must have yelled and cheered them on for the entire six furlongs. It was as exciting as it would be watching Secretariat win the Kentucky Derby years later.

As Smoky and Manteeya were slowed down by their jockeys after the finish line, I turned to Mom and Dad. "Can you believe how Smoky knows exactly where that finish line is? How has he learned that? I swear he loves beating Manteeya right at the wire. I'm so glad you came up for this race. I don't think it could have been any more exciting." Mom and Dad both agreed.

I put my arms around both my horses, and we headed down for the winner's circle. Although I was ecstatic for Smoky, I felt so badly for Manteeya. She had once again run a *huge* race. She wanted to win so badly, and she never gave up trying. As in their last race, the rest of the field was again well back.

When we all gathered in the winner's circle, Mom, as Smoky's registered owner, wasn't sure what to do. As I was busy with Smoky, Heidi and Louise helped her out, and she even got to drink champagne out of the large trophy cup that was presented.

Smoky, with just three races to his credit, had now qualified as a "stakes" winner. In just a few short weeks, he had given notice that he had arrived on the racing scene and that he would be a force to be reckoned with. Little could I have known, even in my wildest dreams, what an *unbelievable force* he would become.

If I thought I couldn't get any *higher* or more excited, I was wrong. The Baby Doe Arabian Cup for mares was slated next. I would again have three entries in the race: Kit, Ninatchka, and Manteeya. Kit was by far the favorite, but before the race, I told Louise and Heidi that Ninatchka had been training really well, and she now looked and felt like a racehorse, so watch out. She didn't disappoint, for it proved to be another thrilling finish, with Ninatchka roaring down the stretch to catch Kit in the last few yards before the wire. It was photo finish. Kit had battled gamely as she always did, but Ninatchka wanted this one, and she was fit and ready. In just a few short months, Ninatchka had changed from a fat and sour mare into a beautifully muscled, determined, and successful racehorse. Her ears were no longer pinned back, and her eyes had lost their threatening look. She was a happy mare now, and she too had come to love this racing game.

Alas, the race meet had to come to an end. Although I hated to see our last race come and go, I knew that I would cherish these days forever. It had been an experience beyond my wildest dreams. My small stable of horses had outdone themselves, and I had come to realize that horses seemed to love this sport just as much as humans. That is what made it so much fun. My horses, especially Smoky and Manteeya, really loved this racing adventure. In addition, I had made the acquaintance of many very special people and had begun friendships that I would cherish to this day.

When the final results were tallied for the race meet, I found that our barn had captured four out of the five top horse awards, with Ninatchka, bless her heart, capturing top honors. I had made top trainer, and Heidi had made top owner for ARA. Smoky had held his own, placing second in the overall horse standings. Indy and Manteeya had both broken their maidens. We had had a blast, and we had won more than our share of races.

At the end of the meet, I thought to express my appreciation to the stewards who had been so helpful and friendly and forgiving of the mistakes that I made. I gave them a box of chocolates along with a thank-you note. It was something that I have never regretted doing as they were so appreciative that they even showed the letter to the governor. They also later told me that in all their combined years of stewardship, they had never experienced such a nice gesture. Most of the comments they received were complaints prompted by disgruntled trainers, owners, or fans and were usually very negative. I began to appreciate the job of steward a whole lot more, and I was very happy that I had made that gesture toward them.

As for Smoky, he would leave Adams County with four races under his belt, earning two firsts, one second, and a third. Best of all, I felt he had developed a lot more confidence in himself and his ability. I was thrilled at the enthusiasm and the desire to win that he had exhibited. This small short race meet had been just what he needed.

All was not as good on the home front, however. All the time and energy that I was committing to racing was creating serious stress on our marriage. It definitely was taking a lot of my time, and even though I tried to make it home whenever I could, I was away too much of the time. Even I had not realized the time, energy, and dedication that racing horses demanded of an Arabian horse trainer. Because our purses were small, we had to be jacks of all trades, and that definitely kept me at the barn during most of the daylight hours. By the time nightfall came, I fell into bed and was sound asleep in no time. It was demanding, but I loved every minute of every day. Well, there may have been moments, but they sure paled in comparison to the highs that just kept coming my way.

So it was that when Silver sp Carter's owners, Mona and Kevin, kept talking about and trying to persuade me to participate in their upcoming race meet in Wyoming, I couldn't resist. I had the bug and found that I didn't really want to quit this newfound enterprise and go home. I had not yet broached the subject of going to the Wyoming meet to Dick and was not looking forward to doing it. This racing bug had hit me very hard, but I also felt guilt about not being at home enough.

But guilt did not win out. Dick and I had some very long and meaningful talks, and we had a great time while I was home. However, after a short stay, I headed up to Energy Downs in Wyoming with all four of my horses in tow. I had to acknowledge that I was hooked. And I was selfish. I loved this sport. I had some good horses that I had spent a lot of time developing. I really hadn't wanted to quit after just getting started.

Smoky would face several new faces at Energy Downs, and one of these horses was a talented gelding named High Ideal. He was trained by Duane and Pat Richardson, and Duane made it known right away when I met him that High Ideal would be the horse to beat at this meet. The big race here was the Energy Downs Arabian Cup, and it was to be run at a distance of six and a half furlongs.

The track announcer gave Smoky a new name that day. He was labeled as the "Colorado Invader." Unknown to me at the time, this would be an endearing term used to introduce Smoky for many years to come. The Colorado Invader did more than invade that day. He demolished the opposition, including High Ideal, by over eight lengths. Manteeya ran a valiant third, coming in behind High Ideal. Smoky led wire to wire for the victory. It was a style that he would become very proficient at and one that would earn him many victories over the next few years.

Then all too quickly, this meet was also over. Mona and Kevin and a few of the others were heading up to Montana for a series of races there. I longed to go with them. Montana had always held a compelling lure for me. I loved the immense expanse of rolling hills with tall grasses and the beautiful peaks of the Rocky Mountains that were found there. But I had promised Dick I would return home, so go home, I did.

On the drive home, however, I kept thinking of how I could arrange going back up to Montana. Once again, I didn't want to quit. I knew I was addicted. What could I say?

As it turned out, Dick was not especially upset or antagonistic when I ventured to talk about Montana and how I would really like to go there. Surprisingly, we ended up totally enjoying our short time together. I realized we both had decided to call a truce and let things fall as they may for this short interval. It was wonderful.

Then I was on the road again. The trip to Montana was awesome, just as I had envisioned. En route, I stabled the horses for the night in a set of pens outside Buffalo, which was just south of Sheridan, Wyoming. The pens were not far from the highway and a restaurant up the road but otherwise were fairly isolated. It had never occurred to me back then to be worried about being a woman alone with four horses. Of course, I had Thunder with me, and I doubted anyone would want to tangle with her. She was such a loyal and protective dog, and I loved her dearly.

When I arrived at Kalispell the next day, some thoughtful and enterprising teenager had already bedded four stalls for me. What a delightful greeting! This kid really knew the secret to making some quick cash. I was tired and not looking forward to setting up stalls. It was wonderful.

This race meet was to be a little more challenging. It was the first of several fair meets where the carnival rides were immediately adjacent to the horse barns and the racetrack. The fireworks display that occurred each and every night wasn't much farther away. It was quite an experience, and I thought my horses were going to crash through their stall doors when the first fireworks went off. The loud noises and bright lights were so darn close. I had to stay by my horses for the duration of the firework displays and try to soothe and relax them. I marveled at how cowboys (and even the Indians in the later stages of our Western expansion) had ever trained their horses and ponies to accept the roar of muskets and rifles firing right next to their ears. I doubted that any of my horses would have made very good frontier mounts for either the cavalry or the Indians.

Because of the conditions (terms) of the races offered, Manteeya would be my only horse to race at Kalispell. She won easily. I was so happy for her as she had worked hard and long for this victory. Her jockey was the bug boy (apprentice) T. J. Francis, and although we were all happy and excited about the race we won that day, we would team up again with TJ, and the outcome would not be near as joyous.

It was only a short trip to our next destination, Missoula. Here, I would meet Pam Roylance and her talented seven-year-old gray gelding, BW Rasputin. Pam was the first person to explain the IAHA (International Arabian Horse Association) sweepstakes program to me. Before this, I hadn't been aware that the IAHA was involved with racing. Their program guaranteed $400 for each win an IAHA horse recorded, and Rasputin had already won quite a bit of money as an IAHA racehorse. Unfortunately, I had just missed the incentive deadline for registering a gelding into the program, and it would now cost me $3500 if I wished to nominate Smoky. I didn't think we could ever make a profit if I had to pay that much as it would take nine wins just to pay back the registration fee. So I decided not to waste the money. If only I could have known what a huge mistake I was making!

Before the day of our first race in Missoula, it had rained a great deal, and the racetrack was very muddy. MCA Maariya was the post-time favorite, but I was confident that Manteeya could beat her. Once again, TJ Francis was Manteeya's jockey. Looking back, I was to wish that I had never even entered this race.

The race started well, with Manteeya racing four wide and going for the lead. But on the first turn, TJ made a terrible mistake by asking Manteeya to drop down to the rail too quickly. Manteeya could not get hold of the muddy track, and all of a sudden, she slipped and fell. Two horses behind her could not avoid her, and they tumbled and fell over her.

My stomach literally turned over inside me as I watched this dreadful scene unfold. A terrible and enormous sickness flooded through me. Forgetting everything else, I frantically rushed down to the track. I hoped against hope that I would find Manteeya without a broken leg. I knew that if that had occurred, Manteeya would need to be put down. I found myself desperately praying to Grampa Saunders. *Please! Oh, please, may she be all right!*

Then I saw that Manteeya and TJ were both up and moving. All four legs were working! *Thank God!* Manteeya, bless her soul, was shaken and covered in mud, but she was in one piece. Miraculously, nothing was broken! We had been terribly lucky and/or very blessed. *Thank you, Lord, and thank you, Grandpa!* I was shaking and wet and cold, but we had all come through this in one piece. *Dear Lord, thank you, and thank you too, Grandpa! I just know you had to have been there for Manteeya.*

Later on, Manteeya came up a little sore because of a bruised hip, but I was so very grateful that was the extent of it—or so I thought. For the time being, we had been terribly fortunate, but this fall and injury would be the beginning of a hip problem that would plague us throughout the rest of Manteeya's racing career.

Kevin Hussein would later tell me that he had been concerned with rookie TJ's daredevil riding. I guess I hadn't paid enough attention to this. I should have been watching some of the thoroughbred races that TJ rode in and picked up on this. I paid dearly for my mistake and knew it sure could have been a lot worse. I vowed to be more thorough and careful in my jockey selection in the future. If I had lost Manteeya in this race, I doubt that I could have stayed in racing. I wondered once again if Grandpa had been listening to my prayers before the race. Had he helped us once again? I really felt that somebody had to be looking out for us. Whatever or whoever had dictated the outcome, I felt so terribly fortunate and blessed.

The upcoming schedule of races was not in our favor. The week following Manteeya's tragic fall, the four-year-old derby, a race that Manteeya had already been nominated for and paid into, was on the card. Now it was just three days away, and I had to decide whether or not to enter her. Although she was responding well to the liniment and bute that we had given her, I didn't want to risk any further injury to her by racing her before she was ready. I also knew that I had to discontinue with the bute medication as any trace of it in her blood sample following the race would not be permitted and would result in disqualification and fines etc. This race would also be her third race in just two weeks, with a tiresome haul in between. Talk about asking a lot from a mare. But Arabians are tough horses, and she was a tough mare when she was fit and sound. The question was—was she physically and totally sound? Or would her hip bruise prove to bother her? Would she hurt herself more if I raced her? Finally, after much indecision, I decided to enter with the option of scratching her from the race if she didn't seem up to par. She would have a new and more experienced jockey aboard.

It proved to be touch and go right up to the time of the race, but Manteeya seemed to be fine and anxious to run. It turned out to be a good decision as Manteeya not only won the race but also beat some very tough colts in the process. One of horses she outran was named Bright Fortune, and he would become a champion sprinter in the years ahead, and even Smoky would find him challenging.

From a pay phone on the fairgrounds, I phoned Dick to tell him about the race. He was always glad to hear from me even if it was hard to converse with all the fair noise in the background. I also had to keep feeding the pay phone at regular intervals, which wasn't an ideal situation.

The rains picked up again, and Smoky almost didn't get to run in the open-stakes race because of a very muddy track. Kevin and I even met with the stewards and called the AJC (Arabian Jockey Club) to discuss canceling the race. However, the skies eventually lightened up, and the rain subsided. Even so, we were all uneasy. We all remembered Manteeya's race, and none of us wanted another race like that.

Everything turned out for the better this time, however. Smoky ran an awesome race, even though BW Rasputin beat him by a length. Smoky not only outfinished the favorite and current champion, Suede, by seven lengths but also put away Silver sp Carter by an amazing ten lengths—and Smoky was still only three! Everyone, including me, was very aware of a new superhorse on the horizon.

With Smoky's race over, our two weeks at the Missoula Fair were up, so we packed and got ready to move on to the Ravalli County Fair in Hamilton, Montana. Here, Spring Fling would finally get on the tote board, running her best race to date and placing third.

Manteeya's race started out as another nightmare. In the race right before Manteeya's race, an accident had occurred, and Manteeya's jockey was injured and raced to the hospital. The pony person who was to take Manteeya in the post parade was our jockey's best friend, so he went to the hospital with the ambulance. Most horses have a pony horse and rider to escort them throughout their prerace warm-up. It helps settle a nervous or excited horse and also keeps the racehorse from running away and using all his energy up before the race. With both her rider and pony person off to the hospital, Manteeya was left not only without a jockey but also without a pony horse.

I was called to the jock's room, where I discovered that the only jockey left that could ride was an older jockey who only rode on occasion. He also weighed in at 140 pounds (twenty pounds over the assigned weight for Manteeya). This never would have been permitted at a big track, but we were at a fair meet, and we didn't have a whole lot of choice sometimes. I also found out that the only pony horse available was a mule. Manteeya hated mules. I chalked this race up as a total loss. However, our new pony person assured me that everything would be just fine, and sure enough, after the initial introduction, Manteeya and her mule got along fine. The post parade went without incident.

The race even began well. However, coming around the far turn and into the stretch, Manteeya ran into a wall of horses. It looked impossible for her to get through. I feared she wouldn't be able to get by all these horses. But just then, a small hole opened up. I saw Manteeya heading for it and watched in amazement as she literally barreled through it. She was free and in the open. My heart sang for her as she raced to the wire for her win. A bystander beside me was aghast; he swore Justin, Manteeya's jockey, didn't have the balls to take a horse through that small an opening. I chuckled to myself. What he didn't know but I did was that Justin didn't have a choice once Manteeya saw that hole and decided to go. Justin was just along for the ride!

Smoky going to post - Energy Downs, Wyoming. 1989
Friend and fellow trainer, Kevin Hussein walking beside Smoky

THE GIRLS....

1. Manteeya with my best friends, Vicki Thorson (purple top) and Susie Witter.

2. Ninatchka in the winner's circle for the "Baby Doe" stakes race

3. Kit Chamanett with some of the ARA team elebrating Kit's win

"B. J.'S TANDY LEATHER FEATURE" BLANKET PRESENTED TO THE WINNER

Ravalli County Fairgrounds September 1, 1989   **LL Manteeya**   Barbara Jagoda Evans . .
Magnificyt. . . . . Place   Race 6   Barbara Jogoda Evans . .
TM Alis Nazzi . . . . .Show   1 Mile + 70 Yards   2:05.2   Justin Dillon. . . . . .

LL Manteeya winning her race in Hamilton, Montana with her overweight jockey and her "Mule" pony.

Photo credits - Steinleys Photography

11 A Restless Wind

Sadly, our year of racing had come to an end. The Ravalli County Fair in Hamilton was the last race meet on the Montana circuit, and we had just run the last race of the meet. It was time to go home. What a wonderful summer this had been. It had been exciting beyond my wildest dreams. Yes, it had its disappointments, its scary times, and its moments of worry and doubt. But the highs had been so overwhelmingly thrilling and rewarding that I knew I was completely captivated by this new endeavor I had discovered.

I marveled at how lucky I was to have been able to do all this and at how so many factors had amazingly come together to allow all this to happen. Never in a million years could I have predicted that my life would change so radically. I knew Mom and Dad questioned my mental sanity and thought I had abandoned my safe and secure world as a teacher for the life of a gypsy. They felt I now lived in a world of unsavory and questionable characters who gambled away their lives and lived from one day to another with no great ambitions. How could I explain to them how totally and unquestionably happy I was? It was the most rewarding, satisfying, and enjoyable life I could imagine. Yes, it was hard work. There was never a day off, and the day began early and ended late. I worked rain or shine and lived a solitary existence in a small camper with minimal amenities. But the thrill of watching the horses that you had invested so much time, love, money, and devotion in win or even just run well in a race was beyond description. It was the most tremendous rush I had ever experienced. I knew I wanted more, but for this year, at least, it was over—*or was it?*

Upon my arriving home, a phone call from Alice brought new possibilities into the picture. Alice was thrilled that Smoky and I had done so well. It didn't hurt that she was receiving 3 percent of Smoky's earnings, and Smoky's earnings were adding up at a nifty pace. Back when Alice and I had first made the trade that was to make Smoky mine, Alice had later stopped by to deliver Smoky's registration papers. At that time, she had also asked Dick if he might be interested in a breeding that she had paid for to a very nice Arabian stallion located in nearby, Loveland, Colorado. She had brought along a picture and a copy of his pedigree to show us. Both Dick and I liked what we saw, and as she had no use for the breeding and because we didn't want to take it for free, I suggested that maybe she would like a percentage of Smoky's earnings in exchange. We all thought this would be another good trade, and we eventually decided on 3 percent of Smoky's earnings. It was such a long shot that she would get anything out of this deal that we laughed about it. After all, Smoky would have to earn a whopping $10,000 for Alice to retrieve her $300 stud fee. That seemed a huge amount of money and totally unimaginable to us. Little did we know!

As I listened on the phone, I heard Alice claim that someone else was also thrilled about how well Smoky and I were doing. This mystery person was a friend of hers who was racing Arabians in Paducah, Kentucky, and his name was Bryan Braithwaite. Alice went on to tell me that every time Smoky won or placed in a stakes race that was sponsored by ARC (Arabian Racing Cup), Bryan received a check in the mail. So naturally, he was pretty pleased and wanted to know all about Smoky and the person who was racing him. He had called Alice to find out what was going on.

I was confused. "Alice, who is this 'Bryan,' and why is he getting checks from Smoky's races?"

Alice replied, "Bryan had SW David on lease when I sent Cyroga to be bred, so he is, in fact, the breeder of Smoky. Evidently, ARC—the Arabian Racing Cup program—pays breeders a percentage of every purse when one of their progeny runs first, second, or third. Bryan had no idea that Smoky had exchanged hands and that he had made it to the races until he started getting these checks. Bryan and I haven't talked or corresponded in a long time."

"Well, that's a surprise and interesting. What else did Bryan have to say?"

"He wants to talk to you. In fact, he gave me instructions to give you his phone number and to tell you to call him. I have to warn you though—Bryan is quite the wheeler-dealer, so watch out." Alice didn't offer much more information other than Bryan had sold a few horses for her.

"Okay, thanks, Alice. I'll give him a call and let you know what he has to say."

With that said, we said our goodbyes and hung up. I was anxious now to talk to this mysterious new player in Smoky's life.

The next day after I had finished at the barn, I called Bryan when I thought that he too might be finished with morning chores. He seemed friendly enough and was fun to talk to on the phone. He reiterated how surprised he had been to receive the much-appreciated checks from ARC and that he was even more surprised when he found out that Smoky was the reason behind them. He asked how I had come upon Smoky and then went on to tell me about Arabian racing in Kentucky. I discovered that he was also the trainer of Ibn Bint Hilyuri, the half brother to Smoky that I had read about earlier.

It was fun talking to Bryan. He was a character and very entertaining. It was obvious that he loved to talk and joke. He also seemed intent upon impressing me and went on to tell me about an upcoming stakes race in Paducah. In his half-joking, half-serious voice, he challenged me to bring Smoky back there and race against some *"real"* racehorses.

I chuckled to myself and thought, *Boy, does he have a big head!* But the seed was planted. I was interested and tempted. In fact, I was *very* interested and *very* tempted. The big issue was how was I going to bring this up to Dick?

I tried to wait for the right moment, but I knew it was going to be hard no matter when or how I approached Dick with this idea. After dinner, I felt I had tell Dick now. There wasn't much time to get ready if I wanted to go back to Kentucky, and the quiet mood of the evening seemed as good a time as any.

Dick was not happy to hear the news. His face and posture told it all. I knew he could hardly believe that I was asking him this. I knew he felt that he had conceded enough already. I had been gone all summer. Ever since my return from Montana, he had been looking forward to a somewhat normal family life with a wife who stayed around some.

But . . . how could I not do this? It was an opportunity to go all the way to Kentucky, to try Smoky against some of the best horses in the east. Smoky was at his peak; he was fit, loved winning races, and was, I felt, ready to show the racing world that he was for real. If I lost out on this opportunity, would I ever have another?

Once again, I made promises to Dick that I wondered if I could keep. Even though Dick had not given me an answer, I quietly started making plans for my trip. I started calling chambers of commerce to inquire about fairgrounds where I might be able to stable overnight during the trip. Dick would overhear some of my phone calls but wouldn't say anything. Ever since the racing had finished in Wyoming, he had tried to make more time for just the two of us whenever I was home. He tried to help me adjust to a difficult home situation, but I think he also realized that he had to let me go. He wanted me to be happy at home and knew that I would not be happy if he tried to prevent me from going. He knew I was unhappy at home, but I never felt he really understood my problem with our relationship. I knew he had to be frustrated and that his life had to be in a turmoil. I felt sorry for him in that regard.

Unhappy and disappointed, Dick finally relented. I knew it was tough for him. I resolved to be as good and as thoughtful as I could be until I left. But it was really for the wrong reasons. I was doing it because I felt guilty, and guilt was not a good reason. In turn, Dick tried to smooth over the rough edges and helped me set up the truck and horse trailer for the long trip. We rigged up an adequate and easy watering system for the horses. It was great having a camper on the truck as I always had a place to stay at night that was close to the horses. I had everything. The only thing I would need to buy on the trip was gas. It was time to go. The wind was not the only thing that was restless in this Colorado town.

12   THE HEARTLAND OF RACING

Well, we were almost on our way. This trip would be farther than I had ever traveled with horses aboard. Not only did I have a big horse trailer, but also, I would be hauling hay, grain, and equipment and had a camper on the truck to live in. Dick had helped me pack wisely and as efficiently as we felt possible, but four horses that were about to run the races of their lives, and a female human needed a lot of basic essentials. We were also trying to save money plus maintain diets the horses were accustomed to, so we had loaded a week's supply of our grain and hay. I would gradually change the horse diet as dictated once we reached Paducah.

The horses knew something was up as I had kept them penned up in smaller corrals the night before rather than leave them in their big grassy pasture. It made it easier and faster to catch and load them for an early departure. Tom, my horseshoer, had freshly shod each of them with new race plates, and Bridgette had written new health certificates. I had already alerted the race office in Paducah that I was coming and had reserved four stalls there. I had also sent ahead copies of all four horses' registration papers and past race performance records as well as Manteeya's and Smoky's nomination fees for their stakes races.

I was excited but a little nervous also. My stomach was a little queasy, but I felt it would settle down once I got a few miles down the road. One by one, with Indy first, I loaded each horse into the horse trailer. It was a blessing that all four horses loaded well and that they were good haulers, especially when they were together. They had bonded well over the spring and summer and were very good buddies. Hay bags as full to the brim as I could stuff them hung in front of each horse to provide nourishment and distraction during the long trip. Smoky was totally content, tied between his two best friends, Indy and Manteeya. Spring Fling had been the last to load. She really didn't have any specific job except to perhaps fill a race for Manteeya in the eventuality there were too few mares to make a race go. It could turn out to be a good investment as I felt Manteeya had a very good chance to win a race there. Sometimes it was hard to get enough mares for a race, and I didn't want that to be the case in Paducah if I was going to haul Manteeya that far.

Dick and I hugged each other for a long time. Then it was time to go. I stepped into the truck, and as I drove out the drive, I turned and waved one last time. I had butterflies in my stomach. I really had no idea what lay ahead.

It was always so great to get the first few miles of a new trip under your belt. It was like the first few minutes of teaching your first class of a new school year. The initial feeling was one of jittery nerves, but once you were into it, everything started to flow naturally. The degree of tension lessened, and eventually, learned skills and knowledge took over. The realization that things were going well and the feeling that you were headed into a wonderful new experience settled in. How lucky we were to be able to do this! It was something Smoky and I loved and shared. We both loved the challenge, the thrill of racing, and the exuberance of winning. There was nothing like it. I just hoped we would measure up to the competition in Kentucky.

I wondered if Smoky could thrill the crowds there as he had done in Colorado and Wyoming and Montana. He had already, in his short career, developed quite a fan base. He was consistent and very competitive and always gave each race his very best shot. In short, he was honest, *and* he was *good!* He had all the characteristics that an avid racing fan loved to see in a racehorse, and he also had many cute and likable personality traits that endeared Smoky to me and those who knew him. He was quite the character.

En route, I was very fortunate to have obtained permission to stay at a very nice fairgrounds in Central Kansas for our first night. Small Western and Midwestern towns that had the luxury of a fairground facility were often very happy and generous in sharing their facilities with horsemen that were passing through. They seldom charged a fee and only asked that you clean up after yourself and the horses. The horses loved these stops as it gave them a chance to run and buck and roll and explore all the interesting smells of a new place as well as search for tender morsels of grass.

This fairground offered a huge outdoor arena as well as several medium-sized pens and numerous small pens and stalls. I opted for the large arena and unloaded all four horses and turned them out together. As each horse was released, it was fun to watch. Spring was unloaded first and waited for Manteeya to join her. Then it was a quick leap up into the air and an immediate roll in the soft irresistible dirt in the arena. Smoky now couldn't wait to be released and showed his eagerness and displeasure at having to wait by whinnying at the top of his lungs. As he was unclipped and backed out of the horse trailer, I knew he would roll as soon as he was released, so I made sure I led him far enough away from the gate and fence so that he wouldn't get caught up in it. He was still rolling when I released Indy, so Indy plopped down right beside Smoky, and as he did, Smoky jumped up. Then realizing what Indy was doing, all the horses dropped to their knees and started rolling as a foursome. What a bunch!

Then it was up and off to the races; around and around the arena they roared. It was entertaining to watch. They were having a ball, and I loved watching them have so much fun. I wondered how many racehorses got to do the things these four did. They were quite lucky, and I knew also that I was very lucky to have four racehorses that got along so well.

When they settled down and started looking for morsels of grass, I decided I'd better attend to setting up water buckets and setting out hay. When they were completely settled and relaxed, I would bring them their grain buckets. In the meantime, I could clean out the horse trailer and pack hay nets for tomorrow's trip. I started to think what it would be like at a big racetrack like Paducah. Smoky and his buddies were headed for the heart of racehorse country. I hoped it would be as exciting and green and beautiful as I anticipated.

The next day and a half flew by, and I couldn't believe it when we were actually in Kentucky. Here we were, right smack in the heartland of horse racing. I knew to expect lusher vegetation the farther east we traveled, but I was totally taken back by the denseness of it. After living for so long in the wide-open spaces of Colorado, I found the narrow roads lined with trees and thick vegetation almost suffocating. It amazed me that I had forgotten how dense the vegetation could be in the east. I was further surprised by the absence of substantial shoulders alongside the roads. It was rather scary in certain places as there wasn't any room at all for avoiding potholes, wildlife, or other unforeseen road hazards.

My thoughts turned to thoroughbred racing. For many years, I had watched the running of the most famous of horse races, the

Kentucky Derby. The excitement and the grandeur of the event always filled me with a great deal of emotion. I envied the trainers and the jockeys and also the grooms who worked alongside the horses who had earned the right to be there. I listened intently to every comment and story that was told on each horse. I marveled at the beauty and the exquisite muscle tone of each equine. I wished that I could be there in whatever role to share the excitement of the day. Back then, it was just a dream. But now I was here. Granted, we weren't at the Kentucky Derby, but we had made it to Kentucky, and we had made it on the tail of a whirlwind. What a year this had been! We had only started racing six short months ago, and here we were, in Kentucky.

True, the Kentucky Derby was not held in Paducah, where we were headed, and the derby was a race that we would never have a chance to participate in. That prestigious race was just for three-year-old thoroughbreds, and although Smoky was a three-year-old, he certainly wasn't a thoroughbred. Thoroughbreds were really the deluxe class of racehorse. They were significantly faster than Arabian racehorses, and they commanded the public attention and therefore raced for much larger purses. The general public was really unaware that Arabians even raced at a flat track. I hadn't even been aware of Arabian racing until a short year ago.

Another fact not widely known is that thoroughbreds would not even exist were it not for the Arabian horse as this is who they evolved from. Back in their history, Arabian horses were the pride and joy of the Bedouins. From their fine animals had come three truly great and renowned Arabian horses that were to become the forerunners of the modern-day thoroughbred. Those three immortal Arabians had been the Godolphin Arabian, the Darley Arabian, and the Byerley Turk. Every racing thoroughbred can literally trace its ancestry back to at least one of these three Arabians. It is in honor of one of these Arabians (the Darley Arabian) that our top racing awards are named after.

My thoughts and reminiscences had made the miles past quickly. We were finally here! As we entered the stabling area, I looked around the facility that was to be our new home for the next several weeks. It was surreal! What I saw was a deluxe barn that contained twenty huge box stalls and a wide center aisleway down the middle. It was by far the best accommodations my horses had encountered in their whole racing careers. We had been allocated the four end stalls, and as our barn was the farthest from the racetrack, it was very private and quiet. There were only four other horses stabled in our barn, and they were at the extreme other end. Next to our barn was a huge grassy meadow where I was allowed to park my truck and camper.

I couldn't believe my good fortune. I was at the biggest, most prestigious racetrack that I had ever been to, and I was allowed amenities that had been totally disallowed at smaller tracks. This unexpected and greatly appreciated arrangement meant that I could sleep, eat, and reside immediately adjacent to the barn in which my horses were stabled. It also meant that I had an excellent and extremely convenient place to graze my horses and let them enjoy the outdoors and some sunshine. I was even able to rope off my block of stalls and let one or two horses out into the aisleway so that they could move around more and even visit each other. One thin rope at both ends of our shed row kept these athletic, fine-tuned horses contained. Looking back on those days, I am flabbergasted at what I did sometimes and am amazed that I got away with it, both in that the horses never hurt themselves and that no one ever really complained about my unorthodox behaviors—that is, until one time when I unwittingly tested the limits. I'll get to that episode later.

Our first day at Paducah mainly involved getting settled in. While the horses rested, I attended to all the paperwork involved with checking in at the race office and horseman's bookkeeper. A new racing license had to be obtained for racing in the state of Kentucky. Each state had its own set of rules and license fees and requirements. A financial account needed to be opened, and original racing certificates with win records needed to be submitted.

The following day, I dedicated to showing my horses around their new surroundings. I decided to start by saddling up Smoky and ponying Manteeya to the racetrack and then around the stable area. Back in those days, neither a helmet or a padded protective chest vest were required when you ponied a horse on the racetrack. Smoky, as always, was excited to see what new adventures awaited him and eagerly headed out with Manteeya at his side. As our barn was the farthest from the track, we walked by many barns on our way.

As we were passing one of the barns, I suddenly and unexpectedly heard a voice to the left and hind of us.

"Magna Terra Smoky, I presume!"

It took me back initially as I really didn't know anybody here, and to have someone recognize not me but my horse was totally unreal. I looked around to see a tall dark-haired man leaning leisurely against the barn wall. Almost immediately, I realized we had just met Bryan Braithwaite.

I laughed and responded, "You must be Bryan Braithwaite," and unknown to both of us at that time, a long and endearing and sometimes difficult and frustrating friendship had begun. Smoky and the man who had started it all had been reunited, and it had been the most unlikely reunion that Bryan could have ever imagined. It would change his life forever. And to Smoky's life, it would add adventures never dreamed of.

Bryan and I had a lot to talk about. He wanted to know all about how I had come to own Smoky, and I wanted to know all about his role in Smoky's beginnings. I found out a lot of things that Alice had never told me, including the fact that Bryan was the person who had the famous racehorse Orzel at his ranch outside of Phoenix, Arizona. Orzel was a gorgeous sixteen-hand-high chestnut Arabian stallion that had dealt the very famous and talented racehorse Comet his only racing defeat. Orzel had also been the stallion that Alice had wanted to breed Cyroga (Smoky's dam) to. However, Orzel proved to be impotent, so Bryan had asked Alice if she would like to breed her mare to the other stallion he was standing named SW David. Alice never gave Bryan a firm yes or no, so Bryan, not wanting to lose a complete foaling year, bred Cyroga to SW David. Bryan said Alice never accepted this change in plans, and as a result, he ended up hauling both Cyroga and six-month-old Smoky back to Alice's place in Nunn, Colorado, without being paid for mare board, breeding fees, or hauling. When I heard all this, I wondered if Bryan should be sharing some of the 3 percent of Smoky's earnings that Alice was receiving.

After we finished our barn chores each morning, Bryan and I began a ritual of daily lunch dates at Bryan's favorite eatery, the Cracker Barrel. I found myself looking forward to these informal lunch dates as Bryan was both very entertaining and informative. He knew a lot more about horse racing than I did, and unlike most trainers, he didn't mind sharing his knowledge and experience. He joked and laughed, and he was fun to be around. We quickly discovered how much we had in common. We even liked the same kind of horses, even down to the bloodlines of Orzel and Smoky (SW David). I started to realize how much fun it was to have someone around who was interested in the same things. It was what I missed with Dick. We started to spend a lot of time together. We would talk and talk, flirting and having a great time. I laughed and laughed, and the laughter felt good.

As days sped by and we awaited our first race, I fervently searched for a place to turn the horses out so that they could buck, roll, and play. Although we had a grassy area beside our barn for them to graze, there was no fence so that I could turn them loose. They loved their free time, and I felt guilty when I could not provide it. I wished that all racehorses could enjoy some turnout time. I felt that it kept my horses happy and relieved the stress often caused by constant stall confinement. More often than not, racehorses spend twenty-two or more hours a day confined to their stalls. It was no wonder habits such as weaving, cribbing, wind sucking, and pacing developed. It could be a very boring life. I loved the trainers who took the time to take their horses out to graze in the afternoons. However, some racetracks didn't even have any place to graze your horses.

In my search, the only place that I could find for turnout was a nice enclosed area on the other side of the racetrack. There was a beautiful bed of flowers in the enclosure that I knew I would have to protect from the horses, but otherwise, it looked like an ideal turnout area. I decided to ride Smoky and pony Indy over first and return for the other two later. I sat down near the flower bed and watched with delight as Smoky and Indy rolled and bucked and leapt into the air in their exuberance with their newfound freedom.

Then suddenly, Bryan appeared. "I knew it had to be you!" he exclaimed.

"What do you mean, it had to be me?" I replied. It wouldn't be the last time Bryan would begin a conversation with a statement that demanded one to ask a question in return.

"Haven't you heard the announcements over the PA system?"

"No, I haven't. They must not carry this far," I said.

"Well, the racing office is trying to figure out what is going on in their saddling paddock and wants whoever is there to get out right now. They are pretty upset to say the least."

"Oh wow, I didn't mean to cause a problem. No one was around, and I thought this was a neat place to let the horses have a little bit of freedom. We really haven't hurt anything, including the flowers."

"Barb, this is the saddling paddock, for Pete's sake. It's completely off-limits to horses and people except for races and scheduled practice schooling. It is especially off-limits to loose horses. You'd better get out of here unless you want to be ruled off the grounds. I can't believe that you are doing this. Yeah, maybe I can! When I heard the announcement, I knew it had to be you and that I had better get over here before they did. Now catch up Smoky and Indy and get out of here."

I did just that. It wouldn't be the last time that Bryan would bail me out of trouble. He did look out for me, and thank goodness he did.

In the schedule of races, Manteeya would be the first to run. It would be a filly/mare stakes race called the Bluegrass Downs Arabian Cup Distaff. I had asked Bryan which jockey he would use, and he had helped me out by introducing me to David Shepler. Manteeya was as ready as I could make her, but it was going to be a muddy track as it had rained a lot of late. I couldn't help but be anxious for her as her last race in the mud had been such a terrible disaster. As an extra precaution, Bryan encouraged me to enlist his horseshoer to nail special mud nails in her shoes so that she could get a better hold of the track. I questioned how these little nail heads could help very much. However, it seemed to be the accepted practice, and Bryan was adamant about having them. I also braided and tied up her tail so that it would not get weighed down with mud. She looked extremely fit and ready.

We were going into this race as the favorite, even though several mares had earned more purse money than Manteeya. Saafari, a gray mare by the famous and prepotent sire Samtyr, was the pick to win within the Arabian betting circle. She had just run second in a stakes race, finishing just behind the much-revered mare, Jessorca. Manteeya had not really faced the caliber of horses that several mares in the race, including Saafari and Abda, had. I wished Manteeya's jockey had been able to make weight as Manteeya would be required to pack his extra five pounds. In horse racing, one pound was felt to cost a horse one length in a mile race. It meant that Manteeya would be giving her opposition a five-length advantage in the race.

Horse racing, especially when you own a horse in the race and have worked with that horse to get it to the point where it is, can be the most exciting thing in the world. It can also cause the most butterflies. I certainly had the butterflies. This race was very special as it would be our first race in Kentucky. I wanted to prove that our horses from the western states were as good as the horses stabled here. Mona and Kevin had also made the trip east and would be racing Silver sp Carter. We had some awfully good horses between us, and we hoped they would prove just how good they were.

Manteeya ended up making all of us very proud. The mud and the extra weight didn't seem to bother her. She beat Saafari by three lengths, and the rest of the horses were well back of Saafari. She broke on top and led the whole race, so she didn't even have that much mud on her. I was so thrilled for her. She had just won her first stakes race, and she had done it in Kentucky. She had extra carrots waiting for her back at the barn.

Smoky's stakes race would not take place for another two weeks. I decided to put him in an open-allowance race to tune him up. It meant that he would be competing against the top racehorses at the track. It proved to be a very tough race, and he ran third. However, he had not only raced against the best but also raced against much older and experienced horses, and he had proved that he could run with them. His stakes race would pit him against his peers (three- and four-year-old colts). That was the race I badly wanted to win.

Bryan had two horses entered, Ziegfried and LP Nouveski. I knew that Ziegfried had a lot of speed and that Bryan would probably use him as a rabbit to get Smoky to use himself up early in the race. That would set Nouveski up to close on a tiring Smoky. Bryan and I had become close friends over the weeks I had been in Kentucky. I had even shopped with him to buy the trophies for the stakes races. However, it didn't mean he was going to let me walk away with any purse money that he himself could use. Right from the start, we were each other's toughest competition, and we were to remain tough competitors for the remainder of our racing careers.

This time, Bryan's strategy didn't work. Smoky took the lead right out of the gates, played Ziegfried plumb out, and never let any horse catch him. He won the race by an incredible twenty-seven lengths. It was like he was imitating Secretariat! It was an unbelievable effort. I couldn't have been more proud of Smoky. Bryan was absolutely stunned and amazed. He had been certain that no horse could outrun his speed horse, Ziegfried. Smoky had not only outrun Ziegfried but also totally demolished him and the rest of the field as well. When all was said and done, however, it was obvious that Bryan was very, very proud of the gray gelding that he had played such an important role in producing. He had felt that SW David would cross well with Cyroga. He had certainly proved that. I chuckled and wondered what Alice would think.

I really didn't think to do any research on SW David until years later, but when I did, I found it very interesting. I really knew very little about him except for some of his pedigree as I had all that from Smoky's registration papers.

SW David (SW for short) was foaled April 7, 1977. His dam was a Sambor daughter named *Sir* WMS Dambra (I wondered if the owner had wished for a colt), and his sire was a handsome stallion named Etiw. Although both Sambor and Etiw certainly could have passed racing genes on to SW, circumstances dictated that he would reach national recognition in the show ring. As he was a strikingly beautiful solid gray who measured 15.2 hands, he soon became a national show champion and, as such, was bred to mares who had excelled in the show ring.

In 1983, SW David produced his first racing offspring, Ibn Bint Hilyuri. Hilyuri, of course, was one of Bryan's top guns at the racetrack, and he would go on to win twenty-two races and over $55,000. SW David didn't sire another racing offspring until 1986, when Magna Terra Smoky was foaled. How ironical it was that an unplanned and unwanted foal would become SW David's real claim to fame. Who would have guessed that such a mating would produce the celebrity who would go on to set record after record on the racetrack and become the most publicized horse to ever run at Los Alamitos Race Course in California?

From 1991 to 1992, Roger Lang, who was converting from show-ring endeavors to racing pursuits, purchased SW for $50,000. Bryan was the broker, so to speak, who facilitated the purchase. It has always amazed me how Bryan showed up in so many of the events in Smoky's story. Roger was to utilize SW as his racing stallion. However, as Roger had been actively engaged in the show ring for so long, most of his mares were gorgeous, had excellent conformation, looked as if they could run, but had the attitude and mentality of the show ring. The resulting foals looked fantastic, looked like they could run, but the desire to win was not bred into their hearts and minds. Later in life, when SW David was finally bred to mares with racing in their blood, he produced some outstanding race and stakes winners, including Soaring Fastneasy, my own Li'l Smok and Lightning Road, and Roger Lang's LP Conquest, as well as Broyuri, Datrya, etc.

Sadly, SW David passed away in 2001 after a bout with colic at Roger Lang's ranch in Fallbrook, California. He was only twenty-four years old. Thank you for your best son, SW.

SW David
(Smoky's sire)

Cyroga
(Smoky's dam)

13 Returning Home

When it came time to leave Kentucky, I found that I had many things on my mind. This time, the racing was *really* over for the year. I was happy it had gone so well, and I was sad to see it end. I knew that I would miss the racing and that I would also miss Bryan. He had added a lot of fun and laughter to my life, and he had taught me an awful lot about horse racing. I wondered what it would be like to return home. I wished in a way that I didn't have to return home. Life was much more uncomplicated and much less stressful with the horses and Bryan than it was with Dick. However, the fact of the matter was that both Bryan and I were married and we had commitments to others. It was some consolation that although we had to go our separate ways, we both knew we would keep in touch and remain friends.

Soon, we were all packed up and ready to leave the Bluegrass State. I would head for Colorado, and Bryan would head for California. It was the end of the first week in October. I reflected over what a year this had been. This time last year, I could never have even dreamed that so much could have happened. Back then, Smoky was still recovering from stifle surgery, and I was wondering if he would end up sound, let alone be able to ever race. I had a broken collarbone and ribs resulting from our New Mexico trip. Manteeya and Indy had only just begun to gallop. Now a year later, I had an amazing stable of four horses who had outdone themselves. We had raced not only in Colorado but also in Wyoming, Montana, and Kentucky. Smoky, as a three-year-old, had run nine races (mostly against horses much older and more experienced than he was) with five wins, two seconds and two thirds. He had earned $10,435. Remarkably, Alice had already earned back her $300 stud fee.

What was truly phenomenal was that my tough and talented mare, LL Manteeya, had topped Smoky's earnings with $11,603. It was a huge amount of money for an Arabian to earn in 1989. She had raced an outstanding fifteen times with five wins, five seconds, and a third. A little later on, I would learn that she had been nominated for a Darley Award. That would be my introduction to the Darleys and to Dr. Sam Harrison, who had not only developed these awards but also instigated the ARC program that really promoted Arabian racing. Had Manteeya not fallen in her stakes race in Montana, she may well have won the Darley for four-year-old fillies. Bunny, who eventually won the award, had raced seven times with two wins and two seconds.

It was with anxiety in my heart and turmoil in my mind that I finally pulled into the driveway of our home in Colorado. Dick was very happy to see me and was very sweet and affectionate. He never mentioned my neglect in calling him very often. He was just happy to see me. I wished I could have been totally happy also, but I already felt a sick feeling in my stomach at having to deal with our home situation.

Bryan called almost every day. He loved talking on the phone. I thought that he had to be a "phone addict," and I started to kid him about always having a phone in his ear. It was fun and very easy to talk with him, and as always, he made me laugh. It annoyed Dick. He started to question the relationship that I had with Bryan. He asked why we didn't laugh and joke like Bryan and I did.

After only one week back at home, I came to realize even more that our strained relationship was impossible for me to deal with. I didn't know if I was right or wrong, but I knew that I had envisioned a much different scenario when we got married. I guess I hadn't looked at the whole picture of our relationship very well.

All during this time, Bryan was trying to convince me to come to California to race. He was sure that Smoky would do well. I was concerned that we might be overwhelmed by the competition there. I knew that I was still a very novice trainer and that I had a great deal to learn. I had never really learned many of the things that really good trainers need to do to care for their horses. I based most of my training on things that I had learned while competing in NATRC, which was an amateur sport with no purse money involved. Racing was the big leagues, with your livelihood dependent upon the results. That is not to say that competitive trail riding didn't teach and instill wonderful horsemanship skills in its competitors. Almost everything I knew about lameness and unsoundness, conditioning and the care of a horse, I learned from NATRC. I gleaned a wealth of valuable knowledge from this sport. What I now had to learn was more of the finer details of care, feeding, and conditioning to compete at a tougher level. I had to become more professional.

I knew that I was very emotionally attached to my horses, and I didn't want to change that. More than anything, I wanted my horses to be happy. To me, this meant having their horsey time just being a horse. I wanted them to have some time to run and play with one another and not be confined to a stall twenty-three hours out of every day. I went to great lengths to make sure they had grazing and playtime. However, my mistake of using the saddling paddock in Kentucky for playtime had been a huge professional blunder. Behaviors like that had to be things of the past.

For a long time, Dick and I talked and rehashed our situation. What we mainly did, however, was defend ourselves against the other. We were getting nowhere. Who was to say who was right or wrong? I just wanted out of it. I finally resolved the issue in my mind. I started to plan for my future, not *our* future. I told Dick that I wanted a divorce. I filed papers the next day before I could have a change of heart.

After that, I felt it would be better to move into Dick's camper that I had used all summer long. I parked it near the barn, and that was how and where I had spent the Christmas of 1989. Dick even helped me move my belongings into a storage unit not far away. I felt that I needed some time to sort out what I needed to do next, and I also wanted to stay around until our divorce was finalized. Dick was not opposed to me staying in his house; however, I thought that was asking too much, and it would make things more difficult for the both of us. I spent my time working with the horses and reading a lot. However, Dick's camper was small and basic, so every once in a while, I spent a night at a local motel and took a luxurious long shower and watched a little TV.

By keeping in touch with Jane Teutsch, I found out there would be a race meet in Holly, Colorado, in the spring and Arabians would be invited to participate. That news was a pleasant and unexpected surprise. This might be just what I needed. Holly was a small farming town located on the very eastern boundary of Colorado. Its biggest draw was a small racetrack that offered quarter-horse racing every spring. Jane and COBRA had worked with track management, and the results were that Arabian horses would be offered several races on the card, including two big stakes races. Lea Brent, who also raced some Arabian horses and lived near Jane, had committed to sponsor two Arabian stakes races with very attractive purses—that is, very attractive purses considering they were for Arabian horses. New hopes and dreams came to life, and I started to plan for that race meet. I rationalized that if I could make enough money at Holly to provide a financial cushion for my horses and myself, we just might be able to make it to California after all. I found a pay phone and called Bryan to tell him the exciting news.

Then I started to itemize the things that I would need to do. I realized that I only owned a two-horse trailer. The horse trailer that I had been using was Dick's. So I went shopping and eventually found a five-horse slant gooseneck horse trailer for $6,500. Even though it was a heavy old thing, it was the best I had come across at a reasonable price. I bought it.

I still couldn't believe it. How could we be so fortunate? Never before had Holly offered races for Arabians. I knew that Jane and Lea had done a lot of hard work to make this happen. Just the same, it was as if destiny had again favored us. Maybe this was our golden-brick road to California.

14 Aurzel — A Lesson in Determination

It was during this difficult and challenging time that all our weanlings needed to be separated from their dams. That meant that Dick and I needed to bring them down from their Stonewall Springs foaling grounds. They needed to begin the process of living away from their mothers, be halter broke, and learn to interact with mankind to a greater extent. Among the weanlings was a bay colt that I had named Aurzel. He was out of my mare Aura Maria and by an Orzel son named Brusally Orselar. Back in 1988, Dick and I had hauled two of our mares down to Showlow (near Flagstaff), Arizona, to be bred to Brusally Orselar in hopes of getting two foals that might make good racehorses. We were both very taken by Orzel (an awesome sixteen-hand stallion) and wanted some offspring with "Orzel" blood. In fact, I named Aurzel as a tribute to Orzel, using the "zel" part of his name as well as the same pronunciation. The "aur" part came from his dam's name. It was very interesting that although I hadn't known of Smoky or Bryan back then, Bryan had Orzel on lease in his barn and, in Alice's grand plan, Smoky's daddy was supposed to be Orzel.

Aurzel was a handsome, personable colt. He had a head start on some of his playmates as I had handled him a lot throughout his first months. He and Aura Maria always came up for treats when we trailered Smoky and the others up for our workouts. He had inherited the quiet, independent, but friendly disposition of his dam, Aura Maria.

Aurzel and his playmates had enjoyed almost a full year running and playing in the scenic foothills of Dick's front-range ranch. It was an ideal place for a young horse to grow up. It offered lush grass, gulleys and hills to run over and through, a sparkling spring-fed creek, lots of trees for shade, and ample sandbars to roll in. It couldn't be beat for developing strong legs and hooves and good lungs and heart, along with agility and endurance. Aurzel was a happy colt, and it made me happy watching him. I hoped he would someday become a good racehorse.

Although Dick and I were facing a divorce, we still worked together on projects that involved the horses. We both wanted to gather up our weanlings together. We hooked up the horse trailer and made the trip up to Stonewall Springs. Aurzel and the other weanlings loaded easily into our stock trailer from the catch pen that Dick had fabricated. They were about to begin a new chapter in their lives.

The day after returning to the farm, I went out to see how our newly weaned colts and fillies were doing. They all seemed content enough, having banded together for comfort and security in the absence of their dams. There had been the usual whinnying and calling for Mom, but as a whole, the weaning process was going smoothly with as little trauma as could be expected. They had been placed in a large semi-irrigated pasture where they could see our other horses and they could watch the daily activities of the farm.

As I approached Aurzel, I held out my hand to offer him a horse cookie (a small biscuit-like horse treat made from oats, alfalfa, and molasses). As he opened his mouth to take the treat, I noticed something amiss with his lower jaw. There was a huge ugly, raw sore on his lower gum. My first reaction was shock as it was so large and so unexpected. I let Aurzel have the treat (which he devoured with relish and no noticeable problem) and thought I'd better catch him up and have a better look.

He wasn't hard to catch as he had already developed a taste for these horse cookies. I gave him a good pat and a rub on the neck. He was a nice colt. He let me have a better look at his mouth, and I winced at what I saw. It looked like what you might expect to see if you saw a gargantuan stomach ulcer. It had deformed his lower jaw, and I thought it must cause him a lot of pain and discomfort, especially when he ate. Yet here he was, acting as happy as can be. Animals seem to be able to deal with a lot of pain and discomfort sometimes. Maybe it's because they don't reflect and worry about it as humans do.

I couldn't believe I hadn't noticed this before. However, when Aurzel's mouth was closed, it was rather hard to detect as his long facial guard hairs and heavy coat masked the enlargement. Still, I felt badly that I hadn't picked up on this before now. What could have caused it? It didn't really look as if a foreign body like a sliver of wood was involved. I wondered if he had taken hold of a metal rail in the cold of winter and it had torn the skin and some muscle away from his lower gum. But I didn't feel that explained the hard enlarged lump. I kept watching him. He had decided I had all the looks at his injury that I was going to get. I didn't blame him; I wouldn't want someone fooling around with my mouth if it looked like that.

Dick wasn't home from work yet, so I went to the phone and called Dr. Carr as I definitely knew I needed her to look at this new development. It was late afternoon when Dr. Carr returned my call. I described the problem, and she too was puzzled. We set up an appointment for the next morning. I couldn't get Aurzel and this terrible sore out of my mind. I slept terribly and was relieved when morning finally arrived.

It was wonderful to see Dr. Carr drive up. I wanted to get this colt over his discomfort and back to normal as soon as possible. It continued to amaze me how friendly and happy he seemed with this obnoxious sore interfering with every bite he took. Once again, he was about as good as any young active colt could be. He patiently let Dr. Carr examine his ugly, red, deformed lower jaw. She had never seen anything like it and was puzzled by it. We discussed possible causes, and although the metal rail idea seemed the most plausible, she was not sold on that cause entirely.

"Barb, I'd like to collect some tissue to examine and even send a sample in to have a biopsy done on it. I really don't like the looks of it, and we need to cover all the bases."

So we asked Aurzel to be good and patient a little longer while we obtained a tissue sample. I talked to him and tried as best I could to convince him that we were trying to help. Bridgette helped by sedating him some. Finally, she had her samples. She would call me tomorrow on her findings. The biopsy results would take longer. She would send that sample to CSU (Colorado State University).

True to her word, Bridgette called the next day.

"Not good news, Barb. I believe we might be dealing with a cancerous tumor. The results from CSU will tell us more. I'll let you know when they come in. There really isn't much we can do until then."

Cancer! I hadn't really thought cancer. This was more serious than I had thought. How had this happened to Aurzel? What was going to be involved now? How serious was this? I went to Dick's tree-nursery office, where he and Pat were working, and told him what Bridgette had found. Dick was very sympathetic. He liked Aurzel and was concerned for him. Dick and I were actually getting along quite well now. We just didn't bring up the divorce issue, and we kept out of each other's way except when things concerned the both of us.

The following week, I got a call from CSU. They asked if I could bring Aurzel in for an examination and possibly some X-rays. They wanted further information on this.

Aurzel was hesitant to load in the horse trailer all by himself, but with a little help from Dick, the two of us were able to lift him up and place him inside. He didn't even seem worried about being alone and went to eating the hay we had placed in the horse trailer for him. At least the growth on his lower mandible didn't seem to slow down his appetite. He was such a good-natured little guy. I hoped we'd find out some good news at CSU. Dick wanted to go with us, so he hopped in, and I started up the truck and headed down the driveway.

Our appointment was at 9:00 a.m. with Dr. Stashak. Several vet students greeted us when we pulled in next to the vet building. I got out and asked where they would like me to take Aurzel. As I opened up the door to the horse trailer, Aurzel was happy to see me. He hadn't even broken a sweat, so I knew the trip had been easy on him. It was to be a behavior that Aurzel would exhibit every time I hauled him somewhere. He didn't really mind if he was alone or if there was company. He was just a happy little soul. For a baby horse, he had a remarkable confidence in himself. The vet students were immediately impressed with Aurzel, and Aurzel basked in their attention. As I filled out paperwork, Aurzel was taken to a large box stall to await Dr. Stashak.

It wasn't long before Dr. Stashak arrived. He was a very handsome, likable person, and he had a nice manner with horses. He greeted Aurzel and went about examining his mouth. As he opened Aurzel's mouth, I asked if I might take some photos with the camera I had brought. I marveled again at how Aurzel cooperated and acted like the model patient. The vet students were equally impressed with him. As he gently examined the extent of the growth, Dr. Stashak explained to both me and the vet students what his observations were. He wanted to do a series of X-rays on Aurzel's mouth and asked if I would leave Aurzel there and call back late in the afternoon to pick Aurzel up.

I didn't need to call back as Dr. Stashak called me. I didn't take that as being good news. He asked if I would stop by his office so he could go over the X-rays with me. I thought, *Oh lord, please let the news be not too bad*. Dr. Stashak didn't offer any information over the phone.

It was not good news. Aurzel had bone cancer, and there wasn't any cure. The tumor was massive and would need to be removed. To contain the cancer, Aurzel would need to have his lower mandible sawed off just in front of his molar teeth. I was sick! To have this happen to this poor little tyke who was so trusting and so kind—it seemed impossible. Surely, I asked, there had to be some other recourse. What about radiation, chemo, or laser surgery? Dr. Stashak said he had hoped one of the other options would be feasible, but he had found the tumor to just be too large for anything else to work.

"How will he eat?" I asked. I tried to control the tears welling up in my eyes.

"Well, there have been other case studies where the lower mandible has had to be partially removed and the prognosis is good. The skin tissue is sewn up over the end of the cut mandible, and the horse learns to scoop up its food. Aurzel will probably need a special diet at first but will eventually learn to eat normal food."

I couldn't believe this was happening. I was heartbroken for Aurzel. I wanted to come out of this nightmare and find nothing like this had really happened. *Aurzel, you poor little tyke. I just want to take you home and for everything to be all right*. But the reality was that it wasn't.

We ended up scheduling the surgery a week from Thursday. That meant Aurzel would have nine days of being a normal horse. *Not really normal*, I thought, *but normal compared to what he would be*. At least he could enjoy the green grass in the hay pastures for a few days more. I took Aurzel home. It was the saddest drive I think I have ever taken.

The days moved slowly. I didn't want the next day to come. I couldn't concentrate on anything. I kept thinking about Aurzel. I didn't really know what to expect after the surgery. I really didn't know what to plan for. I didn't even feel like riding. I had a lot of things to get organized for the race meet at Holly—if I would even be able to go now. What would I need to plan for Aurzel? What postsurgery care would he require? Would it mean abandoning all my plans for racing this year? I had already sold Spring Fling as a pleasure horse as well as my nice pinto mare and a bay filly sired by Dosil. I had planned to take Smoky, Manteeya, Indy, a colt out of Aura Marie and Dosil named Stonewall Country, plus a filly of Dick's named Catcando (Cat) to Holly if I got to go. I planned to train Cat in exchange for Dick caring for my other horses until I could make other arrangements for them after the race meet. Now I wondered if all my planning and hopes would be dashed.

Mom and Dad had even offered me the use of their older camper trailer that they had stored in their backyard to live in at Holly. I had thought that it was wonderful that I would have a place to live and didn't have to try to find a place to rent. Dad had been spending time fixing the camper up and checking the tires etc. Mom was cleaning up the inside and was making new curtains for the windows etc. They said that they would even haul it down there for me. What wonderful parents! Now I had to put all these plans on hold, with the probability that I would have to cancel them entirely. Suddenly, our golden-brick road wasn't so golden anymore.

Because I was the one wanting the divorce, Dick got most of our possessions. I didn't ask for much. With the money I had received from the sale of my house in the Black Forest, I had paid to have his house remodeled, decorated, and furnished. Now that money was gone. I was the one who had wanted the improvements, but now I wished I had the money instead. The only things that were nonnegotiable were Smoky, Manteeya, Indy, and Aurzel. I had paid for them, and they were mine. Dick would also have to make payments to me on the $30,000 that he had borrowed from me for his business. He would not have to pay interest on the loan as he agreed to board the few horses I would have to leave at his place. Any vet and farrier expenses would be billed to me. I didn't argue about anything. I was just glad the divorce was going well with no glitches.

Then the day before Aurzel's scheduled surgery, I got a surprise call from Dr. Stashak. He had been researching Aurzel's problem and had found that a veterinarian at Cal State in California had been successful using massive doses of radiation on a similar horse patient there. It would involve a total of three massive radiation treatments, each ten days apart. He asked, "Would you like to try it on Aurzel? No guarantees?"

I thought that I had never heard better news. I couldn't contain the excitement that I felt. I agreed immediately, no ifs, ands, or buts.

Once again, Aurzel proved to be a model patient, and the first radiation treatment went well. Back at home, he continued to eat well, and I doctored his gum and jaw several times a day. He would need a lot of doctoring after the second and third radiation treatment, but when the time came, I found it was something I could handle without any help from Dick.

Plans to go to Holly were still in limbo. I didn't want to leave Aurzel's doctoring to someone else, so I decided I had better get busy and call someone in charge at the Holly racetrack. I hoped that I might be able to somehow take Aurzel with me. Paul Guerrieri, who was the stall superintendent at Gateway Downs, answered the phone. He had a friendly voice and a kind manner, so I explained my unusual situation to him. I told him that I had horses to race at his race meet but that I also had a weanling colt that needed to be doctored. I asked, if I were to bring panels to set up a pen for him, if I might bring Aurzel with me. Paul was so compassionate. He said that he had the ideal location for us in a barn away from the main barns where Aurzel would hardly be noticed and certainly not a problem. I could hardly believe my ears. I was so thankful. Who else would have ever been that considerate and helpful? Paul had solved one more of my problems. Things were working out so much better that I had even hoped for. Where else and who else would have let me do this? Things had turned full circle, and all I could think was *Yellow-brick road, here we come.*

Destiny, fate, luck—so many things were working out for us, and now Paul had made it happen. Smoky would get a chance to race at Holly, and his performance there would dictate our future plans. Paul was making it possible for Smoky and I to continue racing. Now it was up to us.

AURZEL

Photo #1: Aurzel as a foal with his dam, Aura Maria (spring 1989)
Photo #2: Aurzel as a weanling at CSU Vet Clinic. His tumor is hardly detectable. (winter, 1989)
Photo #3: the tumor on Aurzel's lower jaw
Photo #4: Aurzel at Holly Race Track. He is tied to my 5 horse trailer. (spring, 1990)

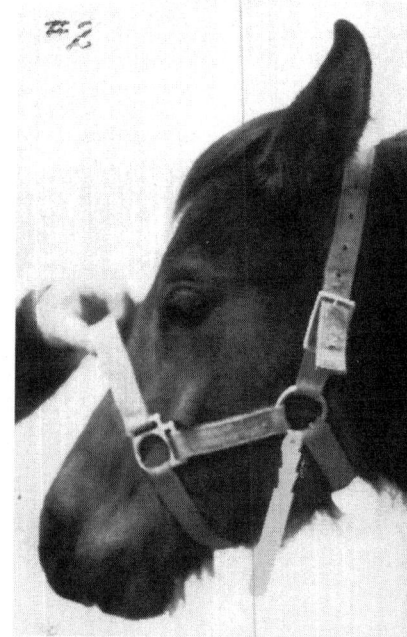

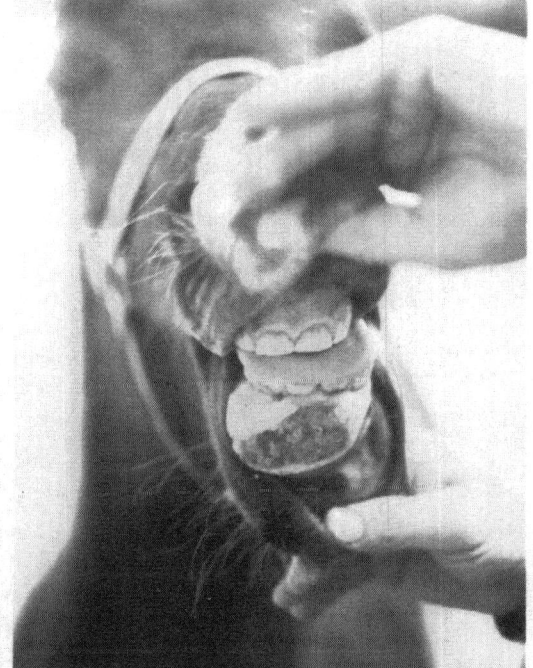

15 On to Holly

It was a gross understatement to say that it was a hectic time. Not only did I have horses to get physically conditioned for racing, but also, the remainder of my things had to be moved into storage. My truck needed to be equipped to pull my newly purchased gooseneck horse trailer, our divorce needed to be finalized, things needed to be planned and packed for Holly, the horses I was taking with me needed to receive their vaccinations and be shod, *and* Aurzel needed to go through his final radiation treatment and doctoring. I was definitely busy.

However, in a way, it was almost a blessing. There was so much to do that I really didn't have time to think about whether I was doing the right thing or not. I didn't have time to mull over the fact that I would be homeless, that I had all these horses to support, and that I was counting on the Holly race meet to provide me with not only an income to cover expenses but also enough extra cash and success to somehow continue racing. Not only was I out of the $30,000 I had lent Dick for his business, but also I had put over $20,000 into remodeling his home and buying panels for the horses' runs and also furniture for our home. I had also invested over $6,000 in some thoroughbred mares that we had hoped to race on the thoroughbred circuit. Dick didn't have any money to pay me back any of it. I found myself wishing that I had not invested so much of the cash that I had received from the sale of my home in the Black Forest into Dick's home and business. I sure could use some of that money now. I didn't realize the worst part of this whole deal was yet to come. On the other side of the coin, if it hadn't been for marrying Dick, I never would have met Smoky, and I certainly wouldn't be racing horses. My life would have traveled a completely different path. I couldn't even imagine it.

It was a big challenge to get ready for Holly. I had to pack for myself, seven horses, and one dog. It involved not only clothing but also saddles and other tack as well as some hay, grain, and supplements to tide me over until I could see what was available in Holly. Even horse blankets, a wheelbarrow, rakes and shovels, wood shavings for initial bedding, feed tubs and buckets, and all the other little things that are needed around a barn had to be packed. And then there were the panels for Aurzel's pen.

The day of our divorce finally arrived. It was done quickly. Neither of us were contesting anything. We had resolved our issues earlier. The judge asked each of us if we were sure this was what we wanted, and we both agreed that it was.

Then as we exited, Dick said to me, "I really never thought you would go all the way through with this. I was sure you would change your mind when the judge asked you if you were sure you wanted this divorce."

I didn't have anything to say. I just looked at him.

Almost immediately, I felt like I had a new lease on life, that this was a new beginning. I felt free, an immense burden off my shoulders. I was excited—nervous too. This had been a big step, divorcing Dick, deciding to leave Fort Collins, and deciding to see if I could make a living doing what I had come to love—training and racing Arabian racehorses. This trip to Holly would really determine if I would go further afield. If I couldn't make enough money at Holly, which was considered to be in the minor leagues, then I had no business even contemplating going on to California. I'd have to reconsider my options. If, on the other hand, my horses, especially Smoky, were as good as I thought they were, we could go to the big city—that is, Los Alamitos, California—and try our hand against the big guns. It was comforting to have Bryan and his confidence in Smoky's ability behind us. He was really the final push. If he wasn't racing at Los Al and constantly pushing me to bring Smoky there, I doubt that I would be considering it now. I also realized that I was very lucky to have such a supportive mom and dad.

Paul Guerrieri had arranged for me to have six stalls plus a camper hookup space near the track. Many of my friends would be racing there, including Crystal Milewski, Mona and Kevin Hussein, and Frankie Rinker. I thought it would be a lot of fun! I knew it would also be a lot of hard work being trainer, rider, groom, and stall cleaner rolled up into one, but it was the way it had to be done to make any money. Crystal and my other friends worked it the same way. And besides that, I wouldn't have had it any other way. I loved the interaction I had with my horses. By working so closely with your horses all day long, you learned each horse's likes and dislikes, when one was off its feed or not acting normal. And by riding them, you knew right away if one was gimpy or sore anywhere, and you knew each horse's habits and way of running. It was fairly easy to give jockeys their instructions when you yourself had galloped their mounts. I wouldn't have liked to be an owner who relinquished her horses to someone else to train. That would take all the fun and challenge out of the sport for me. I wondered how other owners were able to give up total control of their racehorses to someone they often hardly knew. I knew I wouldn't be in this sport if I couldn't train my horses myself.

As it turned out, I was also very glad I had invested in a used five-horse slant gooseneck horse trailer. If I had to, I could actually squeeze six Arabians into it by removing two partitions. Luckily, all my horses got along with one another and traveled well. Even with this tight fit, I still figured that I would need to make three trips to Holly. It was three hundred miles each way, but I could not figure any other way to get everything down there. On the first trip, I thought that it would be best to take my big five-horse trailer with the panels for Aurzel's pen and bedding for the stalls. I could meet Paul, see what the situation called for, and then return for Mom and Dad's camper trailer and my horses. As I had seven horses to handle, my second trip would be with my two-horse trailer, two horses, a load of hay in my truck bed and grain, etc. Mom and Dad would haul their camper down with me on this second trip. I would take the two-horse trailer back to Dick's farm and leave it there. The third trip would involve hauling the five remaining horses and any extras that I could fit in. This would be my heaviest and most challenging load. Thunder, sitting in the passenger front seat, would make all three trips with me. Her companionship was invaluable.

The first trip went as planned. I loved having Thunder with me. She was such a special dog, intensely loyal and dependable. I always felt so safe having her around. When we reached Holly, following the instructions that Paul had given to me over the phone, I pulled into the barn area just past the racetrack. I immediately liked the looks of what I saw. There were several old and weathered brick and wood barns set among some huge old cottonwood trees. *What a pretty site for some barns*, I thought. This was going to be great. Not only was this area secluded and a distance from the racetrack and main barn area, but also, it was adjacent to a large sandy draw and a huge open area where horses could graze and be lounged etc.

I began my exploration of the stalls. Although they needed to be cleaned of manure, cobwebs, and layers of dust and dirt, they were solid spacious stalls. I loved this setup. I hoped Paul would allow me the most northerly barn of six stalls. It was in the best shape, and I would be able to set up Aurzel's pen easily. I started to plan my setup in my mind.

Just then, a truck pulled in. The man who exited was a big friendly-looking man with an endearing look to him. He immediately identified himself as Paul Guerrieri. I shook his hand and asked how he knew I was here.

"Was over at the main track and saw your rig pull in," he responded. "Felt sure it had to be you."

We walked over to the barns together.

"What do you think?" he asked.

"I absolutely love it!" I exclaimed. "This is a wonderful area, and the barns are gorgeous. How come no one has claimed these barns already?"

"Well, no one really wants to be this far away from the track. You will have to walk your horses across that draw and then through that field over there to get to the racetrack. There are more barns like this across the highway, but I felt this area would be ideal for you and other Arabian horses."

"You sure got that right. I think all the Arabian trainers will like this setup." Then I pointed to our left. "I was wondering if I might have that barn."

"Don't see why not. You're the first one here, so you can have what you want."

We talked a little more, with me telling him more about Aurzel. "Would it be all right if I set up Aurzel's pen right here?" I asked.

"Looks good to me. No one at the main track will even know you have him here. Just keep him low profile, and you'll be fine. If you want, you can also have this little storage shed for your grain etc."

"Paul, this couldn't be a better setup. I love it, and I want to thank you so much for being so understanding and supportive. No one else would have or could have done all this. It's made all the difference in me being able to have racehorses at all. I really can't thank you enough."

Paul acted as if it were no big deal, but of course, I knew it was.

"Want to see where you will live?"

"Love to," I responded.

We got in Paul's truck with Thunder in the truck bed and drove across the highway to a small camping area. There were already a number of camping trailers there.

"Thought this space could be for you. Here's the water and electrical and gas hookups. When do you think you will bring your trailer down?"

I explained my plans, and as Paul had to get back to the main track, I returned to the barn area to set up my stalls and the pen for Aurzel. I would soon learn that Paul wore many hats and was the main workhorse behind Holly's racing success. It was almost dark by the time I had finished, but I was very happy with my new home to be. I decided to grab a bite to eat at the local restaurant and spend the night in the front part of my horse trailer, which was a dressing room where I had a bed and a few other essential amenities set up. It was cold out, so I bundled up the best I could. Early in the morning, I would set out for my second load.

The second trip started out badly, with a disaster occurring almost right away. I had my truck loaded plumb full of hay and was pulling my two-horse trailer with Aurzel and Arisya (a new mare Bryan had found for me) aboard. I was supposed to meet Mom and Dad in Colorado Springs to travel in tandem down to Holly. However, about thirty miles out of Fort Collins, my truck lost speed and then died. Luckily, traffic was not heavy, and there was an adequate shoulder so that I was able to coast my rig off the highway.

What do I do now? I wondered. I felt sick. I had two horses aboard and was reluctant to leave my rig. However, as time passed, I realized that was exactly what I would have to do. On the frontage road to my left, there was a farmhouse about half a mile farther on. That looked like my best bet. I hoped the residents would be friendly, helpful people. I reluctantly got out, locked my rig with Thunder left to guard my truck, and started running toward the farmhouse. To this day, I am so grateful to the couple that lived there. They were so kind and helpful. Not only did they welcome me, but also, they drove me back to my truck to see if they could repair the truck themselves.

When this proved futile, we unhooked my trailer, and they used their truck to haul my trailer with Aurzel and Arisya aboard to their place. Once there, they displaced two of their horses to make room for mine, and we went inside so that I could call a tow truck and also Mom and Dad. We ended up towing the truck back to Fort Collins, where it was found I needed a new fuel pump. I found a nearby motel room for the night and called Mom and Dad to tell them what my new plans would be.

The next morning, with my truck repaired, I returned to pick up my horse trailer and horses. I doctored Aurzel and then thanked the couple profusely. They refused to take any financial reimbursement, saying it was something anyone would do.

"That's not true," I said. "I was extremely lucky that my truck broke down where it did."

Later on, I sent them flowers and a thank-you note. It wasn't enough, but I wanted them to know how much their kindness had meant to me.

Mom and Dad were all ready when I reached Colorado Springs. They had their little travel trailer hooked up to their station wagon and were eager for me to check it out. They had spent a lot of time and energy cleaning it up, and Mom had even made new curtains for the windows. It was a cute little outfit, and I was excited about making it a home.

We didn't fare too well on the trip to Holly as the travel trailer kept swaying badly from one side to the other. It was quite windy, and the wind would catch the trailer, causing Mom and Dad's whole rig to cross into oncoming lanes several times. Although we stopped several times along the way, we didn't have any way of communicating back and forth while we were traveling. It goes without saying that we were very relieved when we finally arrived in Holly.

I pulled into the stable area first as I wanted to unload the horses and get them set up in their new home. The stalls were all ready, so all I had to do was fill the water buckets and leave them some hay to munch on.

Just as we were about to leave the stable area for the camping area, Paul pulled in. He had absolutely flawless timing. I introduced him to Mom and Dad, and together, we drove to the campgrounds. The ground was quite muddy from an earlier rainstorm, but we got the trailer situated, and Paul, bless his soul, stayed to help us level up and hook up the utilities. Mom and Dad took an immediate liking to Paul and felt a lot better about leaving me at a racetrack with Paul to look out for me. Even though I was forty-six years old, they were concerned about me being in such a questionable and, in their minds, undesirable environment. They were sure I was going to be among a group of individuals of questionable repute.

With the travel trailer all hooked up, Mom and Dad decided they'd best return home. They dropped me off back at the barn, and we said our goodbyes. I promised to keep them informed and hugged them both. As they drove off, I turned and got in my truck so that I could park my rig where it would be convenient to unload the hay. Once the hay was unloaded, I went to doctor Aurzel, refill the water buckets, and throw both horses some more hay. Thunder and I then headed back over to our new home.

It's so cozy inside this little camper, I thought. *I'm really going to like living here and being at Holly.*

The next morning, I cleaned my two stalls, fed, watered, and walked Aurzel and Arisya, doctored Aurzel, checked with Paul about feeding and watering my horses while I was away, and returned to Fort Collins for my final load.

The final trip went well. It had concerned me a little to be hauling five horses in a new horse trailer. Because it was a gooseneck and a new experience for me, I had practiced pulling my new horse trailer empty around the nursery at Dick's so I would be aware of how much clearance I would need etc. Still, it was nerve-racking, especially traveling through Denver. Several drivers cut in front of me with very little clearance, making us almost stand on our heads. I tried to stay in the center lane to avoid having to slow down for vehicles wishing to exit and prayed that not too many drivers would object to this. This trip seemed to take forever, and I was terribly relieved to finally arrive at Holly. We were all at our home now. Aurzel and Arisya were happy to see us and whinnied happily to their friends. I energetically set about unloading my horses and setting them up for the night. I looked forward to tomorrow.

The next morning, after my initial barn chores, I decided to explore the area on horseback. I rode Manteeya and ponied Smoky. I wanted to check out the nice sandy draw and see where it led to. It turned out to be an excellent area for legging up my young horses; plus, I felt it would provide a nice break from gallops on the track.

I could also take Aurzel for walks there. Next, we rode across the fields to the racetrack. We made a loop around the quarter-mile track and then headed over to the main barn area to see who was around. I ran into John and Robin Hood and was glad to see them. Both of them would again be riding for me.

It wasn't long before Crystal arrived with her horses (she was training Jane Teutsch's horses), and then Frankie and Mona and Kevin Hussein arrived. Crystal set up barn next to me, as did Frankie, but as all the stalls were now full, Mona and Kevin had to stable over near the main track. A new competitor for us, Felix Payne, would be racing at Holly also. Felix was a "big-time" race trainer, having raced in Kentucky and also Delaware. I knew that he would be tough competition. Lea Brent, who was sponsoring both stakes races at Holly, had his horses with Felix.

In the days that followed, I mixed in relaxing rides down the draw with conditioning gallops on the track. I even taught Aurzel to pony, and he enjoyed his trips around the area. He seemed to think he was one of the big guys. His lower jaw was healing well, and he enjoyed visiting with the other horses as I had set up his pen so he could actually visit three different horses in their stalls. The pen was a nice size (thirty-six by thirty-six feet). Sometimes I would rotate the older horses into the pen and could put two horses there at a time so they could roll and visit.

Our first race was to be on April 14. It would be an open-allowance race (meaning it was open to any Arabian horse with registration and race papers in the racing office) going six furlongs. We were all anxious to be racing again.

The day of the race, I spent extra time washing Smoky and braiding his mane. He would be in against a field of very good horses. Felix had entered Lea Brent's stallion, Eden Rabi. Crystal had Jane's good horse, Soaring Michael, Frankie had Rio Hondo and Dynamikc, and Kevin and Mona had Silver sp Carter. I was excited and nervous at the same time. Smoky was a year older and a year wiser. How would he fare against his old rival, Carter, this year?

Finally, the time came for our race. Crystal, Felix, Frankie, and I all led our horses down and through the draw and across the field to the racetrack. Once we were in the saddling paddock, Darrell Seufer, who was the major of Holly and also on the board of directors, held Smoky for me while I saddled him. Although grooms usually did this, I didn't have any, so Darrell offered his help every time we raced, and it was much appreciated. He also led Smoky out for the mount so that I could give John a leg up onto Smoky's back.

I didn't have to say much to John as he knew Smoky well. "Have a safe trip, John. Smoky's ready!"

John gave me a thumbs up, and away they went. I went up in the stands so that I could have a view of the whole race. It seemed the whole town had come out for the races. I knew that quarter-horse racing fans and enthusiasts had come from miles around. They loved their sport. Arabians were an added attraction, a kind of side show. We all knew that and appreciated the opportunity to be here.

Looking across the racetrack, you could see the highway and the trucks and cars passing by. It was very close to the track, and it amazed me that the traffic didn't seem to bother the horses. Other than the highway being almost on top of us, it was a very rural setting with open fields all around. The track itself was quite tiny, only a half mile all the way around. It was designed for quarter horses, and quarter horses did not run far, often only using the straightaway down in front of the stands. This was to be our first race of a brand new year. I hoped we could start it off well.

It seemed to take forever, but finally, the horses were at the gates. They were loading well. No problems. The track announcer had a hard time saying most of the Arabian names, including Smoky's, and so he referred to him as the gray horse. As Carter and Dynamikc were also gray, it was going to be an interesting call of the race.

When they broke from the gate, it was the gray horse in the lead. The gray horse never lost the lead and, in fact, set a new track record of one minute and twenty-one and four-fifths seconds. Smoky had won handily. Crystal had run second with Soaring Michael, and Eden Rabi had run third for Felix. Smoky had once again proven that he was the real thing and a force to be reckoned with. He had even beat his old nemesis, Silver sp Carter.

I ran down to the winner's circle to greet Smoky. What a terrific feeling! We had kicked off the new year with a bang. Smoky was all wound up, and it was hard to get him to pose for his win photo. It was even harder leading him to the test barn. I loved to see Smoky come off a race acting like this. He loved racing, and it showed. His exuberance after a race would become a trademark behavior. He would often walk so calmly and quietly before a race that I worried if he was all right. But after the race, he would literally leap and drag me around. And he was ravenous. If there was any food around, any blade of grass or even a bale of straw, he would grab for it. On the rare occasion he didn't exhibit these behaviors, I knew he had been overstressed and something wasn't right with him.

Our next race was scheduled for the following weekend, and it was one of our two big races, the Brent-Crowley Arabian sprint stakes. Unlike thoroughbred and quarter-horse trainers, we Arabian trainers never thought much about racing our horses in races that were scheduled so close together. We ran whenever we were offered a race that one of our horses would fit. We never played games or tried to avoid racing against one another. We made sure we filled every race that was offered to us. Arabian are tough little horses and didn't have as many feet and leg problems as thoroughbred horses did, and last but not least, the purses were small, so we all needed all the money we could get.

The sprint stakes race was one that Smoky and I had to win if we were going on to California. It and the Sam's Fix Cup race to be held May 5 offered the biggest purses of all the races. These were the races all of us were gunning for. Mona and Kevin would realize that they had to have Carter a little sharper. Felix would absolutely be trying all the harder. It was, after all, one of his owners who was sponsoring both races.

The day of the race finally arrived. Once again, we made our way across the field to the racetrack. Because this was a big race, my pony person had come over to the barn to lead Smoky over to the saddling paddock. I walked off to the side and talked to Crystal, who also had a pony for Soaring Michael.

We were almost to the near end of the track when, all of a sudden, Smoky spooked and pulled the rope away from the surprised pony person's hand. The loose rope spooked Smoky even more, and I watched helplessly as Smoky raced back toward his barn. I knew that if Smoky raced all the way back, there would be little chance that I could manage to run back after him, catch him, and make it back over to the track in time for the race. It was sickening. I was literally watching any purse money we might have won going down the drain. I couldn't believe this was actually happening. *Of all things that could have happened, why this?* I anguished.

Then as if angels had wished it, someone back behind us was catching Smoky as he galloped by. I realized quickly that it was none other than Felix Payne. He had been the last to leave the barn area and saw what was happening. He stood in Smoky's path, put his arms out, and quietly asked Smoky to "whoa." In a totally untypical move, Smoky actually slowed down and allowed Felix to grab hold of his bridle rein and bring him to a stop. I ran back to Felix and Smoky as fast as my legs would carry me. Felix had just saved our day and, in doing so, had probably rescued Eden Rabi's top competition. It had been a totally unselfish action. It showed exactly the kind of person that Felix was. I thanked him profusely. I couldn't thank him enough. Felix acted like it was something that anyone would have done. I knew that was not the case. To this day, I have never forgotten that kindness.

Smoky went on to win that race wire to wire. Soaring Michael again ran second, with Carter improving his performance to race third. Felix ran fourth with Eden Rabi. Once again, I thanked the good Lord and also Grampa Saunders, and this day, I thanked Felix as well.

Smoky's next race wouldn't be until the end of the meet, and it would also be the final race of the meet. It was the Sam's Fix Arabian Cup race, and it would offer the biggest purse of all. It would also be a longer race, going a distance of one and one-eighth miles. To prepare for a longer race, I needed to two-minute clip Smoky longer distances. Two-minute clipping was a term used to describe the speed a horse traveled. Basically, the rider would rate his or her horse to travel a mile in two minutes. Smoky had been set up to sprint. Now he had to go a distance. So I asked Robin Hood to ride Independence Dai while I rode Smoky for our two-minute clip. Indy would be running in this final stakes race also.

We were well into our speedy clip, traveling nicely side by side down the backside, when all of a sudden, I realized that my saddle was slipping backward on Smoky. I knew I wouldn't be able to slow Smoky down with a saddle that was slipping. He was terrible to slow down under the best of circumstances. I also knew that Smoky would most likely panic once the saddle reached his loin. I would probably get kicked or dragged to death if I didn't do something fast. Even though my stirrups were longer than most exercise riders liked, I still couldn't squeeze hard enough to prevent further slippage. I knew what I had to do. I yelled to Robin that I was bailing off, and

I leapt off Smoky. I landed on the track, doing a half roll. It was a reflex action to do this roll, and once again, it saved me from serious injury. I was up almost immediately, waving my arms to let everyone know that I was all right. Soon afterward, Smoky, saddle turned under his belly, was caught up by the outrider. Robin came back to check on me and offered to pony Smoky back to the barn. I walked back to the chute, and Daryl offered me and my saddle a ride back to the barn in his truck. I quickly and gratefully accepted the offer.

Later on, some muscle soreness really set in, but I still couldn't believe how lucky I had been. I had bailed off a horse that was going almost full speed. I never even stopped to think that I might get hung up trying to bail off or that I might break something in my fall. I had just done it. That little episode could have ended our racing at Holly and also ended all further racing plans.

On race day, Smoky once again exhibited his trademark running style and won the Sam's Fix Cup, leading wire to wire. Poor Crystal and Soaring Michael had to settle for second again and Silver sp Carter third. Indy ran sixth and earned $500 for his effort. Smoky had done everything asked of him this whole meet. Manteeya, Indy, and Arisya had won their share of purse money also. I felt I was well heeled.

I called Bryan. When he answered the phone, I casually said, "California, here we come!" Then we both laughed, and I burst into details of the race.

HOLLY, COLORADO 1990

1. Our 2nd trip to Holly with Aurzel and Arisya on board. I stopped at Mom and Dad's so they could join us with their camper in tow.
2. Thunder riding with me in the front seat of my truck.
3. Aurzel and Arisya in the pen I set up for them at Holly. Our stall are to the left. Crystal's stalls are to the right.
4. Smoky (in the lead) racing towards the finish line in his first race at Holly.

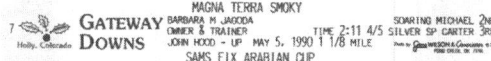
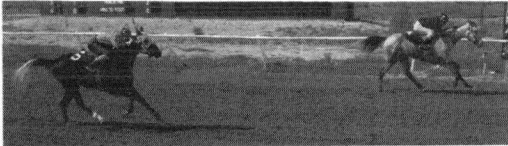

The last and most important race of the Holly Meet:

the "Sams Fix Arabian Cup"

Photo #1. From left to right-John Hood (jockey) Darrell Seufer (major), Brent Lee and his wife and daughter and me

photo credit: Gene Wilson and Associates

16   California, Here We Come

My lord! What a nerve-racking drive. This traffic would be challenging driving a passenger car, let alone a truck pulling a heavy load of horses. In my wildest dreams, I had never imagined how massive LA was with all its suburbs and sprawling sister communities. It seemed to never end. And people were in such a hurry. They darted in and out as if they were the only ones on the road. I wondered if I would even make it to Los Alamitos Race Course without somebody cutting me off and causing an accident. I guessed that most LA drivers had no idea how difficult it was to stop or even slow down a large trailer full of living beings. I kept thinking I must be there, but the cars, trucks, and highway continued to loom in front of me.

I wondered how the horses were faring and hoped that the directions that a friend, Mike Jubb, had given me were completely accurate. I didn't want to get lost in this mess. I tried to maintain the speed of the vehicle in front of me and watched carefully for the exit that Mike had marked for me. I had long since realized that staying in the middle lane of traffic was my best bet for a consistent trip. It allowed faster vehicles to pass me, and I only had to get over one lane when an exit that I would be taking came up. These LA drivers didn't seem to want to be behind a horse trailer or let one in when needed.

It was going on two hours of battling this horrific traffic now. I was wondering more and more if this was where I wanted to live, even if it would be temporary. Susie, my best friend, and I had often discussed how we hated driving through Denver traffic. Denver was a piece of cake compared to this. I couldn't, for the life of me, imagine a racetrack in the midst of all this. All the other racetracks that I had raced at were out in the country or at least at the edge of town, not plumb in the middle.

Then ahead of me, I recognized one of Mike's road marks. It meant that I had about two miles until I came to the exit that I was supposed to take to get to Los Al. I looked for an opening to get into the right lane. Cars were zooming along, and I seriously began to wonder if I would get a big enough opening to get over. I knew with my naivete of driving in such traffic that I required a much larger space to move over than these drivers were used to giving. I kept my right turn signal flashing and hoped that some kind soul would realize my plight. Then I saw an opportunity, and I was aware that a driver had deliberately slowed down so that I might be able to get over. I waved in thanks, not knowing if he could see that or not, and moved over.

I was getting excited now. We were almost there. I wondered what new adventures lay ahead for us and if I had made the right decision in coming here. Smoky and his buddies had done fine in the little leagues, but we were entering the major leagues now. I was even more worried about whether or not I had the savvy to train racehorses at this level. There were so many things I didn't know. Could I compete with the caliber of trainer here? With a sigh of both relief and anticipation, I said a little prayer of thanks for our safe arrival. The entrance to Los Alamitos Race Course loomed ahead.

Well, I was at Los Al, but which way did I go? The grandstands were in front of me, as was a large parking area. A home with acreage and huge eucalyptus trees was to the left, and in the distance, diagonally to the right, were horse trailers parked behind more eucalyptus trees. A van in front of me was going straight ahead, but I doubted that was where I should go as it was obviously delivering food to the restaurant. I decided to aim for the horse trailers. As I did so, I became aware that the racetrack was behind the buildings and no stable area or stalls were visible. I made a wide U-turn in the parking lot and headed in the opposite direction. There weren't any direction signs of any sort, but I now saw rows of buildings that I knew were the horse facilities.

I drove on and came to a stable gate that was closed and locked. There was a narrow road traversing down between the back of the stable area and some railroad tracks. I hoped that I was correct in driving down this narrow road as I didn't want to get into an area where I couldn't turn around. Then I saw that this road led to another parking area. I followed it around and came to another stable gate. The guard came out to greet me. I grabbed my papers and hopped out of the truck. I introduced myself, showed my Colorado trainer's license, and handed over the health certificates and Coggins papers that I knew were required for entrance onto the grounds. The guard confirmed that stalls had been held for me, but he did not know in which barn. While he made a call, I headed back to the horse trailer to open the windows so the horses could better see their new home. They all stuck there heads out and whinnied to their new neighbors. They wanted everyone to know that they had arrived.

In the meantime, John, the guard, had not had any luck establishing which barn had been assigned to me. He finally called over the PA system for Melvin Glaze, the stall superintendent. I was getting anxious to get my horses off the trailer by now. Finally, Melvin arrived. He was a big man and very friendly. I was to follow his truck as I was to be stabled at the far end of the barn area. I was very surprised to enter the barn area and find a two-lane cement roadway leading down between the rows of barns. This was, evidently, both the vehicle and horse path from the barns to the racetrack. In between the barns, which were sturdy cement-block rows of stalls, were walking machines set up to cool horses off after their gallops or races. The barns were large, and there were lots of stalls, but it was a dismal sight. There weren't any grassy areas and very few trees. *Where and what could you do with a horse to relax him?* I wondered. This place was all concrete and buildings. I thought that most of the small fair meets that we had raced at had more horse-friendly stabling than this.

As we came to the end of the barn area (barns 35 and 36), we passed the stable kitchen. It was early afternoon, and most of the grooms and trainers were taking their afternoon break before the afternoon chores. We made a sharp turn behind barn 36 and drove along the length of the barn. Surprisingly, at the end of barn 36, we came upon a huge fenced grassed area with lots of trees. It looked to be part of an old golf course. Along the edge were about twenty portable stalls.

"Well, Barb, this is it. It'll just be temporary until we can get you moved into a permanent barn. Right now, we are plumb full, so you and another trainer will have to share this area for a while. Hope that's all right with you."

"All right with me? This is fantastic, Melvin. I couldn't have asked for more."

I was absolutely ecstatic! How could we be so lucky? We had our own private little world with trees and grass and even some old dirt trails that we could ride along. Melvin looked at me and laughed. He had been scared of my reaction. He felt most trainers would balk at this setup. I think we became friends right then and there.

He told me that the main gate that we had driven though would be locked for security reasons and then proceeded to show me a small opening that I was to use to access the barn area and the racetrack. He was concerned whether my horses would go through the small opening as it had low clearance and was quite narrow. I assured him that it wouldn't be a problem. I don't know if he believed me, but he certainly did in the days to come.

I had hoped that I'd have seen Bryan by now, and I was really hoping that he had bedded four stalls for me. But there was nothing, not even some straw to bed the stalls with. The first thing I wanted to do was let Thunder out of the tack area of my horse trailer. Dogs were not allowed on the back side, and I had stopped and hidden her before I got to the stable gate. She was happy to get out. Then I went about unloading the horses so they could stretch their legs and take in their new surroundings. One by one, I backed them out and tied them to the sides of the horse trailer. Noticing a water spicket right near the stalls, I fetched a water bucket from the tack room, filled it, and offered each horse a drink. Then I began setting up their stalls for the night.

Luckily, I had one bale of shavings left plus a bale of hay and some grain. I inspected each stall and found them to be fairly level and clean. As stalls had never been set up in this area before, there was also grass inside each stall that I knew the horses would enjoy. I chose five stalls at the end, one of which would be used as a tack and feed room. I located my screw eyes and put three in each of the four stalls, two for hanging a large feed tub and one for a water bucket. Then I divided my single bale of shavings among the four stalls, threw some hay on the ground inside each stall, filled the water buckets, hooked one in each stall, and went to get the horses. I set a water pail inside the fifth stall for Thunder.

Now the real unpacking would begin as I would have to move my horse trailer to the back parking lot that I had first seen upon my arrival. Everything I needed for my horses would need to go in the extra stall provided. Before that, however, I thought I should try to locate Bryan, so I put Thunder in the fifth stall, offered her a dog biscuit, and headed for the main barn area.

17   Races to Win Before We Sleep

It was wonderful to see Bryan. I caught him just as he was coming out of his tack room. A huge grin spread across his face, and I immediately realized how very much I had missed him. I ran up to him, and sporting huge smiles, we hugged each other for a long time. I had come to realize by now that Bryan was quite special to me, and I knew that I would never have even considered coming to California if it hadn't been for him. He had been the driving force behind my Kentucky venture, and now here I was in California. I wondered where I would be right now if I hadn't met him. Would I have stayed with Dick? I strongly doubted that, but I wondered if I would have continued with the racing or if I would have returned to teaching.

Bryan had really helped me make the decision to stay with racing and had made the transition to the big leagues possible. He seemed to know all the right people, and he always knew what was going on around the different racetracks. He loved to talk and visit, and it seemed that almost everyone opened up to him and confided in him. He knew the ins and outs of the racing world, and he didn't mind sharing what he knew. He was very proud of his almost innate ability to recognize a good racehorse at first glance. He could see lameness and injuries that the rest of us would be hard put to recognize. It didn't take but a few steps, and he could tell you what limb a horse was favoring and whether the lameness was due to an ankle, knee, hock, or stifle etc. He knew when a horse was tied together correctly and when he wasn't. By that, I mean he could tell if the rear end of a horse was too weak or if the hind leg was too straight etc. for the horse to be an effective runner. Some of the conformation faults were subtle, but his evaluation was generally right on.

I prided myself in being able to pick out a good horse, but I was pale in comparison to Bryan. Trainers, owners, riders, jockeys, and even veterinarians were constantly asking his opinion about various horses, and he was always obliging with his comments. I often chided him that he helped the opposition too much. These same trainers and owners ended up beating him in races because of advice he had offered them. He had done the same for me in Kentucky. He had helped me get Smoky set up for his races, and then I had gone ahead and beat him. I came to the conclusion that Bryan couldn't help himself. He was proud of his knowledge and talent, and I don't think it was possible for him not to have the recognition that this commanded.

Bryan had known I was on my way to California but hadn't known when I would arrive. I had called him when I left Fort Collins, but I hadn't called him en route as it was often too difficult to leave the horses and my huge rig and get to a pay phone. Being that Bryan loved to talk on the phone, he had assumed that I would call him constantly to report my progress. Being that I wasn't a phone person, I had not even really thought to call him en route at all. This trip that had taken me three and a half days to accomplish would have taken Bryan a mere day and a half at the most. Whereas he could travel throughout the night without the need for a rest stop, I couldn't drive very far each day with a full load like I had, nor could I drive well after dark, and I had to plan a stopover after every 350–450 miles of driving.

After our long and fantastically good-feeling hug, we held hands, and as we walked over to his barn of horses, I raved on about my trip and the horrific California traffic I had encountered. Then we loaded up one of his huge wheelbarrows with some shavings and a bale of hay from his shed row, and together, we walked over to see Smoky. Although Thunder didn't acknowledge or accept very many people, she remembered Bryan from Kentucky and was very happy to see him. Bryan thought the world of Thunder, and she sure picked up on that. We checked in on Smoky, and then I finished setting up my stalls while Bryan returned to his barn to finish up his afternoon chores. Later, I joined Bryan at his barn. He had about a dozen horses at Los Al, including, of course, Smoky's half brother, Ibn Bint Hilyuri. He walked me down his shed row and introduced each horse. I recognized Nouveski and Ziegfried and, of course, Hilyuri.

Later, when he was also finished, we drove my horse trailer, along with Thunder, over to the parking area that I had seen when I first arrived. We parked and unhitched the horse trailer close to a lovely line of huge eucalyptus trees. Bryan had thought that this would be an ideal spot to leave Thunder while we were at work in the barn area, and I was quick to agree. Dogs were not allowed on the grounds, and this location was private and quiet and had sufficient shade and even water spickets. I could leave Thunder tied to the horse trailer or, on occasion, even leave her inside the horse trailer. It would only be for the hours that we were actually trackside; other times she would be with us, so I was thrilled that we had been able to find such amenable accommodations for her. It was really important for me to make sure that she had a safe and secure place to stay while we worked with the horses. I showed Thunder around her new area, and then grabbing a suitcase and several other items, the three of us loaded up into Bryan's big blue truck and headed over to Bryan's favorite hangout, the Starting Gate, for a bite to eat. Both Bryan and I were hungry and thirsty, and we had a lot of catching up to do.

As soon as we walked in the door, one person after another greeted Bryan. I quickly realized that the Starting Gate was indeed quite more than just his favorite eating place. Several of the patrons that were the happiest to see him had obviously been there for some time and were not feeling too much pain. Many of them were fellow trainers, and each, in turn, offered to buy a round of drinks to celebrate my arrival. Everyone was very friendly, but I was quite dismayed to see just how much liquor was being consumed. I hoped that this was not a typical day, and I hoped even more that Bryan had not let his drinking issue get away from him. I feared that the Starting Gate might be too convenient a place for Bryan to deal with. I hoped that I was wrong in my initial feelings, but I knew that I was already worried.

I found that I was ready to leave long before Bryan was. I was tired and looked forward to resting and taking a nap. Bryan had already had several beers and was enthralled in conversation with several quarter-horse trainers. I laughed and joked with the rest of them and then less subtly suggested that it was time to leave as I was tired and ready for bedtime. With that, Bryan got up to pay his bill, bid his farewell, and, even though he had consumed half a dozen beers, thought nothing of driving us to his motel room farther down Katella Avenue and not too far from Disneyland. He seemed quite capable, but even so, I was worried at his driving after having consumed so much liquor. I was to learn with time that things would get a whole lot worse before they got better.

The motel room that Bryan was renting proved to be quite private, and we were able to sneak Thunder in without any problem. She was such a good dog and never caused any undue problems. She just liked being with us and was basically up for anything that worked for us. I washed my face, brushed my teeth, and hopped into bed, content to be nestled and held in Bryan's strong and tender arms.

The next morning, after setting Thunder up in her new accommodations, I found myself excited to show my horses their new surroundings. After feeding the horses a quick breakfast, I saddled up Manteeya and ponied Smoky around the old golf course and then did likewise with the other two until all four were exercised. I wanted to stretch everyone's legs without riding any of them too hard as I felt they needed to recover from their trip. I cleaned their dirty stalls and just sponged off Manteeya, Indy, and Arisya for now. I would give them baths later in the day. We had arranged with the local supplier, Gordon Feed, to deliver some shavings, grass hay, and alfalfa later that day. I gave Smoky a bath and took him over to put him on Bryan's walker to dry off. As I was leading him across the pavement, I heard someone ask if that was Magna Terra Smoky.

I was surprised but politely responded, "Yes, it is."

I heard a little snicker and then "You mean that's the horse that everyone is so scared of?"

I was taken back. The comment had not been a compliment. I knew Smoky was not as big nor as muscled as some of the Arabians I had seen here, but the put-down still stung. I continued on to Bryan's barn, and when he came over to greet me, I mentioned the encounter to him.

"Don't worry about them," he said. "They'll be eating those words after Smoky's first race, you wait and see."

I sure hoped Bryan was right.

With Smoky happy on the walker, Bryan and I walked the quarter-mile walk to the racetrack with one of Bryan's horses that an exercise rider was going to gallop. I wanted to see what was going on up at the track, and I also wanted to watch the riders as I needed to pick out a good jockey for Smoky. Bryan pointed out several and told me who they were. Then I noticed a rider whose style, manner, and riding ability I really liked. He was very quiet with the horses he rode and had soft, kind hands. He got his mounts to gallop relaxed and easily and didn't fight or upset them. Bryan told me that the rider was Ralph Pauline.

"Think he'll ride Arabians?" I asked.

"Don't know. Think he will, but you'll have to ask him."

Los Alamitos was primarily a quarter-horse track, and many of the jockeys only rode quarter horses. Some of them felt the Arabians were too flighty and too slow to bother with. In addition, they didn't like riding the long distances Arabians raced. They preferred a burst of speed, going 440 yards or thereabouts.

After the track closed at 10:00 a.m., Bryan and I headed for his truck in the parking lot (vehicles were not allowed backside, where horses were stabled) between the hours of 6:00 a.m. and 10:00 a.m., when horses were going to and from the racetrack. Veterinarians and horseshoers were the exception as their services were invaluable and neither can do a decent job without their vehicle. We then drove to the racing office. I needed to obtain my California trainer's license, turn in my registration papers, and set up my horseman's account. All this needed to be done before I could take a horse to the racetrack. Bryan showed me where the different offices were located and introduced me to Ronnie Church, the racing secretary, Ed Burghart, the track announcer, and Sheila Mays, who managed a multitude of tasks in the racing office. We stopped by to pick up Thunder and then once again headed over to the Starting Gate for lunch. I was beginning to realize just how much time Bryan spent at the Starting Gate. Through no fault of its own, I was already developing a dislike for this place.

The next day, Bryan and I caught Ralph Pauline as he walked a quarter horse off the track. Bryan introduced us. With a firm pat and a few words of endearment to the horse he had galloped, Ralph dismounted, turned his mount over to a waiting groom, and shook my hand. I could tell right away that Ralph was exactly what I had thought he might be. I knew that he was the rider I wanted. I told Ralph that I had been watching him and that I had several Arabian horses that I hoped he might be interested in riding. I also told him that two of the horses were nominated for the stakes races coming up. He was very polite and said he would love to ride them. We arranged for him to work Smoky and Manteeya the following day and Arisya and Indy the day after. I could hardly wait for the next day to arrive.

Finally, the next day did come. Bryan and I walked Smoky up to the gap and met Ralph at the appointed time. Smoky was ready and excited to go. He was a smart little horse, so he knew that he'd get to run fast because he didn't have a martingale on and he had a new rider on his back. I watched proudly and excitedly as Ralph started Smoky off at a brisk trot. When Ralph hit the backside, Smoky was already in a nice fluid gallop. I watched Ralph ease up on his hold of Smoky a little at the half-mile pole and watched as Smoky accelerated to top speed. Smoky was flying. It was literally awesome watching him demolish the racetrack. He was so smooth and fluid and fast! I knew he had put in a good work. He would be ready for his stakes race.

Bryan, ever ready with his stopwatch, had clocked Smoky in 40.3 seconds flat. This was another of Bryan's trademarks. He always clocked his horses' works and often the works of other trainers' horses. Sometimes the official clocker would miss a horse or work, and Bryan always made sure he had a backup time. He was very accurate in his clocking, and it kept him on top of the game as he had a very good memory as well and knew just what horses to be on the lookout for in any given race. Everyone looked to Bryan for official times on their horses' works. He was better than the official clocker because you could get your clocking right away, and it was always very accurate.

As Ralph and Smoky rounded the clubhouse turn and slowed to a stop, I looked at Bryan. "Very impressive! I'm pretty pleased. Smoky is going to like this track."

When Ralph came off the track on Smoky, he turned to me and said, "I've never ridden an Arabian like this one. He can fly. If your other horses are at all like him, I'll ride them all for you."

I couldn't have been happier. I was really excited for Smoky's first race here. It was a big and important race to be run June 9. It was, in fact, the $10,000 Arabian Horse World Open Handicap, going one and one sixteenth miles. Smoky would be running against the likes of Harbor Lites and a fantastic little horse named Charlie Valentine who had shipped in all the way from Delaware. Charlie couldn't have been more than 14.3 hands, but he had the heart of a champion and had already won over $153,000. Smoky, on the other hand, had earned just over $18,000. This race would really be a test for him.

It seemed to take forever, but race day finally arrived. As had been the case in all of Smoky's races, I wore the lucky red jumpsuit that Dick had given me back in 1989. It had become a fixture now, and I didn't dare wear something else for fear of jinxing Smoky. There was a fantastic feeling of excitement in the air, and I could tell Smoky was totally ready for his debut. He was literally dancing on his toes. It was if he were saying, "Just let me at 'em!" I just looked at him and laughed to myself. *What a comic you are, Smoky.*

As I gave Ralph a leg up and wished him a safe trip, out of the corner of my eye, I saw Bryan head out toward the racetrack. I wondered what he was up to as he walked up to the state veterinarian, who was watching all the horses move out before the race. It was the state vet's job to be on the lookout for any horse that appeared to be lame or sore and scratch that horse from the race. Although I didn't know it then, Bryan had watched the state vet pay particular attention to Smoky because of the way he moved in the hind end. As astute as ever, Bryan had realized this and had gone over to talk to him. He knew the state vet and wanted to make sure that the vet realized Smoky always moved that way and that he was perfectly sound. Evidently, he convinced the vet because Smoky got to run. I was unaware all this was going on until after the race. Bryan had once again saved the day for us. It was not the first time he had done so, and it would also not be the last.

Smoky was totally up for this race. He loved this game where other horses got to chase him. He literally pranced out onto the track. I smiled as I watched him. I absolutely loved that he loved what he was doing. It almost made my heart skip a beat to watch him. *What a wonderful life this had become for the both of us,* I thought. *How could I be so fortunate?* As Smoky made his way up the track, I thought back to my time with Twilight and realized that just like Twilight, Smoky was a happy horse. It was exactly what I had wanted it to be. Twilight had taught me well. *Thank you, Twilight. I hope you are well.*

My heart was almost in my mouth as I watched Smoky trot by the spectators and stands in the post parade. Eddie Burghart, the track announcer, was introducing each horse in the exciting and deep voice that made Los Alamitos racing so special. I had never before heard such a wonderful and powerful voice in a track announcer. Ed was an announcer extraordinaire. He knew his horses well, and he brought each and every spectator into a special bond with the horses in the race. Each horse had a tale to tell, and Eddie shared it with the fans. He espoused the talents of Charlie Valentine and defined the challenge that lay ahead for the new invader from Colorado named Magna Terra Smoky. He had the crowd smitten with the race.

As I watched the horses approach the starting gate, I knew that this was going to be the most exciting race I had ever heard announced. Eddie's wonderfully deep voice was met with thunderous cheers and encouragement from the fans. What a stupendous way he had of setting up a race. One felt as if he/she were a part of the race itself. No longer was Smoky called "the gray horse." This announcer not only knew every horse in the race but also pronounced all the names correctly.

Eddie had already set the public up for a great and thrilling race by introducing the favorite, Charlie Valentine, as the determined and talented Delaware invader with winnings of over $153,000 and Magna Terra Smoky as the Colorado Invader, who was unbeaten in 1990 with several track records to his credit.

As the horses entered the gates, Eddie had shivers running up and down my spine. I hung onto his every word as the track crew had the horses brought to and locked up in the gates.

Then I heard, "And they're off!"

I strained to see where Smoky was. The chute for this long race was at the top of the backside, on the far side of the racing oval. I thought I saw Smoky jump to the lead, and sure enough, Eddie announced, "And Magna Terra Smoky, showing early speed, has jumped to the lead. The rest of the field looks content to set just off the early pace."

The horses would be crossing the finish line twice in this race as this was only a five-eighths-mile track. I hoped Smoky would not use himself up too early and think he had to race for the finish line the first time he crossed it. As the horses came past the grandstands for the first time, Eddie continued to play the crowd.

Up above the grandstand, binoculars to his eyes, he was unfolding the story of Smoky's race. "As they cross the finish line for the first time, it is the Colorado Invader, Magna Terra Smoky, full of run in the lead. A patient Charlie Valentine is content to settle in behind the leader. Harbor Lites is waiting behind both the leaders, content to make his trademark late rush."

Then all of a sudden, Eddie was announcing, "And Magna Terra Smoky has no intention of slowing down. He has opened up a two-length lead and is increasing his lead with every stride. Charlie

Valentine and Harbor Lites are being hard pressed to keep up. And Magna Terra Smoky is getting stronger as the race gets longer. This Colorado Invader loves this track. No one is going to catch Magna Terra today."

I was hanging on every word and yelling and screaming in response to Smoky's tremendous burst of speed. Smoky was roaring down the lane. Ralph hadn't even moved his whip.

As he flew across the finish line, I could hear Eddie announcing, "Magna Terra Smoky has just annihilated this field, and he has set a new track record for a mile and a sixteenth. Harbor Lites will run second and Charlie Valentine third."

The excitement was overwhelming. I had been yelling my lungs out, helping Smoky keep his lead down the stretch. The crowd had gone absolutely wild. Smoky had not only won but also demolished the opposition. He had put his doubters to bed and proved he belonged here. He had set a new track record against the best there was. I raced down to the winner's circle to greet him, tears streaming down my face.

I don't remember ever coming down off that high. It had been the most incredibly exciting race Smoky had ever run, and Eddie had contributed immensely to that, I knew. What an exceptional announcer! He made the races at Los Al. I didn't think I would ever forget this day. I gave an extra thank-you to Grandpa. I knew that we couldn't have done it without him.

We reveled in the marvel of Smoky's race for a long time to come. Bryan was especially proud. He was, after all, the only one to have foreseen what a mating between Cyroga and SW David could produce. He had a great deal of confidence in his horse-breeding sense, and Smoky's accomplishments were to his credit. We went on and on in our ramblings about our wonderful protégé. Our little country bumpkin had made it in the big times.

For days, I walked around in a daze, happier than happy, prouder than proud. All my horses were enjoying their time on the old golf course. It was so wonderful for the horses to be able to trot or lope along the nice dirt trails that curved through the trees instead of always having to walk down the cement road to the track.

When we were finished galloping, I would take the horses, two at a time, out to graze. Then one day Bryan came by to tell me that I was spooking the horses that were galloping on the track. Evidently, the horses on the track could see us, and because they weren't used to horses being there, they would shy away. Again, Bryan had heard the news before I did. I knew it was because he had spent so much time up at the track watching his horses as well as other trainers' horses gallop or work.

Not unexpectedly, several days later, Melvin came to tell me that there were four stalls available for me at the end of barn 16. I hoped that our secret little gate would be left unlocked so that I could take my horses over to graze, but of course, it was not.

The end of barn 16 was across from Bryan's barn, and it was also right next to the water-disposal unit that removed extra water from the shed rows of the backside. The pump, when it was on, was extremely noisy. I could never hear the announcements over the PA system if the unit was operating. However, I felt I could sure live with the noise as our rather secluded location allowed me to put up the four lightweight panels that I had brought with me and make a small turnout pen around two of the end stalls. I could let one horse out at a time to visit with one of the others contained in a stall. It didn't bother anyone else, and I never left any horse out in the pen when I wasn't there. I didn't want a horse to get accidentally loose and ruin our last little bit of freedom.

Shortly after Smoky's big race, Manteeya ran her first race at Los Al and finished a very respectable third in a stakes race. Then Arisya raced and beat the champion mares Pacifica and Marahas Mirage on my birthday. What a fantastic birthday present! Even Indy outdid himself, running a close second to Bryan's good speed horse, Ziegfried. When it looked as if Indy might win the race, I thought Bryan was going to go into shock. He could barely accept the fact that Smoky had beaten Ziegfried back in Kentucky, let alone my "filler" horse Indy beating him.

For several days now, I had noticed a handsome and young veterinarian working on horses at various barns as I walked my horses around the backside. I became more and more impressed with him as I watched his kind and professional manners with these horses. I asked Bryan who he was. Bryan said he thought his name was Dr. Moak.

"Do you think he would take on a new client?" I queried.

"Don't know. Why don't you ask him?"

I decided to do just that, and the next day, when I saw him go to the barn behind mine, I stood patiently and waited for him to finish.

"Hi, my name is Barbara Jagoda. Are you Dr. Moak?"

"Yes, I am."

"I'm very glad to meet you. I have to tell you that I have been watching you work on other trainer's horses, and I really like how you work with them. I was wondering if you might consider taking on another barn. I have four Arabian horses."

Dr. Moak looked up at me with a smile on his face. "I'd like that, Ms. Barbara. Just let me finish up a few things here, and I'll be right over. Where is your barn?"

I told Dr. Moak where my barn was, and we shook hands, and the both of us went back to work. I felt that things were really coming together. I now had not only the best rider on the track but also the best veterinarian. Everything was coming up roses!

In the meantime, I decided to put Smoky in an open-allowance race as it was all that was available for him. He faced the champion older horse, News Release. News had already won twenty-five out of his thirty-nine lifetime starts. He was very good. Smoky ran his little eyeballs out but could not beat News. Smoky ran a game second. Unknown to me then, Smoky and News Release would become tough rivals all throughout both their racing careers. News would eventually bow a tendon, and although Judy Rutten, his trainer and owner, would have split-tendon surgery done on him, News Release would never come back to his old form.

Five days later, I again raced Smoky, and true to form, Smoky returned to his infamous winning style, winning an open-allowance race by an astonishing seventeen lengths, He literally destroyed the track record he had set in the Arabian Horse World Open Handicap by a sensational two full seconds. I continued to be on a natural high as my horses kept accomplishing phenomenal feats.

Our next race was the Colonial Ridge Open Handicap Stakes, where Smoky again ran into News Release. Smoky ran gallantly but lost to News once again. It was a very tough field, and he beat many superb horses, including Garland McAlister's great horse, Sayhi Mac, and Bryan's Ibn Bint Hilyuri. It was frustrating though as Smoky ran much faster times in his other races and I felt he could have beaten News Release this time.

A larger problem now faced us. The big and prestigious four-year-old derby was coming up, and it became evident that no one wanted to run their four-year-old against Smoky. The race, worth a whopping $20,000, threatened not to fill. In desperation, Bryan suggested to me that I not nominate Smoky into the race so that horses that did nominate would also later enter the race, thinking Smoky wouldn't be in it. The way our stakes races operated was that about seven days out from a race, the owner of a horse paid a fee, say, in this case, $300. This amount would entitle the nominated horse to be eligible for the race. Then at entry time, usually three days out from a race, another fee of, say, $500 could be paid to ensure a post in the race. A horse that did not pay the nomination fee could supplement in late at a larger fee; in this case, it would be a whopping $5,000. That was a lot of money, and Bryan's plan scared me to death. However, Bryan finally convinced me that I really did not have any other option, and I reluctantly agreed to his plan.

On entry day, even though it appeared that Smoky was not in the race, our plan was not working. Ronnie Church, the racing secretary, announced over the trackside loudspeaker system that the race only had four entries and that the race would not go unless it had a minimum of five entries. I was heartbroken. What a waste of a fantastic purse that all of us who had entries could use a part of.

Unknown to me, Bryan had other plans. He was already down at the racing office consulting with Ronnie Church. Later, I would find out that he, bless his heart, discovered that Jean Pacheco had not entered her good horse, FMR Tikis Shadow. Bryan then returned to the barn area and went to Jeannie's shed row to persuade her to enter. He knew Jeannie well and thought that he could persuade her to change her mind. But Jeannie once again refused. Undaunted, Bryan then decided to tell Ronnie Church what was happening. This race was now worth $25,000 because of Smoky's supplemented entry. Bryan was not about to let that amount of money just go down the drain, especially when he was sure that Smoky had a great chance of winning the race.

As it turned out, Ronnie was very upset when Bryan returned to report that Jeannie still refused to enter even though her horse was sound and able to race. In an unprecedented move, Ronnie picked up the phone and actually called FMR Tikis Shadow's owner, James Wagner, who lived in Florida. The result was that Mr. Wagner was so upset that Jeannie had not entered his horse that he fired her on the spot and entered Shadow himself. He then contacted Felix Payne and asked him to become the new trainer of Tikis Shadow. The race was now on. Bryan had helped me out again, and it would be the beginning of a new and very successful barn for our good friend Felix. I couldn't help but think that the good deed that Felix had done for Smoky and me back in Holly was being paid back at least in part.

Winning the "Arabian Horse World Open Handicap" at Los Al
Bryan is holding Smoky, Felix is to the far left and Louise from ARA is beside me.

Photo Credit: Los Alamitos Race Course Photography

18 The Derby

1990

It was the day of the California Derby. Most horse-racing fans would quite naturally equate the word *derby* with three-year-old horses. For example, the well-known and popular Kentucky Derby is strictly for three-year-old thoroughbreds. However, in the Arabian horse–racing world, derbies are for four-year-olds. The reasoning behind this age discrepancy is that Arabian horses actually mature at a slower pace than do thoroughbreds.

As part of their training, thoroughbreds start galloping as long or late yearlings and are often racing as two-year-olds to be ready for the huge purses that are offered during their three-year-old season. Only three-year-old thoroughbreds are eligible to run in any of the three Triple Crown races, and any three-year-old winning that set of races stands to earn unquestionable greatness. Secretariat was a prime example of this. He demolished his opposition, especially in the third race of the Triple Crown, which was the Belmont Stakes. Arabian racehorses, on the other hand, do not start racing at all until they are three years old. Actually, whatever the breed, it really is a terribly young age to start racing, and the fact of it is that many young horses break down before they even make it to the racetrack. I had been very lucky with Smoky. He had stayed very sound for me after his initial stifle surgery.

Today was going to be a huge day for us. Smoky was going to be racing for more purse money ($25,000) than he had ever raced for before. I know that it was not much compared to thoroughbred purses, but for all of us Arabian owners and trainers, it was a tremendous amount.

I was getting very restless and anxious. It seemed like it was taking an awfully long time for the announcer to call us down for the race. I wondered if there had been an accident up on the track to delay our race. We were always given a call over the loudspeaker so that we would know when we should leave our barn to go to the receiving barn, where each horse would be identified by the tattoo on his upper lip. From there, we would go to the saddling paddock. I had been ready for some time and kept going to the front of the shed row to see if other horses were leaving for the race yet. The water pump at the end of our shed row and next to my tack room had been *brrr*-ing away. I liked the privacy of our stalls at the end of the barn, but the noisy pump was a nuisance.

As I was pacing up and down the shed row, Dr. Goodberry, the veterinarian whom I had originally used when I first came to Los Al, came roaring up in his truck.

"Barb, what the heck are you doing? The race office has been paging for you for the last ten minutes. Your big stakes race is about to be run."

"Oh man, Doc, you've got to be kidding. I've been sitting here ready and never heard an announcement."

"Well, they've paged you about three times, so I thought, 'Where in the devil is she?' I thought I'd better check and see if everything was all right."

"Oh wow! Thanks, Doc. Smoke's ready. I've got to make it up there. It cost me $5,000 just to supplement him into this race."

Even though Doc was no longer my vet, he had the kindness and had taken time out of a busy schedule to check up on me. Bless his heart that he had done this for me.

I was so nervous and panicky that I could hardly bridle Smoky. With my hands shaking, I finally got the bridle on Smoky and grabbed a lead rope. Then I undid Smoky's stall guard. "C'mon, Smoke, let's go."

We took off at a trot through the line of hot walkers that were in between the shed rows. Once we hit the main road, it was all pavement, but I kept Smoky trotting anyway. Our barn was about a quarter mile from the racetrack, and we didn't have a second to spare. Fortunately, Smoky never even batted an eye at this. He had been through enough different things with me that this was all just part of the day. Thank goodness I was in pretty good shape.

Way up ahead, I could just see the other horses heading into the oval for mount-up. The jockeys were being legged up onto their horses for the race that we were the favorite to win and that we might never get to run. Smoky still had to be checked in the receiving barn and be saddled. I started to run faster. It was warm out, and both Smoky and I were breaking into a sweat. I saw Michelle, the identifier, up ahead waving for us to hurry. Grooms and trainers along the way were yelling and cheering us on. Finally, we were within earshot of Michelle.

"Barb? Where were you? You're so late! I don't know if you can make it. Just let me check Smoky's tattoo. Then you make a quick circle through here and get going."

I did as she said and thanked her. As I made my way onto the racetrack, I kicked off my shoes as they were hindering my speed on the soft deep tack and raced with Smoky up to the saddling paddock. I was already tired, and the deep soft dirt of the track made my going even slower. I knew we both looked a mess for this big race, but I just wanted to make it.

"Do we still have time?" I anxiously asked.

Ed Reese, the paddock judge, signaled us over. I handed Smoky off to Ralph Pauline. Ed was anxious to hear what had happened but led me over to the phone to call to the stewards. I was so nervous and tired that Eddie dialed the number for me. George Slender answered the phone.

"Hello, Mr. Slender," I said meekly into the receiver.

"Barb, you are amazing. You know we were just ready to scratch Smoky when we saw the both of you run onto the track. Do you have a good reason for being late?"

As quickly as I could and between my heavy breaths, I told him the story of the noisy water-pump station. Sweat was dripping down into my eyes, and my hands were trembling just holding the phone.

"Well, you've missed the post parade, but you should still have time for Smoky to get warmed up a little. All right, Barb, we'll let Smoky run. Get him saddled up and out on the track as quickly as you can. Eddie can make a late announcement as to his weight and rider. We'll need to see you tomorrow morning. Make it about 11:00 a.m."

My knees were about to falter under me. I couldn't believe it. I was ecstatic. I almost yelled into the phone, *"Thank you, Mr. Slender!"* Then I handed the phone to Eddie. Ralph Pauline had Smoky saddled while I was on the phone just in case we got to go. I waved wildly to Ralph. "Get going! We're going to get to race!"

I watched as Ralph headed Smoky toward Robert Strauss, who was waiting for them on his pony horse. The three of them took off at a slow lope to salvage what they could of a warm-up. I wondered how we could have been so lucky as to have made it and to have so many people pulling for us. The fact that Dr. Goodberry had interrupted his prerace schedule and driven all the way down to our barn to check on us really impressed me. He was a very busy vet at that time of day, attending to thirty-six-odd barns of horses that had races yet to come. Just a minute or two more, and we would have been scratched from the race.

I tried to straighten myself up a little. My hair was wet with sweat, and my lucky red jumpsuit looked as if I had worn it for the past week. I had no shoes. But we had made it! Unbelievably, we had made it! Once again, I couldn't help but wonder if someone wasn't looking out for me from above. I said a silent prayer of thanks to Grampa and everyone else I could think of.

Suddenly, a voice behind me brought me back from my thoughts. "You never cease to amaze me . . . Here you are, the odds-on favorite to win a $25,000 stakes race, and you almost miss it. What in the hell were you doing?"

Bryan was upset, and I knew I deserved a tongue lashing, but I didn't need it right now. "Please, Bryan, I don't need any of this right now. Let's save it for after the race." I turned and walked away as I knew he had a lot more he wanted to say.

It didn't take long before the horses were approaching the starting gate and Eddie was beginning his exciting race commentary. The race that Bryan had fought so hard to salvage for us was about to start. I said a little prayer for Smoky to keep him safe. It had become a habit to do this for each race that any of my horses ran. I would almost feel jinxed if I forgot to say it.

Then I could hear Eddie announcing, "They're all in the gates" and then "They're off!"

Smoky broke a little slowly and trailed behind Bryan's entry, Kimorf. It was an unusual thing for Smoky to do. He almost always broke on top and was the first horse away from the gates. I hoped that Smoky had not used too much of himself before the race.

Then Eddie's voice was announcing, "Kimorf has taken the lead, with Magna Terra Smoky chasing him in second."

I watched and listened as Kimorf and Smoky continued that way down the backstretch. I was getting more nervous. Smoky seldom ran in second place. I hoped that I had not cost us this race.

However, just then, Eddie's captivating and exciting voice broadcast, "But Magna Terra Smoky is not done yet. He is literally full of run on the outside."

And just like that, I watched with awe as Smoky passed and put away Kimorf.

Eddie continued, "And Magna Terra Smoky is by Kimorf, and he is opening up his lead. The rest of the field has their work cut out for them . . . And Magna Terra Smoky absolutely loves this track. He's coming home the easiest of winners."

I was wild with excitement and pride. Smoky had once again annihilated the field, and Eddie was once again announcing that Smoky had yet established another track record, this time for one and one-eighth miles. He had won by an incredible and convincing six and a half lengths. Marise had run second, Kimorf third.

Denise Gault and Marj Barnett, owners of Marise, greeted and congratulated me in the winner's circle. They were most gracious in their loss, and I will always remember that. I know that I looked a bedraggled mess (the win photo would later confirm that), but I didn't care. I had to be the happiest person in the world. What could possibly be more exciting? Nothing could compare to the thrill of watching Smoky run and win, especially today.

Bryan was still upset at me, but I couldn't linger on that. Smoky had won. He had earned over four times what he made in 1989, and I thought 1989 had been a standout year. He had won in spite of me. I kept making such terrible blunders. What a remarkable horse! What other horse could have won a race under the circumstances Smoky faced today? Nothing seemed to interfere with Smoky's determination to win. No wonder the fans loved him. He always gave his racing everything he had. If he didn't win, it wasn't because he hadn't tried. Smoky was true blue. Smoky had the heart, the determination, and the perseverance that every dedicated horse trainer dreamed of having in their horses. How could I have been so fortunate? I thought to myself that the winds of destiny that had brought Smoky and me together in the very beginning were still at work. Whatever force was behind them, I hoped that they would keep right on blowing our way.

Photo Credits: Los Alamitos Race Course Photography

Smoky winning the 1 & 1/8 mile California Gold Cup
at the beautiful Bay Meadows Race Track in California, Ralph Pauline up
photo courtesy of Bay Meadows Race track

Author with Heidi Sommers (ARA) and Bryan Braithwaite
at Los Al Race Track

19 A Bad Decision

By now, Smoky's exciting and consistent racing style was attracting a rather large and loyal group of fans. People came to the races at Los Al just to watch Smoky run. There wasn't a race that went by that we weren't greeted by encouraging comments from fans standing at the rail of the saddling paddock. We even had letters arriving at the stable gate addressed to Smoky and me telling of fan's devotion to Smoky. On occasion, people would even tell me of pets that they had named after Smoky. Then came one of the biggest compliments of all.

It happened as I was combing through Smoky's mane after a bath I had just given him. A truck pulled up beside our barn, and out hopped Bruce Hawkinson. Bryan had introduced me to Bruce sometime before, and I knew he was the trainer of a stable of horses for Doc Allred, who was one of the main owners of Los Alamitos Race Course. I greeted Bruce and wondered what he was doing way back at my barn.

I was impressed and surprised when Bruce commented that Smoky looked well. I didn't really think that he would recognize Smoky out of his racing colors and when he wasn't in a race. I gave Smoky a pat and asked Bruce what I could do for him. Bruce got right to the point.

"Doc Allred sent me down here, Barb. He has admired Smoky for some time now. He would like to buy him."

Bruce's comment totally surprised me. I looked at him and then at Smoky.

"Oh wow, Bruce . . . You've really caught me off guard . . . I don't know what to say. I've never thought about selling Smoky. You know, he's the reason I'm even here at Los Al. He's made all this possible."

Bruce let me ramble on.

"I'm really flattered to hear that Doc Allred thinks so much of Smoky, but racing wouldn't mean very much to me if Smoky was gone. Smoky is what makes this game so much fun. He has given me everything he's got. I couldn't imagine racing without him."

I could tell by Bruce's expression that this was not the response he had expected. He had probably thought that I would be thrilled at the prospect of turning a huge profit on Smoky. Who wouldn't be proud to have Doc Allred interested in their horse, especially when that horse was an Arabian? Doc Allred was a quarter-horse man. He bred and raised some of the best quarter horses around. He had never owned an Arabian, and I don't believe anyone ever thought he would want to own one. I knew I didn't—until now, that was.

I apologized to Bruce again, but I don't think I handled things very well. How could I explain the special bond that Smoky and I had? How could I express my love for this very special animal that had given me so much joy and happiness? I know Bruce liked his horses and he treated them very well, but he was a business man as well. He understood that racing was a livelihood. Horses were to be bought and sold to make a profit. I'm sure he thought that every horse had a price.

"Well, I'm sure Doc will be disappointed. He has admired Smoky for quite some time now. Thanks for your time, Barb. I wish you all the best with Smoky."

"Thank you, Bruce. It has been quite an honor learning that Doc thinks so much of Smoky."

We said our goodbyes, and Bruce drove away in his truck.

I gave Smoky a gentle pat and a carrot from my pocket. "C'mon, tiger, we'll put you on the walker to dry off." As we set out for the walker, I saw Bryan approaching. I knew he couldn't wait to find out why Bruce had been at my barn.

"What was that all about?" he queried as he sauntered up.

"Doc Allred had Bruce come down here to try to buy Smoky," I responded.

"What did you say? Did he offer you a good price?"

"It didn't come to that. I couldn't sell Smoky. You of all people should know that." I clipped Smoky onto a walker arm. "There you go, tiger."

"You didn't even find out what they might offer?"

"What was the point in that? I don't think I could handle having Smoky in another barn. It would worry me to death. He has become so dependent upon the securities that we have formed. How would he adjust to a normal racing routine? He's what makes getting up in the morning so exciting. I love working with him, galloping him, and especially watching him run. It wouldn't be the same without him. We're a team. He has so many quirks. Who else would understand them? Do you think he would be happy anywhere else? Maybe I'm naive and think I'm the only one who really understands Smoky, but he's come to expect certain things that I don't think he would get in other barns. Look how much he loves his walks around the barn area. Who else would take him on those walks? Think how he loves to go down to the receiving barn to roll. Who else would think to do that for him? Who else would set up a pen in the aisleway so he could visit with his buddies? Who else would always reward him with carrots for a good workout or a good race or even a great gallop? Who else would let Smoky stop at the gap three or four times to survey and inspect all the things going on at the track? I could go on and on, but all these things are what make Smoky a happy horse. He races well because he is happy and he loves it. I think that Smoky's heart and his love for racing would slowly die if he couldn't do all the things that he loves to do. And to tell the truth, my heart and love of racing would die as well. Would it be worth it?"

"When you say all that, I guess that you are probably right. I know you love Smoky and that he loves you, but it could have let you start a new life, even buy the ranch of your dreams. Did you think about that?"

"No . . . I really didn't when Bruce was here. But I'm thinking about it now. It would be fantastic to have a nice ranch with huge green pastures. You know how much we would both like that. But to sell Smoky to get that? That just wouldn't be right. I couldn't do it."

With that said, Bryan took me in his arms and held me against him. I sighed and just let him hold me. Later that week, Bryan would report back to me that Bruce had been talking down at the rail. He told Bryan how surprised he had been that I wouldn't sell Smoky.

"Do you know that he even joked that he never even got to make an offer? He exclaimed that there wasn't even any negotiation! He said he had *never, ever* known a horse that didn't have a price!"

We both laughed.

"I bet he thinks I'm really a dumb country hick."

Still, it was a huge compliment to Smoky, and I let it go at that. I couldn't have dreamed it then, but Doc would stay a huge fan of

Smoky throughout all of Smoky's years of racing. Even after Smoky quit racing, Doc would be quoted as saying that he missed the good old days when Magna Terra Smoky was racing.

I could well understand why Doc had been so interested in buying Smoky. During his four-year-old year, Smoky had accomplished so much. He had set four new track records in California, and that was in addition to the track records that he had already set at Holly, Colorado. Smoky had only suffered defeat twice in his four-year-old year, and both times, that was to the older champion News Release. News was setting records of his own, for he now had thirty-two wins to his credit and was challenging the old-timer Sam's Count for the most wins ever to be achieved by an Arabian racehorse. Sam's Count had been retired with thirty-three official wins to his credit.

It was during this time that Bryan began entertaining thoughts of traveling to the East Coast with Smoky. Delaware Park Racetrack was offering purses that were substantially larger than those offered anywhere else in the country. Bryan rationalized that Smoky, who had faster times than the Delaware horses, would have no trouble winning races there. His line of thought was quite convincing, even though I questioned being able to compare times at tracks that were so very different. I worried about the humidity we would face and the fact that we would have to haul Smoky clear across the country to get there.

Bryan kept at his campaign to travel back east. He even offered to do *all* the driving. It was tempting. At this same time, I was receiving very upsetting phone calls from Fort Collins. I wasn't sure why, but Dick was intent upon reneging on a deal that we had made prior to my leaving for California. When I had finished racing at Holly, Dick and I had come to an agreement that seemed to help both of us. I needed a place to leave Aurzel and a thoroughbred gelding that I had purchased. Dick needed a way to alleviate paying interest on the $30,000 that he had borrowed from me to keep his nursery/landscape business up and running. We finally agreed that I could board Aurzel and Kiarctic in one of his pastures, having to pay only for extra hay when needed and for trims, worming, and any possible vet bills. In return, Dick would not have to pay any interest on his loan. It had not been the ideal arrangement as I had really wanted complete severance in our relationship. On the other hand, I couldn't bring Aurzel to Los Al as he was too young, and I wanted a safe and fun place for him to enjoy his early years. Now, however, circumstances were changing this arrangement. I had to get Aurzel out of there. I had to go back to Colorado.

So at a time when I should have been basking in Smoky's achievements, I was instead worried about Aurzel. Bryan and I talked about my problem at length. He saw a way to kill two birds with one stone.

"Why not make our trip to Delaware serve two purposes? We could stop by Fort Collins on the way back."

So it came to be that we would go to Delaware. We were on our way headed east, with Thunder contentedly sleeping in the back seat, when I saw Bryan reach over for a beer from the six-pack that he had neatly tucked in beside his seat.

"Bryan, please don't do that on this trip. I don't mind if you have some beer at night when we stop somewhere—but not while you are driving."

"Don't worry about me. I can handle it."

I hated how Bryan's drinking was such a big issue between us. It especially bothered me to see him drink and drive, and I decided that I had to put my foot down.

"You know, this is my trip with my horses. I am paying you to drive. You wanted to do this. I can't put up with the drinking while you're driving. You know it's wrong, and besides that, it's dangerous. Let's do this trip without the drinking."

"It's only a beer, for crying out loud! Why are you being so unreasonable?"

"Bryan, I'm not going to argue. If you are going to drink and drive, I'm going to back out of this trip. I don't want to go if this is the way it is going to be."

Bryan was ignoring me. He thought I was being totally unreasonable, that this was just another idle threat. "What are you doing?"

We had slowed down for a stoplight.

"I'm getting out. If I have to hitchhike back to Los Al, I will."

I was really hoping that my bluff would work, that he would realize that I was serious. But it took opening the door and actually getting out before Bryan relented. I stood at the curb feeling miserable.

"Okay. You have a deal." He handed me the beer in his hand.

"Do you really mean it? Can you drive this whole trip without drinking while driving?"

"Guess I'll have to."

"Thank you." I got back in the truck and squeezed his hand, and we drove off.

I found myself looking forward to this trip now. I felt that Bryan and I had just established a new rapport of sorts concerning his drinking. I knew that this would be difficult for him. He wasn't used to going very long without a beer. I admired him for having the resolve to change his behavior. I knew there would be some rocky spots ahead, but Bryan was always good to his word, and I felt strongly that he would live up to his end of the bargain.

As the miles sped by and we passed out of California and into Arizona, Bryan turned to me and casually mentioned that he would like to stop by Bob and Nancy's place in Showlow, Arizona, on our way. Bob and Nancy were the couple that stood Brusally Orselar, Aurzel's sire. Bryan had been good friends with Bob and Nancy for a long time. It was just another example of the coincidences that existed between Bryan and me. Back in 1988, Dick and I were looking for a race sire with "Orzel" bloodlines to breed Aurzel's dam and also Hurama, one of Dick's mares, too. In my search for a good stallion, I discovered an Orzel son, Brusally Orselar, standing in Arizona. As he was fairly close and his stud fee was reasonable, we had hauled our two mares down there and thus met Bob and Nancy. It seemed unreal how so many coincidences linked Bryan and me together.

"What?" I exclaimed. "Their place is totally out of our way. What do you want to go there for?"

"I haven't seen Bob and Nancy for ages. It'll be a good place to make our first stopover."

"Bryan, we've just started out trip. I thought we were really going to try to get a lot of miles out of the way while the horses were fresh and traveling well. I don't want to drag this trip out."

"This won't take long. I just want to see Bob and Nancy. They're good friends, and I've not had the chance to visit with them forever."

"Why didn't you do this before? You never even mentioned that you had this in mind. Please don't do this. Let's just continue on."

But Bryan was not to be appeased. I couldn't fathom why he was so intent on going out of our way to see his old friends. I was not happy about this turn of events at all. This trip was not starting out well. Finally, after a lot of bantering back and forth, I compromised. I knew he was adamant about stopping there for some reason he was not telling me. Why in the devil did he have to make this visit now? I was really unhappy, to say the least.

"I don't think I'm going to change your mind, am I? Okay, but I don't want to go up to the house. If we do, you will want to stay and drink with Bob, and then we'll end up staying overnight, and we'll lose a whole day. If we stop down at their gate and park there, I'll let the horses out to graze while you do your visiting."

Neither of us liked the compromise, but Bryan knew that it was going to be that or nothing. I was already upset about the way the trip had started, and now I had to deal with this unwanted stopover. *Was this trip going to end up being a big mistake?* I wondered.

As I unloaded the horses, my mind was still dwelling on this unplanned side trip. I was upset at Bryan and resented having to bow to his wishes. Thunder thought it was a great stop at least and was hunting the area for rabbits. I should have been paying more attention to what I was doing with the horses. In my frustration and displeasure over the situation, I was sloppy in tying Smoky to the side of the horse trailer so that I could unload Indy. In my agitated state of mind, I made the unforgivable mistake of tying Smoky a little too long. I knew better as I did it. NATRC had taught me better than that.

I heard myself saying, "We'll just be a second, Smoky . . . I just need to get Indy out, and then you both can graze."

It was a second too long. In the bat of an eye, Smoky, while scratching his ear, had impossibly gotten his left hind leg over the tie rope. A wreck ensued. Smoky panicked when he realized he was unable to put his hind leg down. I dropped Indy's lead rope and rushed over to try to untie the lead rope from the horse trailer. I couldn't get near the rope.

Bryan was yelling, "Let me in! I've got to cut the rope."

Bryan tried to find a space where Smoky's thrashing wouldn't injure him. It seemed to take forever, but finally, Bryan succeeded in cutting the rope. Smoky lurched back, holding up his left hind leg. I cringed at what I might find.

Bryan was cursing. "I can't believe you were so f——ing stupid. If we had stopped at the house like I wanted to, none of this would have ever happened. But no, you had to have your way. Now look what you've done!" He kept up a screaming criticism.

I felt badly enough without any of this. I lashed back. "None of this would have happened if you hadn't insisted we come down here in the first place, so shut up!"

I reached over for Smoky. "Let me have a look, Smoke. How bad is it?"

Smoky didn't want me messing with his leg, and he tried to hobble a few steps on it. He wasn't putting much weight on it. *Not good*, I thought.

Finally, I was able to get a good look. It didn't look all that bad right now . . . but it was a rope burn, and rope burns tended to get rawer and sorer as time wore on.

Bryan and I were both still so upset that it wasn't going to do any good to try and talk right then.

I wanted to put some ice on the burn but didn't think Smoky would tolerate that very well. I ended up putting a Furacin wrap on the ankle and gave Smoky a couple of bute to ease the pain and swelling.

We were both visibly upset and hardly talking now. Bryan took off walking up the drive to see Bob and Nancy while I lamented over my stupid mistake. Smoky and Indy were happy to graze, but I knew that I would probably pay dearly for my blunder.

When Bryan returned about an hour later, we were both more amenable to conversing. We discussed what might be best for us to do. I fluctuated between returning home and proceeding on. When it came down to it, we really didn't know the extent of injury to Smoky. In addition, a substantial nomination fee had been paid for Smoky's big race back in Delaware, and we were both really loath to give up on our big plans. However, I also had an awful feeling that this trip was not starting well, and I wondered if it was an omen that maybe it was not meant to be.

In the end, Bryan persuaded me to continue on. "We can always turn around later if things do not get better," he rationalized.

I loaded up Smoky and Indy, and we continued on down the road. As nightfall approached, we both kept a lookout for a place to stop for the night. As we drove through Socorro, New Mexico, we came across a young boy driving some sheep. We slowed to a stop and asked him if he might know of a place where we could turn our two horses out for the night. It couldn't have worked out better, for he offered us a pen at his little farm. It was quite the sight, watching Smoky and Indy bed down among the pens of sheep for the night. They seemed quite happy, however, and enjoyed exploring their new digs. Smoky was favoring his hind leg some, but he still managed to run about and buck and play. At least it didn't seem to be any worse. Later, I caught Smoky up, redressed his rope burn, and gave him another bute tablet.

The next two days went without episode. Then, as we approached Louden, Tennessee, Bryan turned to me and said, "Sam Harrison's place is just up ahead. You'll like meeting him and seeing his place."

I was looking forward to that. I had heard so much about Sam and all that he had done to promote Arabian racing. He was quite a character to hear Bryan describe him. I was also looking forward to turning the horses out in one of Sam's pastures so that they could graze and move around.

Sam turned out to be the character Bryan had described, and he was also quite the charmer. We enjoyed good conversation and a great dinner at one of Sam's favorite restaurants.

Although Smoky was still favoring his rope burn, it did not appear to slow him down. He ran and played and bucked like a youngster. As I watched him having so much fun, I couldn't help but wish that we were going into this venture at 100 percent. I wished that I could turn back time and do the stopover at Bob and Nancy's all over again.

Finally, we arrived at Delaware Park. We had made the long trip in great time thanks to Bryan's tenacious ability to drive for endless hours at a time. He had also kept his promise not to drink and drive. He was quite proud of that, and I was proud of him.

I had never been to Delaware, let alone Delaware Park before. Bryan had. He had raced superstars here such as Brusally Gaysar, Ibn Bint Hilyuri, and Brusally Orlen. Orlen was to become a major player in our breeding program many years later. It was to be a sad fact that neither of us realized the tremendous potential that Orlen had until it was really too late.

As we entered the drive, I couldn't help but feel that it was such a nice setting for a racetrack. There were lush manicured lawns and huge trees lining the road as it wound its way to the stable gate. At the horsemen's gate, Bryan recognized and chatted with the guard, and after signing the horses in, we proceeded to the receiving barn, where we were to be temporarily stabled until further accommodations could be made for us. It turned out to be the ideal situation for us. It was quiet and peaceful, and Smoky and Indy were the only horses in the huge long barn. The shed row was surrounded by nice green grass and was completely fenced. It meant that Smoky and Indy could be turned out to graze and it wouldn't interfere with anyone. We had our own little private world until race days when other horses that shipped in would also be stabled here. Even Thunder was able to get out and explore the area.

"What did we ever do to deserve this? This is absolutely wonderful!" I exclaimed.

Bryan shrugged and laughed. "I was hoping that this was where they would put us. All the regular barns are evidently full."

"Well," I ventured, "the horses are going to think they died and went to heaven. Let's get them out."

As we unloaded Smoky and Indy, both horses looked around at their surroundings. It was so cute. I couldn't tell if they were expecting to be home or not. We walked the horses around a little to show them the area and then turned them loose to roll and play.

"Smoky's still favoring his left hind. This trip might still be for naught."

"Hard to tell. But I sure wish he looked better too," Bryan replied.

Just then, Indy and Smoky took off. They tore around the area, and Smoky's rope burn seemed to be bothering him less. I just loved watching the both of them have so much fun.

Bryan and I got busy setting up two stalls. When we finished, Bryan turned to me. "Well, let's catch up Smoky and Indy. I'm hungry, and I'm betting you are too, and we still need to find a motel room for the night."

"Sounds wonderful! Let me grab their halters."

I gave Indy's halter to Bryan, and we started walking toward where the two were grazing.

"Dang, I think these two like this green grass a little too much."

Smoky and Indy had watched us approach, and as we got closer, off they went.

"Obviously, they don't want to be caught." I laughed. It was great watching them enjoy their new turnout so much, and I thought it was kinda cute until I began to realize that they were really serious about not being caught.

"Guess I'd better go back to the shed row and grab a bucket of grain. Looks like we need some friendly motivation here."

I ran back to the barn and returned with a bucket of Omolene and some carrots. "This ought to do the trick."

I shook the bucket and held out the carrots for Smoky to hear and see. Smoky let me almost get up to him, but just then, he swung around and, with Indy following, took off. They both ran clear around to the other side of the shed row.

I turned to Bryan. "This is going to be harder than I thought."

Slowly, we walked around the barn to where Smoky and Indy were now grazing. This time, we didn't even get close before they took off again.

"Do you get the idea that these two would like to spend the night out here grazing?" I half-jokingly said to Bryan.

But it wasn't a joke anymore. We had to catch these two up. We couldn't leave them out. They weren't even supposed to be running loose here at all.

"Man, if anyone sees them out like this, we might be in a lot of trouble. How are we ever going to catch these two?"

Finally, it was Bryan who devised a plan.

"I think we can get those two. There's a manure pile behind the barn with a wall along one side and a fence on the other side. If we can get them going in this direction and keep them along the fence, we can trick the both of them into running into the manure pit. It's a perfect blind alley."

I chuckled. "Okay, let's give it a try. But we better make sure it works the first time. They won't fall for it a second time."

Bryan was looking over the situation. "Why don't you stand out to the side so they stay along the fence and I'll head them toward the pit?"

Smoky and Indy took to running almost immediately, and we were hard-pressed to get in the right positions. Indy was so intent on watching Bryan that he hardly realized that he was running plumb into a dead-end trap. Smoky was right on Indy's heels. We quickly blocked the only exit.

The result was precious, and I wished that I had had a camera at that instance. Smoky's head went up as he saw the dead end. He whirled around, and with a look of total surprise and disappointment aimed at Indy, he registered his disgust. It was ever so obvious that he felt his partner in crime had carelessly led them both into a trap from which they could not escape. To this day, Bryan loves retelling that story, and we can both still remember that infamous look on Smoky's face.

Sadly, Delaware did not turn out to be a good racing experience. Smoky's rope burn still bothered him in spite of all that we and our veterinarian tried to do. It did not help our cause that Smoky was high weighted for his first stakes race. Although he was only a four-year-old, he was assigned the incredulous and unrealistic weight of 130 pounds in a field of mostly older horses. I could not believe that this was happening. I felt that Delaware Park was favoring its local resident horses and went to visit the racing secretary to vent my concern.

To my dismay and utter amazement, the racing secretary bluntly stated that the weights that he had assigned were just and fair. He iced the cake by adding, "Weight doesn't really make any difference anyway."

I couldn't believe what I was hearing. The whole rationale behind assigning weights to racehorses was the established fact that one additional pound of weight literally cost a horse a length in a mile race. Smoky would be carrying up to fifteen pounds more than some of the other entries. I protested and argued, but I realized he had no compassion or even time for a lowly Arabian horse trainer who was a woman and an out-of-stater, to boot. It was an insult, and I knew even then that he would never have dared say what he did to a male trainer.

I got up and left. I knew that there wasn't any point in arguing the issue with him any longer. I couldn't wait to find Bryan.

"I can't believe he can get away with this. What can we do?" I ranted at Bryan.

"Not much, I'm afraid. That racing secretary doesn't much care about Arabians in the first place, and he certainly doesn't care about one that doesn't stall here and support the whole meet. You can either scratch him from the race or use it as a practice race for the big four-year-old stakes race that we really came here for. You've paid the nomination fee, so if Smoky is all right, I'd race him."

Bryan's response wasn't what I had wanted to hear, but I knew that he was right. In the end, I decided to test the competition and race him. It would at least give me an idea of what Smoky could do here.

Smoky ran a poor seventh. He was not right. He had too many obstacles against him. I felt his rope burn still bothered him even though he was no longer lame. He had endured a long trailer trip clear across the country, and he had not been able to condition for the race at all during that time. In addition, I had not anticipated the extremely deep cushion of earth at the Delaware track. Smoky was used to racing on a lightly cushioned fast track. It was like he had come from running on a hard dirt road to running in the sand along a dry beach. I had asked the impossible of him. I let the pressure of coming so far, Bryan's assurance that he was better than the horses here, and the money I would lose dictate an unwise decision.

Even so, Smoky came off the race in great spirits and shape. His rope burn looked no worse. Because he was feeling so spry, I decided to race him back six days later. Finally, I made a good decision as Smoky ran an outstanding race and beat a very tough field of horses.

The four-year-old stakes race did not have such good results. I realized that I had had no idea of the exceptional caliber of four-year-olds that called Delaware Park home. Monarch AH, a very talented Wiking son, was touted as the strong favorite, and he proved his prowess and authenticity. He demolished the rest of us in the race. Smoky ran a good race but placed fourth. Fourth does not pay well.

That was to be our last race here. I realized that I had accomplished nothing by bringing Smoky back east. We had come a lot of miles, wasted a lot of time, missed a lot of races in California, and spent an awful lot of money. I had not shown the Delaware crowd the true Magna Terra Smoky, and I had wreaked havoc with his great racing record. Why had we decided to be so greedy? I knew that I would be glad to be on the road home again.

This bad dream was not over quite yet, however. I still had to deal with Dick. As we headed out for California, I wondered what Dick was really up to and just what he would demand. Before we left Los Al, I called a trainer and NATRC competitor whom I had ridden many miles with. She had such a kind way with horses, and her home was not far from Dick's farm. I had asked her if she might have room and time to start light work with a young colt. She said that she did. So at least Aurzel had a safe place to go.

While I had been setting up those arrangements, Bryan piped up, "Why don't we call Alice and see if we can rest Smoky and Indy at her place while you meet with Dick? I'm sure that she'd love to see

Smoky again, and I haven't seen Alice since I delivered Smoky to her when he was six months old."

"Hey, that sounds like a great idea. It'll give me something to look forward to. I've been absolutely dreading the meeting with Dick."

So it was that at least some plans had been laid out. Now I just had to hope that Dick didn't have something up his sleeve.

We came to Alice's place first. I was anxious to see how Smoky reacted to his old stomping grounds.

"Think he'll remember this place?" Bryan queried.

"Oh, I'm sure of that. Smoky doesn't forget much, and this place was a huge part of his life."

Sure enough, as I lowered the ramp and backed Smoky out of the trailer, a loud and piercing whinny rocked my ears.

"Dang, Smoky, did you have to do that right then?" I laughed.

I looked over at Bryan. "Does that answer your question?"

Alice was striding over. We had called her en route to let her know when we would arrive.

"My, Smoky looks good. He's grown and filled out too. How did you do in Delaware?"

"Not good, Alice. I'll tell you all about it. You sure look wonderful."

"Bryan, how the heck are you doing? It's been ages!"

Bryan gave Alice a big hug, and they laughed and carried on. Eventually, Alice and Bryan took a break from their bantering.

"Thought you could put the horses in this corral. It's big, and it's safe." Alice pointed at a large wooden corral next to her cow barn.

"That'll be great."

Smoky and Indy were both anxious to be set loose. To roll, I imagined. As we let the two loose, it was almost an automatic response. The ground was deep loose dirt and ripe for a good back rub. We all three laughed.

"I'll get them some hay from the barn. The stock tank is already full of clean water," Alice stated as she headed for the barn.

We finished setting up the horses for the evening and headed toward Alice's home. We had a lot of things to talk about.

The next day, Bryan and I drove to Dick's farm. Bryan was so gracious to have come with me. He wanted to make sure that everything went all right. Neither of us knew what to expect from Dick.

I reluctantly made my way up to the house. Dick answered the door. New agreement papers were set out on the table, a beautiful wood table that I had bought and paid for. We said our formal amenities and got down to business. I was not happy about the changes that had been made in our agreement, but I knew I had to sign them to get Aurzel. I knew that I should fight this, but to do that, I would have to stay in Colorado. It would take time that I didn't have, and it would take more money. I had horses waiting for me back in California, and Smoky and Indy had to be looked after. And in the meantime, I still wouldn't have Aurzel.

So I signed the new modified loan agreement. Dick signed Aurzel over to me, and I walked out. I never wanted to see that man again.

20 THE DARLEY AWARDS

No award meant as much to the Arabian racing world as earning a Darley. This treasured trophy and honor carried no monetary prize with it, but its very name signified the best of the best. In its fourth year of existence, it encompassed everything its creator, Dr. Sam Harrison, had envisioned. To win a Darley assured one's place in the record books and thus the associated immortality of the achievement.

Dr. Sam Harrison was very well liked and respected by members of the Arabian racing world. Several years before, Dr. Sam, as he was affectionately called, had recognized that the Arabian horse-racing industry needed help. In fact, it had needed help badly. In response to a dire and downward spiraling situation, he had devised the Darley Awards to recognize outstanding Arabian racehorse achievement, and he had also established the ARC (Arabian Racing Cup) program, which was patterned after the Breeder's Cup of thoroughbred racing. His ARC program was designed to monetarily reward Arabian race winners and their owners and breeders. By initiating this, Arabian purses were able to grow, and this encouraged more breeders and owners into the sport of Arabian racing. So the sport that was once badly ailing was now growing and prospering.

This year, to my delight and amazement, Smoky had been nominated for a Darley Award. What an accomplishment from a colt that had such a tenuous beginning and who had been marked early on to never achieve anything! I was so thrilled and happy for Smoky. This nomination signified, more than any other single thing, that he had beaten the odds. It signified that the little guy could make it if given the chance and the encouragement. For me, it was going to be even more of a special event because the Darleys were scheduled to take place at Los Al Race Course. It meant that I could afford to attend the ceremonies and that I could be present to perhaps see Smoky earn the recognition that I felt he had worked so hard for.

But my elation did not last long. An error came to my attention when a list of horses that were nominated for each Darley category was published. The list that came out named the five horses that were nominated in each category and also the earnings for each horse. Smoky was in the four-year-old category along with his main rival, a colt by the name of Shakil Rakkad. Smoky and Shakil had both had a phenomenal year and were very close in all regards, especially in total monies earned. However, what was really upsetting was that the amount of money printed next to Smoky's name was incorrect. There was an error of over $4,000. The chart showed Smoky earning $57,478 for the year compared to the $61,728 he had really earned.

With this error published and given to the voters, it made the second-leading money earner, Shakil Rakkad (with $61,222 in earnings), look as if he had earned almost $4,000 more than Smoky. The actual fact was that Smoky had earned over $500 more than Shakil. Smoky and Shakil had run the same number of races (an amazing fourteen races for each horse), with Smoky earning ten wins and two seconds and zero thirds compared to Shakil's eight wins, one second, and two thirds. The incorrect information given on monies earned for each horse was crucial. This was usually the deciding factor in who won the Darley. This incorrectly printed information was what the delegated voters were using to determine the winners of the four-year-old Darley Award. I couldn't believe it. Was this an accidental error, or was it deliberate? Smoky was once again the little guy fighting for his rightful place among the big guys. I wasn't going to let this injustice prevail. I carefully thought out what I needed to do.

The first thing I did was call the AJC (Arabian Jockey Club) and obtain a detailed printout of Smoky's races and earnings. Right away, I found the error.

"Look at this, Bryan. They haven't even given Smoky any credit for the monies he earned in this race at Los Al. I know I have the results of that race here somewhere."

Bryan had been almost as upset as I was over the information printed on Smoky.

"And look at this. Even with that error, the AJC shows Smoky earning $59,578. How did Sam's committee ever come up with $57,478?"

Bryan checked the information. "So there were actually two errors! Either someone was really careless, or they didn't want Smoky to win this award."

"That's what I'm wondering too. Look here . . . This is the result page for the race in question. Smoky actually earned $2,250 for that second place. So altogether, he should have the amount of $59,478 recorded by the AJC plus this $2,250 that they omitted for his second-place finish. That totals $61,728 in earnings, not the $57,478 shown. I need to call the AJC and get their mistake taken care of and then call Sam."

I did get AJC on the phone, and after checking their records, they called me back and acknowledged their error. Dr. Sam was more difficult to reach, and even after numerous attempts, I was not able to contact him. So I decided to put everything in writing and send him a letter. I thought Dr. Sam would wish to make things right and was confident that he would do so before the voting took place. I asked Dr. Sam if he would be so kind as to publish the correct information and get it out to the Darley voting committee before a vote was taken.

The written response I got back from Dr. Sam was devastating to me. Very matter-of-factly, he informed me that just to get nominated for such an award was an honor. He went on to say that no system was perfect and that the source of information he used for money earned was by far the best he knew of. He trusted the source and said he would stand by them. He was not about to change any information on the voting ballots because of data found by one individual. He wanted me to be a good girl and keep quiet so things could get done.

I turned the letter over to Bryan for him to read. Bryan had listened to my livid exclamations as I read Sam's letter. He knew I was angry and very upset.

I couldn't wait for Bryan to finish reading the letter.

"Can you believe this? I can't apprehend that Dr. Sam actually wrote this! It's unreal! I really expected an honest response and an apology. Instead, I get this! Man, so much for Sam and the Darleys!"

Bryan put the letter down.

"I can't believe this either. It isn't right. Sam is making a huge mistake."

Up to this time, I had totally respected and valued the Darley Awards and had held Dr. Sam in very high esteem. Now I thought, *What a farce the Darleys really were!* Were they meant for only big and important people and big and important horses? I did not know many of these big and important people personally, but I did know some of the people, organizations, and magazines that voted for Darley Awards.

"I'd better get busy, Bryan. I'm going to write everyone I know—people, magazines, racetracks, etc.—that are voting on these Darleys and let them know the real facts. And I'm going to enclose a copy of my letter to Sam and also a copy of his response to my letter. They haven't heard the last of me. And maybe they are going to wish they never heard of me."

Bryan, bless his soul, even called Sam. I listened to his conversation.

"Sam, I'm calling you as a friend. It's about Magna Terra Smoky and the four-year-old Darley Award."

I heard a pause in the conversation, and then Bryan was restating, "Sam, did you hear me? I'm calling you as a friend. I'm not trying to criticize or be judgmental, but for your sake and the Darleys, I think the record needs to be set straight. You are a good friend, and I've known you a long time. I'm just asking you to do the right thing."

Bryan looked over at me. "Sam hung up on me," he said in a hushed voice.

That year, even though the Darley Awards were to be held right in my backyard, I did not go. I had not received any reply to any of my letters. Not one. Not even from Ray and Jane Teutsch. Not even from the *Arabian Horse Magazine*. Not even from ARC, Sam, or Los Al Race Course. I was thoroughly disappointed and even more disgusted. I thought my input had no impact. I did not want to waste my time or money attending something that was a farce. I did not want to support a program that would not listen to honesty and the facts.

While others enjoyed the festivities of the Darley Awards up in the grandstands, I brooded back at the barn. Bryan decided not to attend the Darleys also but had gone up to the track to watch the races. Suddenly, he appeared in his big blue truck. Silently, he walked over and handed me a copy of the Darley Awards booklet that he had obtained.

"I really have no desire to see that," I said.

"Think you should, hon . . . You might be surprised."

Bryan evidently wanted me to see something, so I took the program and opened it.

"They've listed Smoky's earning correctly. Someone read your letter and got things changed."

"Isn't that something? Wouldn't it have been wonderful if someone had had the balls to call me and tell me about it? But not one person did. I'm glad the information is changed and Smoky is represented correctly, but it doesn't really change the fact that no one wants to buck Sam and own up to the mistake. It's just been silently glided over. Sam can't repair what has been said and done. I really don't care if Smoky wins the Darley or not anymore. Darleys don't mean the same to me now. I just want Smoky to have the credit that he is due. At least the people attending the Darleys will read the correct data on Smoky. They'll know who the best horse is."

Later that evening, I learned that Magna Terra Smoky had rightfully won the Darley for four-year-olds. Whatever had transpired behind closed doors, I never heard. I had fought for and earned the victory for Smoky, and that was all that mattered. However, I never did hear a word of apology or regret over what had almost taken place. Although I would care for racehorses for another fifteen years, I never did attend a Darley Award ceremony.

In spite of the Darley debacle and in spite of Delaware, 1990 will always be a favorite year in my memories. Smoky was on top of his game. He loved what he was doing, and I loved watching him do what he loved doing! Smoky ran one more race after the Darleys and ended the year with an amazing fifteen races, of which he had won ten and place second three times. He had earned an incredible $65,204, an outstanding amount for an Arabian horse in 1990. His only races that had results that were off the chart were his two stakes races in Delaware. Those black marks should have been against me, not Smoky. It had been my negligence and my fault that he had run subpar in those races. I wish that could be recorded in the record books. I should never even have attempted to run Smoky in those races. It's something I will always have to live with. It was a *very, very* poor judgment call.

Then again, maybe that needed to happen. Maybe things were going too well, were too easy. Something had to bring me back down to earth. And bring me back, it did. It was a humbling experience, more humbling than most people knew. For I knew the terribly wrong thing that I had done. I had run a horse that was not 100 percent, and I had known it. We had been fortunate. Smoky could have been badly injured trying to protect his rope-burned ankle. I wondered how I would have dealt with that. I realized that I, like a gambler on a winning streak, had been addicted to the winning. I had gambled with the thing most precious to me. Thank goodness I had been given a second chance. Yes, 1990 had been a good year. Sometimes the worst times have the most to teach us. If I learned from my mistake, then perhaps a lot of good had come out of the Delaware trip.

The final awards of the year, the ARAC awards, reaffirmed just how awesome Smoky was. ARAC stood for the Arabian Racing Association of California. These awards were held in the huge Penrose room at Los Alamitos Race Course, and both Bryan and I did attend this awards ceremony. No one knew ahead of time who had won any awards except the ARAC board. It turned out to be a sweep for Smoky. Not only did he earn Four-Year-Old Champion of the Year, but he was unanimously named Horse of the Year. Smoky's sire, SW David, earned Sire of the Year, and Smoky's half brothers, Broyuri and Ibn Bint Hilyuri, both trained by Bryan, earned Three-Year-Old and Five-Year-Old Horses of the Year. I couldn't hold back my tears of pride, and neither could Bryan.

My letter to Dr. Sam Harrison and the Darley Awards Committee
concerning the incorrect recording of Smokey's earnings
for Darley Award voting   Dec. 20, 1990

12-20-90

Dear Sam & the Darley Awards Comm.,

I have debated about writing this letter as I realize how much of your time, energy & devotion goes into arabian racing & the Darley awards. You have created the world of arabian racing for the rest of us so I hope this letter does not come across as being ungrateful.

I guess my disappointment lies in the fact that I don't feel Smokey had a fair shot for a Darley award. It seems to me that the Darley Racing form should provide an accurate detailed account of each horse yet the figure of $57,478.⁰⁰ attributed to Smokey in the category of "Horse of the Year"

-2-

is over $4000 short of the $61,728.⁰⁰ recorded by the Daily racing form. It is $2000 under the figure accredited to him for 4 year old colt/gelding. Should these figures perhaps be checked before being sent out for votes? Smokey had a 2nd place finish on 7-8-90 & yet earned $0?

Shahil Hakkad is a good horse & I have no qualms about him winning out over Smokey. But I do have a qualm when Smokey may have missed this recognition through no fault of his own. His earnings of $61,728 top Shahil's accredited earnings not visa versa.

Sincerely,
Barbara M. Gogole

21   1991 AND RIO HONDO

The latter part of 1990 had given me a sneak preview of a new challenge on the horizon. Although Bryan and I were good friends and romantically involved, we were also each other's fiercest competition. On one hand, it was a good thing, for it pushed us both to perform better. On the other hand, we would have been a totally awesome force had we pooled our resources and worked as a team. I guess we were both too independent and too competitive to be able to work together.

To add to that, we each had very different methods of training, and neither of us would compromise much in the way we did things. I felt that Bryan left too much responsibility with his grooms and that he left his barn too early and too often to go drinking with his buddies at the Starting Gate. Bryan was a very social person. I was very quiet and would rather spend my extra time with my horses. Both Bryan and I realized that Smoky would never have become the horse he was with Bryan as his trainer because Bryan would not have taken the time that I did.

On the other hand, Bryan got horses to work that I never could have. He had a way of working with difficult stallions that I never had. They respected him and acted on their best manners with him. He knew how and when to discipline them, and they raced well for him. I enjoyed watching him in the saddling paddock with these stallions as they always looked so quiet and well-mannered. I babied my horses probably to the extreme. It worked well with the mares and geldings I had in my barn. I knew I did not do well with stallions and did not have any in my care. I liked to brush, saddle, and gallop my horses and also personally care for their legs and backs etc. each morning after their workout. Each horse was attended to in an individual manner.

I seldom—actually, almost never—wrapped a horse's legs. I preferred to rub down their legs and backs with rubbing alcohol or a liniment and to apply mud to their legs without a wrap. Bryan wrapped almost all his horses' legs literally every day. Although I could spot many lameness issues etc., I galloped my horses to feel out a problem, whereas Bryan could see a leg or back problem that a horse had with just a glance.

I spent so much time attending to my horses that I did not have time to visit up at the rail of the racetrack. As Bryan did not gallop his horses and his grooms cleaned his stalls and did all the leg care, Bryan had time to visit and socialize up at the track. By doing that, he saw which horses looked sour or lame. He knew which horses had good workouts and which horses to be on the lookout for. He knew when a new horse arrived, and he loved to gossip, so he learned and shared all the little things that were going on around the racetrack. He knew the current romances, who was broke, who had problems, and what they were. Everyone confided in Bryan. He was easy to talk to, and he joked and teased with everyone. The women looked forward to the teasing, and the men looked forward to hearing Bryan's comments on the horses. Bryan was a walking encyclopedia on horses, and everyone wanted a part of that encyclopedia. What I knew of the goings-on around the racetrack, I inevitably learned from Bryan.

Bryan was getting low on good horses, however. He wanted a superstar like Smoky, and so to that end, Bryan cultivated a new client named Bob Rudolph. Rudolph was a flashy individual who had the money to buy good horses, and like Bryan and me, he loved to win. As a child, Rudolph had come down with polio, and it resulted in a crippled leg. He always walked with a limp. He seemed personable, but there was something about Rudolph that bothered me. He liked to flash his money about too much. I often wondered if it was done to compensate for this deformity or if there was more to it than that.

"Rudolph will be good for the sport," Bryan would counter when I would voice my concern. "We'll be able to get some good horses now," he would say.

With Bryan's eye for a good racehorse and Rudolph's money, they would make a team that Smoky and I found hard to beat. Bryan's first acquisition for Rudolph was a gorgeous dark chestnut gelding named Rio Hondo. My friend since Holly, Colorado, Frankie Rinker, had found, like the rest of us, that racing in California was a lot more expensive than it had been in Colorado and Wyoming. She was broke, and so in her dire financial state, she decided to sell Rio in both his and her best interests. Although Rio Hondo had never been a huge threat to Smoky when Frankie owned and trained him, he became a formidable foe under Bryan's auspicious handling.

Bryan and Rudolph also teamed up to buy another of Smoky's rivals, the lovely and talented Silver sp Carter. Carter was obtained in a $5,000 claiming race. When I learned of Bryan and Rudolph's intent to submit a claim on Carter, I swiftly and worriedly hunted down Mona and Kevin to warn them of the strong possibility that they might lose Carter should they race him in the $5,000 claiming race. Mona and Kevin were sick about the idea of losing their star performer that they had raised and trained and loved through the years, but it was another situation where the expenses of racing had emptied the pockets of owners trying to race their own horses. Horse racing proved to be an expensive proposition, even when you did most of the work, including the training, galloping, and grooming of your horses plus the cleaning of stalls etc. It was hard to earn enough purse money to stay ahead of expenses. Horse racing was not called the "sport of kings" unjustly.

During this time, Rudolph soon became Bryan's major client. I became more and more concerned about this and cautioned Bryan about putting all his eggs in Rudolph's basket. My gut feeling of distrust for Rudolph didn't go away. I watched as he flashed his money about even more boldly, often bringing wads of bills out of his pocket to pay for a $5 lunch or make a bet at the windows. He would boast about how much he had bet on a race and flash his earnings around for all to see.

Perhaps some of this showy behavior could have been attributed to his resentment involving his limp and could be accepted as just that. But I felt that he loved the way he could buy people off. He seemed to feast on the trainers who needed money. He appeared to love the control and power that money brought him. He could be both very charming and very devious. Sometimes I did not really know what to make of him, but I knew that I really didn't trust him and was scared of what he might try to do with all his money. I would find out in the years to come that I had every reason to be wary and afraid.

To my dismay and frustration, Bryan shrugged off my concerns. Bryan was drinking even more heavily at this time, and we had a number of very vocal arguments about this. He wouldn't admit to how much he was drinking. He spent a great deal of time over at the Starting Gate and would argue that he knew exactly what he was doing as far as Rudolph was concerned. I certainly didn't agree, but every time I attempted to bring the matter up, another bitter argument would ensue. It seemed that all we did was argue anymore. Gone were the days of fun, humor, and teasing. To further compound the issue, Rio Hondo had already beaten Smoky in a race last December, and if I kept harping on Rudolph's credibility, I knew Bryan would eventually mention something to Rudolph, and the two of them would be merciless in their accusations that I was just a sore loser. I felt that Rudolph was certainly not a person that one wanted as an enemy.

It was during this time that I had the fright of my life. Bryan and I were living in a motel room down near Disneyland, so each morning, we would load up Thunder in Big Blue (Bryan's big dually truck) and drive over to where our horse trailers were parked under the eucalyptus trees at Los Al Race Course. I had my large five-horse trailer set up for Thunder to stay in (or stay tied to) while we worked at our barns during the morning hours. She was a fantastic dog and never caused any problem staying there and never seemed to resent being left. She had food, water, and shade and always knew that we would be back to free her in a few hours.

Then the nightmare happened. Bryan and I returned to the horse trailer to find Thunder gone. I knew right away that something terrible had happened, and I was beside myself with concern. Even if Thunder had gotten loose, she would never have left the horse trailer. She never wandered from the place I left her, even if she was not tied. I anxiously examined her tie rope.

"Bryan, the clip isn't broken. Someone had to take her. But how could they get close enough to her? She is so protective of her area."

"Let me see that. Do you think the clip came undone?"

"I don't see how it could . . . and I know Thunder wouldn't just leave."

I was becoming more and more upset.

"Well, let's search the area before we do anything else. She's bound to be around here somewhere."

I didn't feel we would find her, but the both of us went in opposite directions calling and searching. Bryan walked toward the main road, Katella Avenue, as I searched the parking lot of horse trailers and vehicles.

Please, Grandpapa. Please, dear Lord . . . Help me find Thunder. I don't know how I will manage without her nor her without me.

We searched and searched and called and called . . . but no Thunder. I knew Thunder would not wander. I was very afraid that somehow, someway, someone had stolen her.

When Bryan and I both returned to Big Blue, I turned to him and said, "I wonder if the Humane Society could have picked her up. Maybe someone complained about her. I think I'd better get a phone book and look up the addresses of the Humane Societies in the area."

So we got in Big Blue, picked up my little green Datsun from the parking lot, and drove across the street. There was a phone booth just down from the Starting Gate restaurant and bar. The phone book had been removed.

"Dang these California people. They can never let anything be."

"Come on, babe, let's go inside and use the Starting Gate's phone book."

The Starting Gate people knew Bryan well, so it was no problem. I found two local Humane Society locations, jotted down the addresses, and left Bryan at the Starting Gate while I went to visit both. I did not want to just call either location as I wanted to be physically present to make sure Thunder was or was not there.

My fears and chagrin really escalated when I found that neither facility had picked her up. I was getting very worried now. I didn't know where to look or who to call. I went back to the first facility I had visited and asked where else I might go to look for Thunder.

"Well, there is a small facility that sometimes works your area. You might try them. They'll be closed by the time you get there, but here is their address and phone number."

"I wonder if I might I use your phone to call. This is a very special dog, and I am really worried."

She smiled and said, "Of course. Good luck!"

As I dialed, I prayed that I would hear good news, but no one answered. Evidently, if anyone was there, they thought that it was too late in the day to be answering calls. I knew I would have to suffer and worry through the night. It was going to be a long sixteen hours until I could find anything out.

After a totally sleepless night, I went to the barn early and got things underway. Bryan had said that he would take care of everything else for me, so I left so that I would arrive at the Humane Society just as they opened. It was a difficult place to find. I wondered how people even knew of its existence.

When I arrived, the gate was still locked. There were several parked cars inside, so I waited—not very patiently—for the facility to open. Finally, someone came to the gate. I almost pounced on him.

"Hold on," he cautioned. "I can't really tell you anything. You'll have to ask at the desk. Sarah will know if we have your dog."

"Thanks," I said as I rushed toward the building.

"You must be Sarah. I'm looking for my female German shepherd. Did you happen to have any come in?"

"You might be in luck. We had one come in yesterday. Let me call Sam, and he'll take you on back to where she is."

I knew the minute I saw her that it was Thunder. I was so happy and so relieved. I called to her, and she jumped up, wagging her tail and whining. She looked as if she had been through some kind of ordeal, but she was alive and well.

"Thunder, Thunder . . . you can't imagine how happy I am to see you! I don't know what I would have done if I hadn't been able to find you."

Thunder was one in a million. She was the most loyal, faithful, and intelligent dog I had ever owned. I put my arms around her and held her to me. I hugged her and hugged her, and she in turn smothered me in kisses.

As we enjoyed our joyful reunion, I stopped a moment to reflect on the blessing bestowed on me and to thank Grandpa and, of course, the one who had surely made this possible, God Himself. Life was wonderful again.

Back at the track, racing continued. Smoky's first race of the new year was the mile and one sixteenth California Cup Stakes. Vals Starburst looked fit and ready, and he was. He defeated both Rio Hondo and Smoky. Seven days later, Smoky returned to top form, winning a six-furlong open-allowance race in the track-record–breaking time of one minute and 18.3 seconds. I was in hopes that this race would set up Smoky to put away Rio Hondo in the final stakes race of the season at Los Alamitos, but it was not to be. Rio Hondo ended up defeating Smoky in a dramatic photo finish in the Gold Rush Stakes. Smoky fought so valiantly. I was so proud of his effort. I only wished he could have stuck his nose out that extra two inches.

It was a bitter defeat for me as Rudolph was merciless in his teasing. It wasn't that I minded being teased; it was just the manner that Rudolph did it. He knew how much I lived for Smoky and his races and that I had a hard time of it when Smoky lost, especially if he had run his heart out. It seemed to me that Rudolph enjoyed seeing people hurt or suffering and that he got his kicks out of rubbing it in. I tried to laugh about his teasing at first, but it became so annoying that I knew my true feelings about his teasing showed through. So he teased me all the more. It was a never-ending cycle, and it didn't help that I didn't like Rudolph. I really didn't want to be viewed as a sore loser, but I sure hated losing to Rudolph. He totally rubbed me the wrong way, and Rudolph did everything he could to egg me on. Up until now, I had really enjoyed horse racing. Rudolph was putting a huge damper on that.

Smoky had run three races in a three-week span. He had run against the best horses the West Coast had to offer. True to form, he had given me his best effort every time he set foot on the racetrack. But Smoky was not 100 percent, and I didn't know what to do for him. Even Dr. Moak was baffled. I have often wondered how much greater Smoky could have been if I had only known how to read the signs he offered and, if at that time, I had had the experience and knowledge to know what to do for him.

With Arabian racing finished in California for the season, we were delighted to be offered some races at Turf Paradise Race Course in Phoenix, Arizona. I had never been to a racetrack in Arizona and was excited to see what Turf Paradise was like. When we arrived, I immediately liked what I saw. It was warm and sunny, and the air was fresh and clean. The roadways throughout the stable area were dirt instead of the pavement we had to endure at Los Al, and there were grassy areas to graze the horses. As soon as I had the horses settled in and my chores finished, I set to weeding and watering a grassy area between our barn and the racetrack so Smoky and his stablemates would have a special area at which to dine. Turf Paradise featured a lovely mile track and also a turf racecourse in addition to the dirt track.

The first race for Smoky was the Scottsdale Cup at a mile and a quarter. In addition to Rio Hondo, he would face another rival that I hoped we could beat, and his name was Shakil Rakkad. Smoky was able to defeat Rio Hondo this time, but Shakil would trounce Smoky by a devastating nine lengths. After the bitter battle between Shakil and Smoky for the Darley last year, it was a tough loss to stomach.

Again, another lesson that I would not learn until many years later had allowed this defeat. It was a lesson that took a long time for most of us on the West Coast to realize. None of us really understood the tremendous advantage that Delaware horses had over the rest of us. The heaviness of the Delaware racetrack coupled with the humidity on the East Coast fashioned a tough opponent to beat. Horses shipping to Los Al or Turf Paradise literally felt they could fly over a racetrack that had a lighter base and with very little humidity in the air, and fly, they did. They whipped us soundly and went back home smug in their superiority. Shakil had shipped in from Delaware and had been fit and ready. He and his entourage loved it here at Turf Paradise.

Things did not get better for us as Rio Hondo came back to revenge his loss in the Scottsdale Cup and defeated Smoky in a mile race on a sloppy track. Another reversal, and Smoky, undaunted by his previous defeat, avenged his loss by winning the Arabian Cup Handicap, putting away both C Patriot and Rio Hondo. Frank Quesada had ridden Smoky in all his races at Turf Paradise as Ralph Pauline hadn't wanted to leave California.

Throughout our stay at Turf Paradise, my groom for the meet was the most unusual person I believe I had ever hired. His name was James, and he wore jeans and a large black top hat to go with his wild beard and sunglasses. He looked like a character out of a Charles Dickens novel, but he was good with the horses and quite dependable.

About this time, I was introduced to two horses that Bryan owned but was not racing. I really liked both the horses and, finding out that Bryan was looking to get rid of them, asked Bryan what he wanted for them. He priced them at $500 each but told me that the bay who was named Jaf Orphatyne had terrible suspensory ligaments, and he had never been able to hold them together well enough to race him. He recommended passing on the bay. The other horse was a gray named Murphy. The problem with Murphy was that he had never been registered, so it would cost $500 to get that done. After a few days of mental debate, I decided to buy Murphy as he seemed to love life and was a happy horse. Because of his personality, I named him Ona Natural High but often just called him Murphy as it was easier to say, and the name Murphy also suited him.

Soon afterward, I began galloping Murphy on the racetrack. He was a nice mover and showed a lot of promise. He also was a handful and full of himself. It was during one of these morning gallops that I felt Murphy getting away from me. He started galloping faster and faster and would not come back to me when I tried to slow him down. He was also headed for the outside rail and would not respond when I tried to pull him toward the inside rail. I realized Murphy was out of control. I did everything in my power to regain some control and/or some sense of steering, but nothing worked. My arms felt like rubber from the exertion of trying to slow him down. As we approached the on-and-off ramp to the east side of the track, I realized Murphy had every intention of exiting the track at full bore. Directly ahead, I saw a large building and realized that Murphy was heading straight toward it. He seemed to be oblivious to the building's presence. I knew I had to bail, and I did.

Bryan later told me that I regained consciousness long enough to tell the medics, who rushed onto the scene, to find Bryan Braithwaite. It was the last thing I said for quite some time.

Later, when I finally awoke, I was in a hospital bed. Bryan let me know what had transpired. I had suffered a concussion, fractured my collarbone, and cracked some ribs. (Was this an Indy repeat?) He said the doctor also feared that I had ruptured my spleen and possibly a kidney. It hurt to move, and I felt terrible. Later that day, I was told that I might have to have my spleen and a kidney removed. Before Bryan left, I made sure that Bryan promised not to let them remove anything if I lost consciousness.

"Don't sign anything. Don't authorize anything," I implored again. "I want to know more. I need some proof!"

Although I had problems with some of Bryan's behaviors, he always proved to be an honest-to-goodness true friend. He was always there for me when I really needed him. Here he was again, cheerful and uncomplaining, watching out for me. What would I ever have done without him? He not only comforted me and tended to my needs in the hospital but also automatically took over the care of my barn of horses. It gave me great peace of mind knowing that my horses would be looked after and taken good care of. That included even Murphy, who, by the way, had come out of the debacle just fine.

The next day, I was scheduled for a dye test to determine the condition of my kidneys. Having been a biology teacher for over twenty years, I asked if I could watch the flow of the dye on the monitor. I was relieved to see the dye flow successfully into and out of each kidney without any problem. I looked at the technician, who hadn't yet said anything and excitedly reported that everything looked fine to me—so would I be able to go home now? In response, he informed me that that would be up to my doctor.

Later that day, when my doctor visited my room and I excitedly asked if I would indeed be able to go home, he replied that my kidney did look to be fine but that I was terribly anemic and that he would talk to me about this when my iron levels were up in a normal range. So the next time Bryan visited, I ask him to bring me some of the Red Cell iron supplement that we fed to our racehorses. Unknown to the doctors and nurses, I drank what I thought were massive amounts of this terribly tasting brown liquid. Four days later, my iron level was up, and I was released. I thought I should tell other trainers that Red Cell really did work!

By the time I got out of the hospital, the race meet at Turf was over. However, a race meet at my alma mater—Holly, Colorado—had decided to offer a couple of stakes races for Arabians. After hashing things over, Bryan and I decided it might be a good move to go to Colorado to see if we could pick up some extra money. After checking things out, we found that we could stable our horses and train them at Pikes Peak Meadows, just south of Colorado Springs. It was a very nice facility that our old friend and competitor, Lea Brent, had bought and renovated in 1990 with the intent of promoting Arabian racing in Colorado. However, after one year, he had faced an enormous debt load and had to shut the track down. In spite of this, he had kept it open and available for training and boarding. It was a great opportunity to be back in Colorado and to see my parents and friends again. Grass was abundant for grazing the horses, and there were numerous outside pens that I made good use of.

With some of Smoky's earnings, I had bought a half brother to Smoky while in Phoenix. He was a very good-looking gray stallion that looked as if he could run. He and Smoky became good friends, and I would put them in adjoining pens where they would stretch their necks over the top rails and jaw at each other for hours on end.

Back at the barn, however, it was the same old story. Bryan was still drinking too much. He would rush through his morning chores so that he could head over to the local bar to join his newfound buddies for a round of drinks. When I would try to address the issue, he would get very upset and stomp off. Our relationship became very strained. I felt that I could no longer even talk to him without one of us ending up in a huff. In the meantime, Scott, his groom, was left to take care of the horses. Unknown to either of us at that time, Scott was being paid by Rudolph to report any training issues or problems back to him. As Scott was not one to overexert himself, he soon became unhappy with the situation at Bryan's barn. Rudolph would end up hearing about all this activity.

Being left on my own most of the day, I found myself questioning why I stayed with Bryan. All I ever seemed to do was nag at him when we were together. I felt frustrated and angry and was lonely for companionship. Bryan seemed to enjoy being with his bar mates a whole lot more than he did with me.

Out on the track one morning, Murphy ran off with me again. I thought that I had changed his tack sufficiently to prevent this, but his mind was made up. He was headed directly for the outside rail. As it looked as if he would collide with the rail and probably tumble head over heels on top of me, I elected to bail off once again. This time, I flung myself over the rail and ended up rolling down the hillside. Other than a few cuts and bruises, I was not badly hurt *this time!* Looking back to this incident, I wondered why I didn't just give up on Murphy and give him back to Georgia (Bryan's ex-wife), who had owned Murphy as a youngster. Bryan had told me that Georgia had liked and spoiled Murphy and that she was the reason for Murphy's erratic behaviors. To me, the two seemed perfect for each other.

During this time, Thunder was not doing well. She was getting old and elected to stay at the barn when I rode horses to the track or around the rows of stalls. One morning, after having galloped a horse, I returned to find her lying in the tack room. As I approached, I could tell something was terribly wrong. I knelt down; she lifted her head to me and died in my arms. I knew she had held on just long enough to say goodbye. I was terribly sad and heartbroken. She had been such a wonderful dog, a truly faithful friend, the best pet I had ever had. I cradled her in my arms and wept.

Later, Bryan and I buried her under a lovely elm tree that guarded the entrance to the racetrack. At Bryan's suggestion, we found and planted some beautiful purple iris above her grave, and we said our goodbyes to her. Bryan had loved her too. We would both sorely miss her.

Shortly after Thunder's death, Bryan and I traveled to Holly for the two stakes races. I had decided to race KHArisya in the Eden Rabi Distaff, and Bryan planned to run Rio Hondo and Snickers in the colt stakes. I had decided against running Smoky as once again, he was just not moving right.

Smoky was a complex horse to figure out. Periodically, he exhibited little signs that something was just not right with him. He seemed to do his best when he had continual, consistent exercise. If I felt sorry for him and just put him on the hot walker to try to give him a day of rest, the next day, he would act stiff and would not move quite right. He never was really lame; his gait was just little uneven. I figured that he had a slight case of tying up. In the olden days, it was referred to as "Monday-morning sickness" because it happened in workhorses that worked six days a week and had Sundays off. If these workhorses were fed the same ration on Sunday, when they went back to work on Monday, they would show stiffness and pain in their hindquarters. It would often be difficult for them to move. It was caused by the rapid breakdown of the glycogen that had a chance to accumulate in the horse's big muscles on their day off. When a horse was worked consistently, the glycogen didn't have a chance to build up. On Monday, after being fed a full ration on Sunday, the glycogen that had built up would be broken down more rapidly than usual, causing large amounts of lactic acid to form. Lactic acid destroyed muscle tissue. The kidney could also be damaged trying to remove the lactic acid. It could be a serious problem.

Knowing that much about tying up, I always made sure that Smoky got some form of exercise even on his day off. His grain ration was also drastically reduced, as was it for all my horses on off or easy days. Bryan never reduced his grain rations on days off. It always irked me that he did this and that he always seemed to get away with it. To add insult to injury, he always fed a *lot* more grain than I did and still got away with it. On the other hand, it really irked Bryan that I didn't feed more grain. He insisted grain made power. I couldn't argue with that. I knew that it did. But when I tried more grain, I suffered the consequences. How did other trainers manage to feed more grain than I was able to offer my horses? Smoky was a tough problem to figure out. I wanted to give him more grain so that he had the energy he needed, but no matter what grain mixture I tried, when I did, we both certainly paid the price. I wondered if this problem hadn't started that day back at Dick's farm in Fort Collins when he supposedly developed laminitis. Was it really laminitis? Or could he have been tying up? So little research had really been done on tying up at that time. Did his body start going haywire back then, or was it a condition he was born with? I knew that I would probably never really know.

Smoky had Bryan and me baffled today. First of all, he had been galloped the day before. He had not had the day off. Second, when I grained my horses, I always added electrolytes to help prevent tie-up. So neither of us really knew what to make of Smoky.

What made it more difficult for me to figure Smoky out was that he was only exhibiting the problem on his left side, and it was so slight that Bryan and I thought he had a slight stone bruise or a sore shoulder. We brought out the hoof testers and could not find any problem with his foot. His shoulder felt fine. I sure wished that Dr. Moak was here to check Smoky out. Tying up can fool you. Sometimes when a horse tied up, he looked stiff and lame in the front end when it was really the big hindquarter muscles that were the problem area. Smoky didn't have enough of a problem to determine what his problem was. It was enough of a concern though that I didn't take him to Holly with us.

When we had arrived at Holly, it was raining cats and dogs. There was only one covered stall left. The rest of the stalls were open pens and did not have any protection from the cold and the rain. Talking it over, Bryan and I decided that the best arrangement we could make was to put Arisya in the covered stall and then put the two geldings, Snickers and Rio Hondo, who knew each other and got along well, in two separate large divisions of the six-horse trailer. That way, all three would be kept dry and they could still move around. Mona and Kevin arrived later, and all that was left were open pens. They were forced to put their horses in these unprotected pens. We felt so sorry for them. Even with their blankets, their horses were shivering and unhappy.

The next day, Arisya ran a fantastic race and demolished her opposition. However, it was a different scenario in the colt race. Ever since Adams County, when I wrote the stewards a thank-you note and took them chocolates at the end of the meet, they had looked out for me. Smoky had been nominated, but I had not entered him in the stakes race at Holly. The stewards were sure something had happened when Smoky was not entered in the colt stakes race, so they entered him for me. They even put John Hood up on Smoky for me. When Bryan entered Rio, he requested John Hood for his rider as he knew Smoky wouldn't be in the race. However, since the stewards had put John up on Smoky, the racing secretary, thinking he was doing the next best thing, put Markel Harden on Rio Hondo. When Bryan learned of the turn of events, he was quite upset. He tried but was unable to finesse a jockey change.

So as the horses and riders made ready in the saddling paddock, Bryan told Markel about his race strategy. His riding instructions to Markel were to have Rio Hondo come from off the pace. His other entry, Snickers, would challenge the pace and be sent after the speed horse, who happened to be Creator LTD. However, Markel, for whatever reason, ended up chasing Creator with Rio Hondo. It was not Rio's racing style, and Creator LTD ended up winning the race. Rio Hondo finished second, and Snickers was third. Bryan was livid. One thing Bryan did know was his horses. Rio always ran from off the pace. He was a locomotive coming down the stretch if he had been saved and relaxed early on. Everything had gone wrong for Bryan as far as this race went.

Afterward, of course, Scott relayed the whole scenario to Rudolph. Not surprisingly, Rudolph was very upset. He believed that Bryan had been more interested in helping me than him. When Bryan phoned Rudolph, he didn't buy any of Bryan's story. He just understood that Arisya got the warm stall and won and Rio was left in the horse trailer and lost. He demanded that Bryan return to California at once with his horses.

When we returned to California. Bryan found that Rudolph had engaged Garland McAlaster as his new trainer. Bryan learned most of the story from Garland, who told him of the deal Rudolph had made with Scott. Evidently, Scott was told that Rudolph would help him get a trainer's license and he would get to train Rudolph's horses if he kept Rudolph informed of all activity that went on while in Colorado. When we returned to California, Scott found out that Rudolph was not true to his word, and he remained a groom, now under Garland. Garland was grateful for and liked having the horses but hated having to take Scott on as a groom in the bargain. For Bryan, it was a very dismal time. To his credit, he handled it well.

Back in California, our first races were at Bay Meadows. Arisya raced well, but Smoky only managed two seconds and a fifth. I couldn't see that Smoky had any residual problem from Colorado, but I continued to wonder and worry if Smoky still had a problem that I had just not figured out.

During this period, I had decided that Smoky could not maintain his winning ways if he always tried to win races wire to wire. Even Bryan was putting two horses in a race—one to challenge Smoky early on and the other to make a late run at a tiring Smoky. Trying to win all his races wire to wire was giving Smoky's opponents a tremendous advantage. Other trainers soon picked up on the fact that Smoky would always be the speed horse. Therefore, some of them worked at trying to tire Smoky out early with a speed horse that they never intended to win the race with and then catch Smoky in the stretch run with their *"big"* horse.

Bryan would hardly talk to me when he learned that I was trying to teach Smoky to race from off the pace and save himself for a fast closing finish. He was infuriated that I would change Smoky's style when he had won so many races and set so many track records racing out front. My arguments were to reach deaf ears. However, I knew in my heart that I had to do this. We might lose a few races in the transition, but I believed it would make racing easier on Smoky and also lengthen his racing career. As I was the one who always galloped Smoky, it was fairly easy to secretly work on our new game plan. So that it would remain our secret, I galloped Smoky first thing in the morning when very few individuals would be there to see anything. The clocker was not up and at work at that time, so I really had a free rein. I would watch like a hawk for horses that might be working and set Smoky up to chase them down the lane to the finish line. Eventually, I enlisted other riders and friends so that I could further practice our new strategy. Even then, most trainers didn't have any idea what I was up to.

Our first real opportunity using this new racing style came at Pleasanton in the California Gold Cup Handicap. I put Rick Norton in the saddle for this race. Rick was excited about getting to ride Smoky and was very happy to attempt to bring Smoky from off the pace as I wanted. Smoky was in post position 10, and as the horses settled in the gates for the break, I hoped and prayed that Rick would be able to get Smoky to break from the gates nice and easy. I was excited and tense at the same time. I glued my eyes on the starting gate. It seemed to take forever, but finally, the gates flew open, and a wave of horses emerged.

I saw almost immediately that Smoky was not in the lead. He had broken from the gates without his trademark bolt for the lead. Rick had got him to relax, and he had emerged in the middle of the pack. I watched as Rick eased Smoky over toward the rail in fifth place. As the horses progressed down the backstretch, Smoky moved into fourth position. He seemed to be moving easily and listening to Rick. Smoky was a little more forward that I would have liked, but he was not the leader of the pack. He was not in the lead, and he was not fighting to be there. However, to my great concern, the front-running horses had fashioned a wall that I was afraid Smoky would have a hard time getting through. It was a nightmare for any trainer who had a horse that raced from off the pace.

I saw Rick swing Smoky to the outside. He had elected to circle the group. It would cost Smoky valuable ground, but waiting for a hole to open up had not appeared to be an option. I was yelling and screaming encouragement, but I was also afraid that Smoky wouldn't have enough time or enough ground to reach the wire first. But Smoky wasn't done, and neither was Rick.

Smoky continued circling the field and was now challenging for the lead. Four horses raced and battled for the finish line with barely a half length separating all of them. Then just before the wire, Smoky dug in like he had done so often while battling Manteeya and drove for the wire, finishing half a length ahead of his challengers. He had done it. Smoky had won coming from off the pace. He had thrilled the crowd with his dramatic finish, and he had shown that he had learned his lesson well. What an athlete! It was a race that Rick Norton talked about for years to come. He was so ecstatic that he had won, that he had followed riding instructions to a T, and that he had felt the fantastic surge of power when he had asked Smoky for more. He became one of Smoky's biggest fans that day.

With the Pleasanton meet now over, we returned to Bay Meadows outside San Francisco. I hoped that we could reverse the losing streak Smoky had posted at this racetrack, but it was not to be. Smoky came charging down the stretch after the lead horses but lost to Vals Starburst by a head. It was an exciting race. I just wished the outcome could have been "a head" better. Then we were off to Ferndale, where Smoky won his first race and then lost his second race to FS Orion, whom he had beaten easily the week before. It was a very frustrating time for the both of us, with this back-and-forth success and defeat.

Next, we were back to Smoky's favorite racing oval, Los Al. However, Smoky only managed to post two wins in his next nine starts. His last win came in the Charles Pollard Handicap (with jockey Severiano Martinez up in the saddle), where he set a new track record for one and one sixteenth miles in a dead heat for the win with Sinbad Sam. He had even defeated Rio Hondo. I was elated by the effort and determination Smoky had shown, only to be shocked to learn that the purse for the race was less than that for an overnight race. It was a fact that I had learned not from the ARAC board but from a jockey the next day. Although the race had been advertised as a $10,000 stakes race and we had paid $150 to enter, Smoky earned less than if we had just run in a regular allowance race that cost absolutely nothing to enter. Many of us had even bypassed a higher-paying handicap race (the Oasis Overnight Handicap) to honor Charles Pollard's memory and support the stakes race named after him. Our race had drawn the top horses around, including Rio Hondo, Vals Starburst, and FS Orion. It had posted a ten-horse field for the betting public. I decided something had to be done to right the situation. I wrote a letter of protest stating the glaring injustices of the race and asking ARAC to rectify their mistake. I argued that this had been an exceptional race. It featured our top horses, had a ten-horse field, and featured a very exciting dead-heat run in track-record–breaking time. The race had advertised a $10,000 purse, and that is the amount that should stand. At entry time, the Charles Pollard Stakes had offered a larger purse than the Oasis. After the fact, the Oasis Handicap paid more. The Oasis had a smaller entry fee than did the Charles Pollard, yet it paid more. It had attracted less talented horses to boot. The Charles Pollard Stakes Race had been badly represented. I gave a copy of my letter to all Arabian horse trainers who had entered a horse in the Charles Pollard and to members of the ARAC board. Eventually, ARAC added $1,000 to the purse. It was done to keep me quiet or pacified. It still didn't meet the advertised purse or right the situation to my way of thinking. but I knew I wasn't going to get any further with my protest.

The year 1991 came to a close, with Smoky having run an amazing twenty races during the year. Although I felt it had been a very discouraging and disappointing year, his statistics were not that bad. He posted a record of 20 (6-7-5)3, meaning he had run twenty races with six firsts, seven seconds, and five thirds with three stakes wins. He had earned $40,013. He had set two track records, one at six furlongs and another for one and one-eighth miles, and now boasted a lifetime record of 44 (21-12-7) with earnings of $116,253. He won the Darley for Older Horse of the Year and also the ARAC award for Older Horse of the Year. He also won the Finish Line Trophy for Older Horse and was also one of five horses nominated for Sprinter of the Year. It was not at all bad for a subpar year, but I didn't feel really good about it. We, including Dr. Moak, had not been able to pinpoint or fix Smoky's problem, and there was, I knew, a problem.

22 Wind and Sand

It was a new year, but racing would not pick up for us until the middle of April at Los Al. For the next few months, trotters and pacers would inhabit our barns here and we would have to go elsewhere. We hoped to be able to race once again at Turf Paradise, but unfortunately, there had been a change of management, and amid a great deal of conflict, the decision was made to discontinue offering Arabian racing. This meant a long dry spell for us.

Bryan and I spent a lot of time talking over the options that we had available to us. We both agreed that we wanted a facility that was not too expensive as we would not have any purse monies coming in. However, we felt we needed a facility that had some form of track so that we could train our new young horses and get them at least accustomed to the feel of a racetrack. My usual requirements were to have access to some turnout areas and to have some grass for the horses to enjoy once in a while. After mulling over several options, we both felt that the Fairgrounds in Kingman, Arizona, would meet our needs and desires the best. To its credit, Kingman was fairly close, was not too expensive, had a racetrack, provided a place to park Bryan's fifth wheel, and had turnout pens and arenas, some grassy areas, and a warm climate. It was also only twenty-five minutes from a ranch that our friend and fellow competitor, Roger Lang, owned. It seemed like the ideal vacationing spot for us and our horses. Never could we have suspected that this innocent move to Kingman, Arizona, would so drastically change both Smoky's and my life forever.

So we moved in with high expectations and good feelings about our new dwellings. I loved the open and airy arrangement that the long rows of outdoor stalls offered. The horses could visit through the chain-link fencing that provided the separation for the upper half of each stall. Smoky loved being able to visit with his friends, and all the horses seemed very happy in this new arrangement. There was a huge rodeo arena where several horses could be turned out together to play and frolic, and there were a number of rodeo pens on the inside of the racetrack where horses could roam through the aisleways and nibble on the clumps of grass growing there. Everything seemed perfect.

However, the wonderful amenities that Kingman seemed to offer turned out to be a lot less than ideal. The restless winds that flew down off the California mountains and across the plains never seemed to stop blowing. These huge currents would sweep up the sand into dust devils and sometimes create huge billowing clouds of red dust that caused everything not nailed down to fly around in a state of frenzy. The sand got into everything. I found my hair full of it and my face covered with it after a morning of galloping and working with the horses. Several of the horses, including Smoky, had runny and/or irritated eyes. At least twice a day, I would wipe away the slime and gunk that had collected in the corners of their eyes. Then I would follow this up with a squeeze of clear eye if it seemed to be needed. I frequently did the same thing for my own eyes.

As it was Sunday, I had decided to make an easy day of it and turn all my horses out in groups of twos and threes to play in the arena while I cleaned their stalls. Most horse owners and trainers had already fed their horses and left. Because of a freak accident that had occurred a week earlier, I was functioning with a broken arm. It had slowed me down as far as galloping horses, but because we owned a kind and gentle pony horse, I was still able to pony some of my gentler horses, and I was still able to clean stalls and brush horses etc. The accident had involved none other than my persistent and aptly named disaster horse, Murphy. He had somehow cut his left knee during the night, and I had called the local veterinarian to come out to stitch the cut up. I had debated having the knee stitched as knowing Murphy, I felt he would never let the stitches alone long enough for the cut to heal. In addition, I knew that the knee was a terrible place for stitches anyway as it is such an active joint. But in the end, I had felt the wound was just too long and gaping to leave it to heal without stitches.

As the incident would pan out, it was unfortunate that I had made the decision to have the cut stitched up. Dr. Burrows, who was mainly a dog and cat veterinarian, had given Murphy a little too much tranquilizer. Murphy became very unsure on his feet, and he stumbled. At that instant, I realized that Murphy was going to fall and crash into the corner of the concrete-block base of a shed row of stalls. Instinctively and stupidly, I tried to steady Murphy. It was a huge mistake as he lacked the ability to steady himself even with my help. He fell forward, catching my right foot. Now we both had lost our balance, and as he lurched forward, he knocked me completely down, falling on top of me. I lay trapped there, not able to get up or move Murphy. Dr. Burrows just stood there looking at us. I didn't know whether to be hurt or angry.

"Help get this horse off me," I said in frustration. "Grab him by his halter and front leg and flip him over or at least raise his head and neck up enough so that I can get out from underneath him."

I couldn't believe that I was the one having to direct the proceedings. It seemed like an eternity, but finally, Dr. Burrows managed to lift Murphy enough that I was able to crawl out from under him. I slowly got to my feet. Everything appeared okay except for my right forearm, which was aching and tingling. I found it hard to move that hand or fingers.

"Are you all right?" Dr. Burrows asked.

"I'm not sure . . . I know I'll be stiff and sore tomorrow. I think my arm got the worst of it. How much tranquilizer did you give Murphy? He still can't stand up."

Eventually, Murphy did get up, and together, we managed to get the knee stitched. Since the injury was in such a bad location, I knew that if Murphy acted up or was allowed too much exercise, he would tear the stitching job apart. Even with my arm aching, I was more concerned about him than I was about myself. I knew my arm still ached, but I felt a couple of ibuprofen would take care of it.

True to form, Murphy tore the stitching apart. However, I kept the wound doctored, and it was looking better each day. In fact, I thought, the injury would have healed just as well without any veterinarian. On the other hand, my arm hadn't fared so well. It had caused enough pain and discomfort the day after that I decided to visit a local clinic. There, I found out that it was broken and I would need to have it cast. I was beginning to wish that I had never seen Murphy and had never decided to buy him from Bryan. All he seemed to be was trouble.

Having my arm in a cast had slowed me down. The cast extended beyond my elbow, so I couldn't bend my arm. As I couldn't gallop my horses now, I often just walked them or turned them out to play. It was Sunday, a slow and easy day for most of us. I had already put CJ and Smoky out to play and was going to collect them so I could put a new filly I had recently bought, named Kaleidoscope, out for some playtime. Bryan and I were hardly talking, having argued the night before. We had both clung to our feelings of animosity into these morning hours.

It wasn't a very pleasant day as the wind was really blowing. It made most of the horses a little fractious and excitable. As I went to lead Kaleidoscope out of her stall, she suddenly bolted and then pivoted to the left. It was all done in a fraction of a second. Before I could even react, she had smashed my left arm against a large ill-placed metal post that happened to be in exactly the wrong place. It took a moment for me to realize that the lower half of my forearm was hanging at a forty-five-degree angle from the rest of my forearm. It had happened so quickly that it took a while for the pain and the realization of what had happened to register.

I remember looking down and thinking, *Oh man, I can't believe this.* I had enough wits about me to realize that Kaleidoscope had run into the stall beside hers, so I closed the stall door with my right hand and latched it. I was anxiously trying to remember where Bryan was and if he was even still here. I cradled my left arm in my right arm and tried to keep calm as I called for Bryan. Everyone else had left by now. It had been too windy to do much of anything, so everyone had just done the minimum and left for the morning. Then I felt a rush of panic as I realized that even Bryan was gone.

I was more worried now as I headed out for the parking lot where our fifth wheel was parked. I prayed that Bryan would be there. If he wasn't, I hardly knew what I would do. A wave of sickness overtook me. I was beginning to feel faint and wondered if I could make it much farther than the fifth wheel if Bryan had left.

"Please, Bryan, be there," I cried silently to myself. I knew I needed help badly. I certainly couldn't drive a car in my condition, and I didn't know how far I would have to walk to find someone.

As I drew nearer to where our fifth wheel was parked, I felt a flood of relief. Big Blue was still there. It meant that Bryan was still here too. Tremendously relieved, I called out for his help. The door to the fifth wheel opened, and Bryan appeared.

I don't remember ever being more happy to see Bryan.

"Oh, babe, am I ever glad you are still here! I think I've really done it this time."

Bryan had only to glance at me to figure out what was wrong. "Oh my god, what did you do?"

"I think I broke it," I replied.

Bryan rushed to my side. He gently grasped my right arm and steadied me. "That's pretty obvious. C'mon . . . We'd better get you to the hospital."

Forgotten was the argument of the night before. I felt rather guilty as I had caused the argument, and here I was, asking the same person whom I wouldn't even talk to an hour ago to help me. Bryan just acted like the true friend that he was. He tenderly helped me into his truck. I could hardly manage to get in, even with his help.

"We'll need my purse, babe. It should be in the closet on the bottom shelf."

Bryan went back to the fifth wheel and picked it up, and we sped away to the hospital.

It was a short drive for which I was grateful. My arm was tortured with pain now, and I was feeling very woozy and sick to my stomach. It seemed forever, but we finally arrived at the hospital emergency entrance. I knew it would be painful to get out of the truck. Every little movement made me cringe with the pain. I tried to keep my broken arm as motionless as I could while Bryan tried to help me move sideways along the seat and down to the pavement by holding my right side and other broken arm. I wished I didn't have to move, but of course, that wasn't going to happen. I had to get into the hospital. I clenched my teeth and went for it. I thought I could handle pain. But this was something else.

Once I got down out of the truck, I thought that I would never make it to the door, but we finally made it to the emergency room and the receptionist's desk. By now, I was turning white, and Bryan asked if he could complete the paperwork so I could be helped quicker. He gently sat me down and got my wallet out of my purse. I sat and waited, glad that Bryan was taking over but anxious to get some sort of pain medication into my body and get my arm immobilized. A terrible nauseous feeling had permeated every cell of my body. I realized that because we hadn't arrived by ambulance, my injury was not considered critical, and therefore, I would probably just have to wait my turn.

Bryan finally finished up the paperwork and came to sit by me. "Doing okay, babe?" he asked.

"I'm trying to hang in there but wish someone would give me something for the pain. I can't believe how this hurts! Would you see if I have some ibuprofen in my purse?"

Bryan picked up my purse from the couch beside him. "Where should I look?" he asked.

"There should be a small round green plastic container somewhere in the bottom of my purse."

He searched and rummaged around. "This it?"

"Yes. Are there any rust-colored round tablets inside?"

Sure enough, there were.

"Save three and dump the other pills in my purse. You can use the pill container to get some water."

Bryan dumped the pills and went to the water fountain. He was soon back, and I gratefully downed the pills and water.

"Hope that helps, hun."

"Me too," I responded.

It seemed to take forever before someone finally came.

"Oh my, what have you done?" the nurse queried as she swiveled the wheelchair around so that I could get in it.

"Think I broke it pretty bad. Do you think I might have something for the pain?"

"Let me check, and I'll have them bring something back."

I thanked the nurse. The ibuprofen hadn't cut the pain at all. With that said, I was escorted back to an examination room.

"I'll be right back with something for your pain. Then we're going to have to remove your jacket and sweater by cutting them off."

When she returned, I gratefully swallowed the pills, and she began cutting. It was one time I didn't object to having my clothes cut off me. I sure hadn't wanted to try to take them off over my head. All the same, and even though I only had to move my arm a slight amount so that she could slide the cut clothing out from between my arm and body, I still felt a horrible rush of pain and then nausea.

"There, it's all done," she said as she patted my right shoulder. "The doctor should be right in."

The nausea and pain subsided as I was allowed to steady and hold my arm motionless against my body. I knew my arm would have to be moved a lot more before all was done, however. The doctor still had to look at my arm, and I still had to go through all the X-rays. Several paramedics and staff members stopped by to offer their condolences, but it seemed like ages before the doctor finally arrived.

"Well, young lady, what have we here?"

Dr. K introduced himself and, looking at the report, commented, "So you had an accident with a horse, did you? Well, we'd best get some X-rays of this break. Let's get you back to the lab."

Then he left, and an orderly wheeled me down to the X-ray room.

Darn, I thought. *I think I'm going to be in for another wait once I get to X-ray.*

Sure enough, I did have to wait again. Finally, the X-ray technician was ready. If I thought I was in pain before, it was nothing compared to the terrible sickness I felt flood every nerve cell in my body as they lifted my arm to put a plate under it.

"*Owww!*" I cried. "I can't do this. It's too much! I'll never get through these X-rays!"

I wanted for it to be all over and for my pain-racked arm to be stabilized in a cast and pain medication working to block out the terrible pain. This was taking an eternity. I closed my eyes and tried to think about anything but my arm. I kept trying to think, *This too will pass, and it will all be over soon.* It was something I tried to think every time I was in a situation I didn't particularly like. It always seemed to help me through rough times.

After a whole lot of pain and what seemed like an eternity, the X-rays were finally all taken. I was so relieved that this, at least, was done. I was wheeled back to the examination room, where I again waited. I held my arm to me as still and quietly as I could, but nothing seemed to help. After another long wait, the X-ray technician showed up and said the X-rays were ready. I was wheeled into an office where Dr. K eventually appeared.

"Well, you've suffered a very bad break, I'm afraid. Thought you might like to see. This is your lower arm. As you can clearly see, both your radius and ulna are broken clear through as slick as can be. These edges are totally smooth. That's not good, I'm afraid. It means that there isn't any way to repair your arm by simply casting it. The break is *too* clean. There just isn't any rough or irregular surface to encourage or facilitate a solid heal. We're going to have to use bone grafts and plates and screws to repair the breaks."

I just stared at the X-rays. I had known it was a bad break and knew, without really admitting it, that it would take surgery to mend my arm.

He questioned me about insurance. I thought to myself, *This is going to be expensive!* As I really didn't know what my insurance would pay, especially since it was out of state, I asked if the surgery would cost more being that it was Sunday.

When he replied, "Yes, it will. Sunday accidents can be very expensive," I knew that it would be more than I could really afford right now, so I asked if I he could immobilize my arm in some manner and give me some pain medication to tide me over so that I could wait until Monday to have the surgery done.

"Are you sure that's what you want to do?" he queried.

It was obvious that he couldn't believe what I was requesting, but he finally said that he could do that. He would schedule me for early Monday morning.

It was another painful procedure to put on the temporary cast, but once the bones in my arm were immobilized and I was given more pain medication, I felt 1,000 percent better. Bryan was aghast that I was postponing the surgery until the next day. However, when I told him the difference in cost, he understood a little better. I knew if it was him, he would not have waited.

The next day, I was admitted to the hospital for my surgery. This time, I was put totally under for the procedure as bone grafts needed to be taken from my hip. I didn't feel a thing, and it was wonderful. Before I knew it, the surgery was done, I was waking up, and my arm was set. It felt so good to have my arm in a solid, immovable cast. As the initial pain medication wore off, my hip where they had removed bone for the graft actually hurt more than my arm. But the pain was very tolerable, and I didn't mind it at all. My arm had been taken care of, and that terrible pain that I had never wanted to endure again was gone.

The following day, I was allowed to go home. Bob and Nancy (Brusally Orselar's owners) came up to visit and, thinking it would make me feel better, whisked me away to Laughlin to enjoy a big steak dinner and to do a little gambling. It was one time I really didn't feel like gambling. I really just wanted to lie down and sleep, but they had been so kind and thoughtful. How could I not enjoy their company and their kindness?

As reality settled in, I realized that I couldn't even comb my hair or dress myself. In fact, it was very hard to do anything with two arms that you couldn't bend at the elbow. It was a frustrating time, and once again, if it hadn't been for Bryan, I don't know what I would have done. He cooked all the meals, tended to the horses, and even patiently washed and combed my hair, even curling it. He helped me get dressed and, of course, undressed, which, he joked, he didn't mind doing at all. He actually even did a very good job of setting my hair, which I knew was a very challenging job for him. Again, there was not a single grumble. There was no complaining at all. Bryan just took over, making me feel better with his never-ending dry sense of humor and comforting presence. I don't think I could have asked for a more patient and caring helper.

For the remainder of the time we spent in Kingman, Bryan and Severiano, a friend and jockey from Los Al, took care of my horses for me. When it came time to move back to Los Alamitos in California, I once again realized just how fortunate I was to have Bryan there. I never would have been able to make the move back to Los Al without him. Smoky's eye had still not stopped weeping, and I was getting anxious to be back at Los Al so that Dr. Moak could examine it.

When we had arrived back at Los Al, both Dr. Moak and Dr. Goodberry came by as we were unloading the horses. They were dumbfounded by my two broken arms, couldn't believe my predicament, and, of course, had all sorts of questions. I could hardly wait to tell the both of them about Smoky's eye, and Dr. Moak immediately went to Smoky's stall and set about examining it.

"Looks like a small scratch, Barb. Can you see this? Probably caused by that blowing sand you said you had in Kingman. I think we can get it cleared up. These drops should take care of it. I'll check back tomorrow."

Smoky's eye seemed to improve, but it still wept. It bothered me that I was unable to doctor him myself and had to rely on Bryan or Severiano to do it.

There were two races coming up for Smoky. The first was a four-and-a-half-furlong open-allowance race, and the second was the Sierra Knights Sprint Handicap. As I was unable to gallop Smoky or even lead him up to the races or saddle him for races, Bryan became the official trainer for Smoky. He was quite pleased with the situation until Smoky ran. Smoky only managed to run second in both races, losing to horses he had beaten badly in the past. Bryan had been sure that once he was training Smoky, he could improve Smoky's racing ability by leaps and bounds. It really bothered him that he had not been able to garner a win with him, and he comments on that to this day. I was a little miffed also as I felt Smoky should have won both races.

I handed Bryan a hacksaw and asked him to cut the cast off my right arm. We ended up using every tool we could find, but we finally got the cast off. It was not a good move. Even though I wrapped my arm when I was up and about, it caused me a lot of pain for several years to come, and my wrist never did regain the flexibility and strength it had before. I felt that I had also damaged a nerve when I broke this arm. My left arm, which had a much more severe injury, would heal completely with no side effects. But at least I could do a few more things for Smoky and my other horses and I could comb my hair and dress myself. I also went down to the racing office and had Smoky's racing papers put back in my trainer's file.

Smoky's eye did not get better. In fact, it was getting worse. Dr. Moak changed medications, now to be given on a more frequent timetable. As Bryan and I had moved to a ranch in Norco that was sixty to seventy-five minutes from the racetrack and had other horses to take care of there, I reluctantly left Severiano in charge of administering the eye drops during the evening hours. Looking back, I wished that I had stayed in a tack room at the track so I could have at least supervised the procedure. Even with one cast off, I couldn't do the job by myself, but I would have been there to make sure the drops were administered on schedule and that everything was done in a clean and sterile fashion.

Smoky's eye not only didn't get better but also started to develop an ulcer on the surface. I was really getting worried now as Smoky's eye wasn't responding to even the new drops. When Dr. Moak stopped by as he did each morning, he expressed that he was worried also.

"I'm going to call Chino Vet Clinic, Barb. I think we'd better have a more thorough diagnosis here. I'll make arrangements to have him admitted. When can you leave with him?"

"Let me check with Bryan."

Bryan just needed time to give instructions to his grooms, and we took off to pick up my horse trailer.

Chino Veterinary Clinic was a highly respected equine facility, and when Bryan and I had arrived and met the two veterinarians, Dr. Vachon and Dr. Liskey, we knew why. They were both very personable and professional and got right to work. They examined Smoky's eye and took specimens for culturing. Closer examination revealed that two of the three layers of cornea tissue enclosing the eye had already been eaten away by the culprit invader, be it bacteria, fungi, or whatever. Smoky's eye would need to be sewn shut to support the remaining layer of corneal tissue. He would need to remain at the clinic and be administered antibiotics until results were obtained from the lab. The spectrum of antibiotics was meant to cover all suspected culprits. Smoky was not at all keen about being there, let alone staying there, but I knew it had to be done. I hugged him around his neck, gave him a carrot, and told him I'd be back the next day with more.

As I was able to drive my Datsun in spite of one arm in a cast, I arrived the following day with all of Smoky's favorite treats. The only thing he seemed to want were the nectarines I had brought. His eye had been stitched shut and was covered with bandages. I asked if I might take him out for some grass. That brought Smoky to life. He loved being outdoors, and he loved eating grass. He literally dragged me around from one lush patch of grass to another.

"Take it easy on me, Smoky," I pleaded. "This isn't easy with one arm still in a cast." But I was happy that he was being Smoky.

With each succeeding visit, however, I could tell Smoky was steadily regressing. I worried for him. In spite of pain medication and antibiotics, he was not feeling well. I inquired to the point of being a nuisance as to when the results of the cultures would come in.

Finally, the news: the culprit was a fungus named Aspergillus. It was a fungus that I was quite familiar with. My seventh-grade life science classes had often examined slides of it under the microscope. The medications that Smoky was on combated Aspergillus. *Good news*, I thought.

However, the next day when I came to visit, Smoky was hooked up to an IV drip from the ceiling. I was absolutely shocked at what I saw. It was one of the most depressing sights I'd ever seen. Smoky was standing, head drooping, in a semidark box stall. IV tubes ran from the side of his right nostril and the left side of his neck to a coiled yellow tube that ran to an IV bag that was supported from the ceiling of his stall. The right side of Smoky's nose was skewed to the right side because of partial paralysis as a complication from injections he had been given. His right eye was covered by gauze bandages and the black cup of a one-eyed set of blinkers. His body sagged like that of an old horse. His good left eye was half closed and dull. His head was hanging down, and his lower lip hung almost lifelessly, with saliva dripping from it. He was a picture of dejection and was totally disinterested in anything going on around him. He barely acknowledged that I was even there, and when he did, it was with such a terribly sad expression that I covered my face with my hands and almost cried. Smoky had absolutely no spirit and hardly any life. He oozed with depression.

Tears swelled in my eyes. I had never seen Smoky so completely listless. I put my head on Smoky's wither and cried. Through my tears, I whispered to him, "It should never have come to this. I'm so terribly sorry, Smoky."

When I was finally able to stop the tears, I wiped my eyes and dried my face. The more I looked at Smoky, the more I felt something else, something different, had to be done. I had seen and heard of horses going into a state of depression and anguish over things like this, and they had died. Smoky looked like one of those horses.

"Smoky, this can't go on . . . We have to do something different for you, or you're not going to make it, are you? I'm going to leave for a little while, but I'll be back. We're going to get you fixed up, big guy." I gave Smoky a gentle pat and moved through the narrow stall opening. I pulled the stall door a little more shut but not all the way. I wanted Smoky to be able to see out if he wanted to.

The barn area was empty of people. Barn chores had been done for the day. I went directly to the receptionist's desk and asked if I could speak to Dr. Vachon or Dr. Liskey. She told me that Dr. Vachon was not on duty and that Dr. Liskey was in surgery but that he should be finished shortly. I said that I would wait.

About forty-five minutes later, Dr. Liskey came out. I asked him if he had a few minutes to talk about Smoky. He did. Both he and Dr. Vachon were excellent in the rapport they established with their clients. Both worked long hard hours, and I often noticed shadows under their eyes. Still, Dr. Liskey acted as if Smoky was his most important patient and he had lots of time to spend on him and me.

"Dr. Liskey, I'm really worried about Smoky. I've seen Smoky and other horses too when they've been sick or down and out, but I think Smoky's past that stage. This whole thing plus the confinement and the strange environment is doing him in. He's not eating. He's so dehydrated that he has to be on IV fluids. He's been tying up. His face is partially paralyzed, and now he doesn't even respond to people or other horses. He doesn't care what's going on around him . . . He just stands and stares. I think he's losing the will to live, and I'm scared. I think we need to open up his eye and see what is going on. I'm thinking that maybe we even need to take his eye out."

Dr. Liskey had let me ramble on without interruption. When he realized I was finished, he responded, "Let's take a look then, Barb. I'll schedule him for first thing in the morning, say, eight o'clock. Can you be here?"

"You bet I can. Thank you, Dr. Liskey!"

The next day couldn't come soon enough, but it finally arrived. After slowly moving Smoky to the surgery room and administering some local painkiller, Dr. Liskey carefully unstitched Smoky's eye. I was so glad that he was allowing me to see things for myself. However, I wasn't prepared for how horrible it looked. What I saw was a huge blob of thick green snot.

"Oh my lord, he's never going to have vision out of that, is he?"

"It's difficult to say, Barb. I've seen worse, and they've recovered some vision . . . but it'll be a long haul. He may just see light and shadows."

I thought, *Just light and shadows? Is that all that that might come from this? Was all this pain and suffering worth it for that?*

I knew what needed to be done now.

"Dr. Liskey, I really do think we're losing Smoky. It's not worth having him suffer so much for the little we'd gain. I feel we've got to take the eye out. He can't stand much more of this. I think the pain has too much of a hold on him. He's a fighter, but this thing has him whipped. I'd like to ask you to take out that eye."

It didn't take him long to answer. "All right, Barb, I'm in agreement. We'll get it on the schedule for tomorrow."

Almost immediately, a flood of relief spread over me. I knew that I was making the right and the best decision. I thanked Dr. Liskey and walked back to Smoky's stall. He was still standing listlessly in the same place and position as he had been in when I left. I entered his stall, but he didn't even acknowledge my presence. I moved to the far side of the stall and stared silently at the shell of an animal I knew as Smoky.

Again, I could hardly wait for tomorrow. I wished that the surgery could be done right now. I didn't want Smoky suffering any longer. Would tomorrow ever come?

Tomorrow did come, finally, and by the time I got to the clinic, the surgery was over. I was grateful for that. I had not wanted to see Smoky the way he had been again. Smoky was recovering in his stall. He was still coming out of the effects of the anesthesia. Dr. Vachon said that everything had gone well. I just sat and watched Smoky.

When I arrived the following day, I couldn't believe the difference. Smoky was a completely changed animal. He was alert, his head was up, and he recognized me. He wanted out the stall door. I was absolutely amazed and elated. What a *difference!* I was happy beyond words. I knew that I had absolutely made the right decision. Smoky was back! I put my arms around his neck, and for the longest time, I just hugged him.

After that, each day showed a remarkable improvement. Even the facial paralysis was going way. The dull look in his good left eye vanished. On June 15, my birthday, Smoky was released to go home. I had never had such a wonderful birthday present.

Ona Natural High (Muphy) posing for his racing supplement

-1991-

Thunder's grave at Pike's Peak Meadows

Smoky winning at Beautiful Turf Paradise in Phoenix, Arizona

pictured left to right are me, Frank Quesada (jockey) and James, (my groom) holding Smoky

Roger Lang's initial farm lay-out Kingman, Arizona

Some of our stalls at the Fairgrounds in Kingman. Pictured are Smoky and Kaleidoscope

< 1992 >

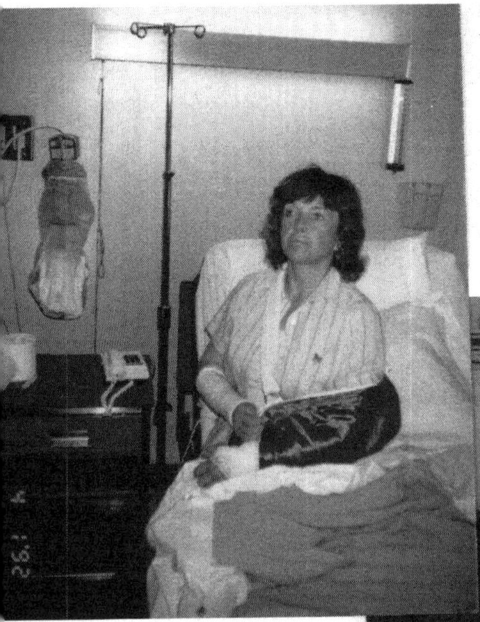

Resting in front of my 5 horse slant Horse trailer...watching Bryan and Sevriano do all the work

Looks like I am about to cry at having 2 broken arms

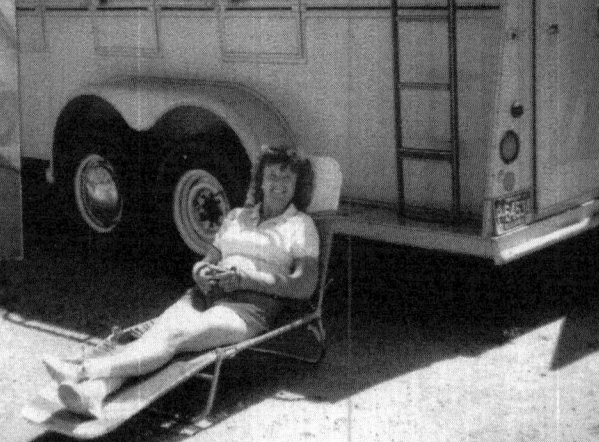

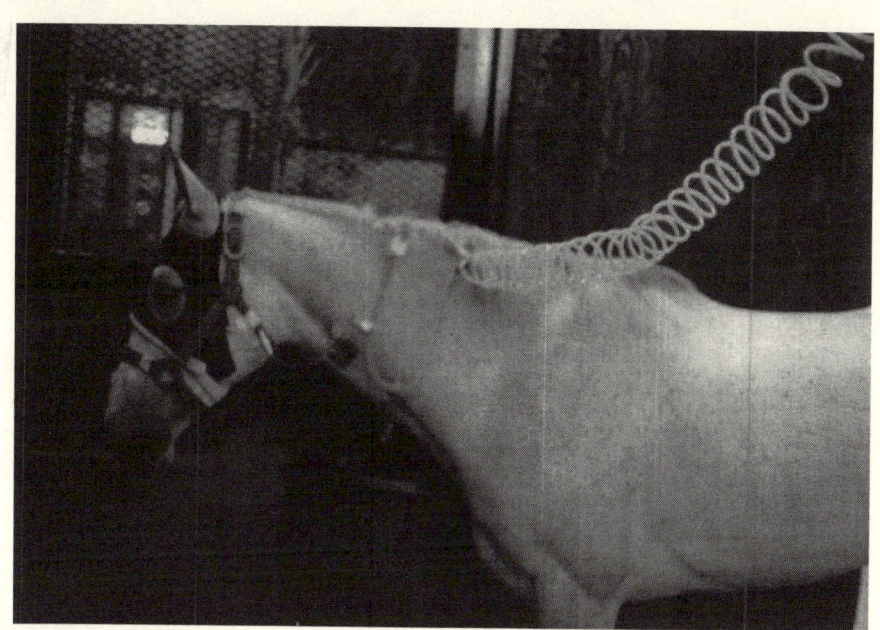

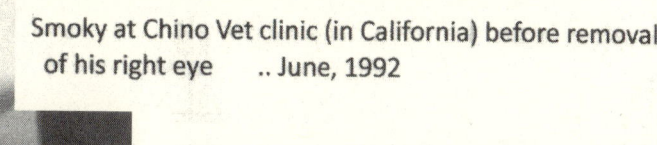
Smoky at Chino Vet clinic (in California) before removal of his right eye .. June, 1992

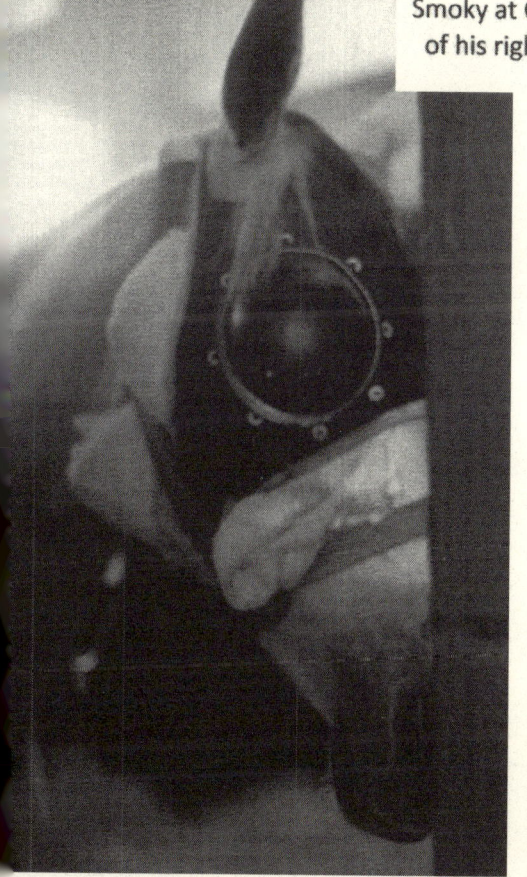

23 His Undaunted Spirit

1992

Bryan had traveled with me to pick up Smoky as I really couldn't manage driving a truck and hauling a horse trailer with only one good arm. When we stopped to check in at the Los Al stable gate, I hopped out to open Smoky's side window. Almost immediately, he recognized where he was and let out a jubilant whinny. It made my heart sing to hear him so happy. As we drove onto the grounds and pulled into our shed row, Smoky could hardly contain himself. He knew he was truly home now, and the responding nickers of welcome from his stablemates had him beside himself with excitement. He was anxious to get out of the trailer and be back where he belonged, back with his buddies and back to a life that he so dearly loved.

As Bryan let down the ramp and undid the butt bar, I wondered if Smoky would have any difficulty backing down the ramp straight and quietly with his right eye removed and still bandaged. I walked up beside him and talked as reassuringly as I could to him.

"I'm here, Smoky. I'll help you back out of here. Everything will be fine! Just let me guide you."

I let Smoky turn his head to the left to look behind him. He was a little hesitant to move. He wanted out of the horse trailer, but this was a new feeling for him. He would have to put his trust in me. I didn't want Smoky slipping off the right side of the ramp, so while Bryan stood by the right side of the ramp to move Smoky over if need be, I gently pushed on his shoulder and asked him to back up.

"You're doing a great job, big guy," I reassured him. "Just take a few steps slow and easy, Smoke."

Very slowly, he took a small step and then another. I wished I had two good arms so that I could be a little more natural in backing him down the ramp. As he took his next step, his left hind foot felt the downhill slope of the ramp. I saw his hesitation and then watched as he picked his back foot up quickly.

"It's okay, son, you've done this lots of times before . . . Just a little more, and you'll be down and out."

I patted his neck and put a little more pressure on his halter and lead rope while pressing on his shoulder. He responded to the pressure and my reassurance, and very slowly, he backed down the ramp. He was not at all sure of himself, and I admired the trust that he was placing in me. It took a few more hesitant steps, and then he was on the solid, secure dirt of his shed row. He had done it. As if to herald his accomplishment, he let out a loud hello to everyone. Bryan and I laughed and congratulated him. Smoky was back!

I tenderly rubbed his neck and walked my very proud and excited patient around the area to let him see all his stablemates as they looked out from their stalls. It was wonderful to see Smoky so alive and so full of himself. He was gorgeous, I thought, with his head held high and his neck arched and his hooves barely touching the ground as he danced and pranced in his jubilation. I let him totally enjoy his reunion parade. I was so glad to have him back. My heart could hardly contain all the happiness I felt.

As we continued Smoky's triumphant march around the area, I found myself anticipating the next step. At some point, I had to get Smoky to enter his stall. How would Smoky deal with entering a confined space that offered a very narrow entrance? I decided to walk him up to his stall and just stand him there and let him look in. I could tell right away that he wanted no part of the narrow opening. It was obvious that he didn't trust anything to the right of him, especially the right edge of the stall door.

"I need to be on your right side, don't I, Smoky? I need to let you know when things are safe on that side of you."

So very quietly, I passed in front of him so that I was in front of but also to the right of him. I offered him a carrot to put him at ease. He grabbed it but also tried to pull me to the left and away from the stall door.

"No, no, Smoky, that's not the idea. I want you to know that I'm right here. I won't let this side of the stall get you. I'll be your right eye. You take care of what's on your left, and I'll watch the right." I let him relax and then turned him to the left away from the stall. "I'm going to lead you up to the stall straight on, Smoky, so that you can see the whole opening. I'll be on your right, and I'll go in just ahead of you."

I was glad it was daylight and the sun was bright so that he could see the interior of the stall and it wasn't just a dark hole. I stayed on his right side and just ahead of him enough so that he could see me with his good left eye. The bandage was quite bulky over his right eye, and I knew he was afraid of hitting it as well as being afraid of this new half world he could see.

"It's okay, Smoke. This is where the right side of the stall door is . . . I won't let you get hurt by it. Come on now. You can do it."

Smoky stepped gingerly forward.

I patted his neck. "Good boy!"

Slowly, he took another cautious step. He was coming in. He was going to trust me and my judgment. Then suddenly, he was in. We had just mastered another huge obstacle. I felt a tremendous sense of accomplishment. However, Smoky immediately attempted to whirl around to escape. This was a typical Smoky behavior, and I was ready. Quickly, I responded by preventing his whirl, and then slowly, I turned him to the left so that he could look out. I wanted him to remain in the stall but also feel comfortable. If he could look out and see his friends and the stable area, I knew it would do a whole lot to put him at ease.

I scratched and petted his neck. "You did it, big boy! What a champ! I'm so proud of you."

Bryan and I fussed over him and offered him another piece of carrot, but he was still too tense to think about eating it. I kept petting him and talking to him. Bryan put his stall guard up, and we let Smoky survey his kingdom, for that's how he thought of it, I'm sure. All my other horses followed and looked up to Smoky. He was their leader, and he was home again. It felt so very good to have the kingdom all together again. Long live the king!

With my left arm still in a cast, I had lots of time to dote on Smoky, and in the days that followed, we spent a lot of quality time together. Since I couldn't ride, I decided to spend as much time as I could helping Smoky adjust to having just one eye. Each day, I would halter Smoky, groom him, and take him for walks around the stable area. At first, Smoky was very hesitant; however, I constantly made a point of being on his blind right side. It was amazing how much confidence he gained when I led him from that side. I became his seeing-eye dog for that side of him, and eventually, he came to trust me unconditionally.

Pretty soon, he was walking so fast that I had a hard time keeping stride with him. Friends, grooms, trainers, and veterinarians alike would voice their hellos or wave their greetings, and his walks grew to be a habit in their daily lives.

Then I started to notice that Smoky started choosing the direction that he wanted to take his walks. He would literally drag me off in the direction of his choice just like a big dog eager to get some exercise and see the sights. This little habit really made me chuckle, and of course, I let him have his way. Little did I know that this would become one of Smoky's favorite pastimes for the rest of his racing career. He would love to explore and go for walks at every racetrack he was at from that time forward. He learned to know where all the grassy areas were, which, unfortunately, weren't very many at Los Al.

Somewhere along the way, I thought to let Smoky lead the walks. An old habit from endurance riding came into play. Many times on a fifty-miler, especially on the uphills, I would dismount and tail my horse up the hill at a walk or even a trot. What this involved was running or walking behind your horse with a lead or rein in one hand and his tail in the other. A well-trained endurance horse would follow the trail and turn or stop on command and, without a rider to carry, could conserve precious energy. I couldn't think of a better way to build Smoky's confidence. His eye was healing well, and he was becoming more full of himself. He needed more mental and physical diversions.

Smoky took to this new game as if he himself had thought it up. He was taking me for walks, and he loved it. Each day, he would set out on his mission with zeal and know exactly which direction he wanted to go. I wondered sometimes if he lay awake at nights planning his daily itinerary for his walks. The only place he didn't want to go was back to his stall. People enjoyed watching him walk by with a definite purpose in his stride and his trainer in tow. It really was quite a sight. He would drag these walks on and on, and they became longer and longer. I enjoyed seeing him so happy, and I always felt badly when I'd have to say, "That's enough for now, Smoky . . . We have to go back. I have to take care of Indy and Manteeya and the others. We'll walk again this afternoon, okay?"

During this time, Smoky's eye was healing very well. Dr. Moak eventually removed the last bandage for good. I fashioned Smoky a special set of one-eyed blinkers that Smoky wore for a while, mainly for my peace of mind more than anything. Eventually, those too were laid by the wayside. People often asked if I thought of getting Smoky a glass eye. It was something I had thought I might do in the beginning, but as Smoky grew more and more confident and seemed so happy, I thought it best just to let things be.

It was during this time that I *finally* got the cast off my left arm. What a relief! However, my arm was very weak, and I was very tentative using it at all. I had to get it back in shape and used to doing some work again. Smoky and I would continue to mend together.

It wasn't long before I realized that Smoky was ready for more exercise and more adventure, so I started taking him up to the receiving barn near the racetrack, where he immediately took to rolling, after which he would jump up with a big leap into the air. His eye had healed over so well; no amount of dirt or dust could bother it now. I had thought to ask the attendants in the receiving barn if we could do this before I brought Smoky up there. I didn't want to repeat my Delaware mistake. They were tickled to have Smoky come visit but did ask me to keep my activity low-key and not make it public knowledge. I readily agreed.

As Smoky developed more and more confidence, I began lunging him in circles, first with his good eye toward me and eventually with the missing eye toward me. At first, he really didn't feel comfortable lunging to the right, but we just did a little bit more each day. Soon, that too became comfortable for him.

Then the day came when I decided to ask Robert Strauss, who had been Smoky's regular and faithful pony horse person before his eye surgery, if he would have the time to pony Smoky. Smoky really liked Robert and his black pony horse, so the transition from hand-walking to ponying was easy. If Smoky had to lose an eye, I was so glad that it had been his right eye. So much training was done on the left side of a racehorse. Even a pony horse always stayed on the left side of a racehorse. Robert just walked Smoky around the stable area and down to the receiving barn. I tagged along to watch. Then Robert began trotting Smoky in circles in the receiving barn. Smoky was adapting so well that I started to think he might like to trot around the racetrack. Robert and I both thought he needed the exercise and that he might really enjoy it. The only place he got any real exercise was doing circles in the receiving barn, and that got old after a while.

It was so cute when Smoky realized he was going to go on the racetrack. His whole demeanor changed. He looked beautiful. His head went up, and his tail flowed up over his back, and he actually started prancing. He was ready! He actually wanted to do this! I was amazed and delighted. Good old Smoky!

As soon as Smoky was on the track, he stopped and just looked and looked. Robert and his pony horse stopped with him. Robert talked to him and just let him keep on looking. Smoky must have spent ten minutes just looking and watching. Jockeys and trainers coming onto or exiting the track called out to Smoky in greeting, and he seemed to bask in the attention. This behavior of stopping and intently looking and watching was to become a habit that started on this day, and Robert and I were always happy to accommodate it. It tickled the both of us that he enjoyed studying the activity of the track that much.

Eventually, Robert asked Smoky to move on. There were about five or six more stops before Smoky reached the gap. The gap is where the main track and the on chute to the track join. Robert just let Smoky do his thing. Then as easy as can be, Robert had his pony horse and Smoky trotting. Smoky looked like he was showing off. It was ever so evident that he was happy to be back. We had been a little concerned that Smoky might feel uneasy about horses coming up from behind on his blind side, especially if they were galloping, so Robert kept him close to the outside rail where the only horses that would be on Smoky's blind side were those that were backtracking and exiting the track. Horses and riders that were backtracking had to walk or trot (no galloping), and Smoky could see these horses coming toward him, so it didn't pose a problem as there wasn't any big surprise element.

What fun it was to watch Smoky make his return trip around to the backside! That first day, Robert didn't take him across the gap. We didn't want to risk having a horse come up the chute and pass Smoky on his blind side. Robert stopped the two horses halfway down the back side, turned to face the track, and again just let Smoky stand and watch. Then they came trotting back. As they passed the grandstands on the front side, all of a sudden, Smoky kicked out his left hind leg in pure happiness. I had to chuckle. Even Smoky's endearing trademark kick-out was back.

As the days passed and Robert continued ponying Smoky to the track, I began to have notions of *maybe*, just *maybe*, racing Smoky again. Other horses had raced again after losing an eye. Luckily, Smoky had lost his right eye. I reasoned that he could always see the inside rail and know where he was. If I raced him on the outside of the field of horses, he would always know where they were also. The next step then was to have Robert pony Smoky with a rider up. I would have loved to be that rider, but my weak left arm dictated otherwise. So I enlisted Frank Quesada for the job. Frank had been riding and winning on my other racehorses during Smoky's ordeal, and he was very quiet and kind with the horses. I could trust Frank to work with Smoky and Robert.

Smoky was sure he was in a race. Why else would he have both a rider and a pony horse? He was extra proud and extra excited today. However, he still had to stop and survey all the horses and the things that were going on once he stepped on to the track—and he had to do this several times! Finally, the threesome was ready. Smoky looked so fine trotting around the track with Robert and Frank. It was *so* obvious that he was *so* happy, and I was *so* happy too. Smoky kicked out this left hind leg extra high today.

It wasn't long before Frank and Smoky were galloping beside Robert with no lead attached. Then shortly after, Frank was galloping him without Robert and his pony horse, and always, Frank kept Smoky closer to the outside rail as Robert had done. The next step, I thought, was to have Smoky gallop in company, and who could be better company than Indy? Indy was so good for Smoky. Smoky trusted Indy so much that we were able to have Indy even gallop on Smoky's blind side. I could hardly believe that Smoky was adapting to all these new things so well. He was the last horse that I thought would be able to adapt to losing an eye. He was amazing. Old thoughts returned—*If only Alice and Larry could see him now!*

As time passed, I felt that the moment had arrived to put in an official work. I was anxious to see if Smoky could hold his speed and also if he could handle the pressure. I decided it would probably be best to work him in company—with Indy again, of course. They would work three eighths of a mile or three furlongs. I directed Frank to let Indy's rider gallop head to head with Smoky for the first quarter mile, and then Frank was to urge Smoky on the last furlong so that Smoky would be racing alone in the lead. We would see how Smoky handled the speed and also how he handled being alone at the wire.

It turned out that it was a piece of cake. Smoky never gave any indication that he had ever been away from the track, let alone lost an eye. He ran straight and true to form. He came trotting back, one happy camper. Later, I would find out that he worked the fastest Arabian work of the day—an amazing thirty-nine seconds flat.

I had a race in mind for Smoky. It was the Samtyr Sprint Handicap to be run at four and a half furlongs on July 25. I wanted to work Smoky one more time (this time out of the starting gate), and if everything went well, we would enter that race. Six days after having posted his bullet work for three furlongs, Smoky would blow us away with an amazing four-furlong work in 51.4 seconds. Smoky was ready physically. I hoped he was ready mentally too.

Exactly one month and ten days after being discharged from Chino Vet Clinic, Smoky was back at the races. What a remarkable recovery he had made! It was amazing to me not only that he was back but also how quickly he had returned. I was so proud of him. However, if I thought I had been nervous for Smoky's very first race back in 1989, it was nothing compared to how nervous I felt today. This was to be Smoky's first race with a missing right eye. I hoped and prayed that I had made the right decision in bringing Smoky back. Even so, I had to admit that he looked absolutely fit and happy out there in the post parade. Eddie Burghart welcomed Smoky back and even honored him by announcing Smoky's past accomplishments and what had transpired during the past two months.

Smoky was not to be the favorite today; rather, SGR Orzel, who had shipped in from Delaware, was the favorite at two to one. I knew that SGR Orzel would have that "Delaware" advantage and would be very tough. KA Czubuthan was also in the race, along with the speedy sprinter Shahzabro and Bryan's speed horse, Broyuri. It was a very tough field for Smoky's first race back.

Even though I had told Frank not to try to win if Smoky didn't appear to be 100 percent physically or mentally, I still worried that Smoky might get boxed in or cut off by other horses. Thank goodness we had drawn the outside post position. We would leave from gate 8, and Smoky would be able to see all the other horses. Our plan was to have Smoky break easy and run wide. We would sacrifice a lot of ground this way, but we felt Smoky didn't need any surprises on his blind side.

As they approached the starting gates, butterflies had my stomach feeling like I was on a ship in a storm. I clenched my fists and prayed to everyone up above whom I felt might be watching today. It included Grandpa, my old competitive trail horse, Brandy, my friend, Sue Bretag, who had sadly died of cancer, and even Thunder—to please help Smoky have a safe trip. This little prayer ritual had become a comfort for me, and I did it before each of Smoky's races. This time, however, I kept repeating it and repeating it, and I definitely asked more people etc. to help out.

The horses were at the gates. I watched the horses being loaded in the gates on one of the TV monitors. Smoky appeared to load nice and quietly.

Then Eddie was announcing, "And they're off!"

Broyuri and Serprimo went right for the lead, as was expected. KA Czubuthan and SGR Orzel were close behind pressing the pace. Smoky had broken very slowly and was at the back of the pack.

Eddie was announcing, "And Magna Terra Smoky is racing eighth and last. He can see them all."

Our plan was 100 percent on target so far. I was feeling a little more relieved. Thank goodness I had worked so hard to change Smoky's running style. He could sit back and be relaxed and then make his bid, if he wished, at the three-eighths pole. Down the backstretch, Broyuri and Shahzabro had opened up an impressive lead. Smoky was racing wide and was now in sixth place.

Eddie had just announced, "And Magna Terra Smoky will have to pick it up."

It was as if Eddie had given Smoky the official cue, for all of a sudden, Smoky exploded, and he was in the hunt. He had gone from sixth to third in a matter of precious seconds. Now we were crazy, out of our minds, cheering for Smoky. He was honing in on the frontrunners. He had run wide the whole trip and had completely circled the field, and still, he came.

Bryan was yelling, "Go, Smoky! Get 'em, Smoky! *Go, go, go!*" and I was just as loud and excited.

Eddie was focused on Smoky now.

"And here comes Magna Terra Smoky . . . like a tremendous machine . . . He is narrowing Shahzabro and Broyuri's lead with every stride. Now he's head and head with the pair . . . He has caught them . . . Magna Terra Smoky is in the lead!"

It was the thrill of a lifetime for Bryan and me. Smoky was back. Eddie's announcing had sent waves of excitement through the crowd, and Smoky's unbelievable charge down the stretch had brought tears to my eyes. I felt so much pride that I thought my heart would burst. That this was happening was more than I could ever have hoped for or dreamed of. Smoky was absolutely unstoppable. It didn't go on deaf ears either that Eddie had used an expression on Smoky that was famous for describing Secretariat in his phenomenal Belmont Stakes victory.

But wait . . . The race was not over. Smoky had the lead but, in doing so, had automatically dropped down to the rail. The jockey on KA Czubuthan (who had chased Smoky down the lane) was not going to miss the opportunity presented. He swung KA to the outside and was rapidly closing ground on Smoky's blind side. I helplessly realized that Smoky probably didn't have any idea where Czubuthan was or how close. I put my hands to my face and pressed them against my cheeks. How could those last few yards seem so incredibly long?

Hang on, Smoky. Please hang on!

The finish line was just ahead, and suddenly, Eddie's voice resounded even over the roar of the crowd as he let out an exuberant "Magna Terra Smoky has done it! He has won! Magna Terra Smoky is back!"

Amazingly, Smoky had won his comeback race. He had proven to everyone watching that he truly was a great racehorse. He had shown not only courage and determination but also plain old-fashioned guts. Bryan and I, along with many race fans, ran down to greet Smoky in the winner's circle.

What a wonderful feeling to be back in the winner's circle with Smoky! Even Robert was there. He had very quickly left his pony horse in the care of another pony person and had hustled through the onlookers to be in Smoky's win picture. We turned Smoky so his hollow eye socket would be facing the camera. This was one photo that I would treasure for the rest of my life, and I wanted it to show that he really had won without his right eye.

While we were basking in the public's eye and I was accepting Smoky's victory blanket, the official time for the race flashed up on the tote board. I looked up and was in total awe. The posted time was an unbelievable 57.1 seconds. Smoky had just run the fastest four and a half furlongs of his life. It was an amazing full second faster than he had ever raced before. He had run wide, circled the whole field, and still posted the win, and he did it in almost track-record–breaking time. He had surpassed all the expectations I could have ever hoped for.

As we left the winner's circle and made our way to the test barn, it felt like I was walking on clouds. Smoky was more excited than I had ever seen him. He was one very happy horse, and I was one ecstatic horse owner. Tears rolled down my face as I put my arm on Smoky's neck. It couldn't be any better than this.

July 1992

Robert Strauss ponying Smoky after the loss of his right eye

Smoky taking me for a walk on the Los Al backside after losing his right eye

Photo Credit: Los Alamitos Race Course Photography

24 A Cold and Relentless Wind

1992

I have often wondered if I hadn't broken both my arms about the same time that Smoky lost his eye if I would have spent so much time with Smoky during his recovery. There were a lot of other horses in my barn, and I always felt that I had to gallop all of them to keep on top of their progress and also so I could assess their mental and physical condition. With two broken arms, I was unable to do this and so gave Smoky an amazing amount of attention and time. He basked in the attention, and I rejoiced at his recovery. His unbelievable ability to bounce back and win his first race with one eye had been the most amazing thing I could ever have hoped for. He absolutely loved racing. I was so glad that I had decided to keep working with Smoky and that somehow fate had again intervened to choose this path for us. It made me realize also that sometimes things that seem so devastating at the time can actually turn out to be blessings in disguise.

As I looked over the condition book of races for the following weekend, I was surprised to find another race that Smoky fit. Smoky had run through all his conditions long ago, so unless a race was offered that included an extra factor (such as nonwinner of a race over one mile for the current year), he never got to race unless a stakes race was planned. If I raced Smoky again, it would mean that he would only have a break of seven days between races. Although thoroughbreds often needed at least two weeks between races, many Arabians were able to race more frequently. Smoky had often raced with such short breaks in the past, but now he had an extra handicap, and I wondered if it might be too much for him.

"I really don't know what to do, Bryan. What do you think?"

"Why would you give up the opportunity? Smoky's in fantastic condition, and he sure came back off that race last weekend in good shape. If you pass this one up, when might you get another race for him? They don't offer that many races that he fits unless they're stakes races, and there aren't any stakes races coming up."

"Yeah. I've thought about all those things too. I just don't want to overstress him. This race is a lot longer, a mile and one sixteenth. That's quite a difference from the four and a half furlongs that he just ran."

Bryan contemplated my worries.

"All Smoky had last weekend was equivalent to a really good work. You would have probably worked him five furlongs to set him up for this race anyway. All you've done is set him up perfectly for this longer race. I don't think you can afford to pass this race up. This longer race will give Smoky a better chance to get the positioning he needs. He can afford to race a little wide and see the whole field. I think it'll be great practice for him if nothing else."

"You're right about that, and Los Al doesn't offer that many long races. I'm not sure I have him super fit for this longer distance, but I also don't know when I'll get another chance for such great practice."

It was great to be able to toss ideas back and forth with Bryan. I could always trust him to be completely honest. He never had an ulterior motive. He loved and admired Smoky, and he looked out for Smoky's interests, more so now that Smoky had lost an eye. Bryan had been completely thrilled as well as totally surprised that Smoky had handled the loss of his eye so well. He, along with most other trainers, had felt that Smoky would simply be retired.

"All right then. I'll put him in the race. Do you have any horses to enter?"

"Got two for other races. Want to go up to the racing office and enter?"

I smiled, walked over to him, and gave his hand a gentle squeeze. Together and hand in hand, we made our way up the road to the racing office.

Later that day, after entries closed and the race office had had time to schedule races that filled and type up the official race list, Bryan and I stopped by to pick an entry list. Smoky's race had filled, and as I looked at the entry sheet, I recognized our main opposition immediately. KA Czubuthan, that gorgeous chestnut stallion trained by Robert Knight, was again among the entries. I knew that "Czub" absolutely relished this longer distance, which meant that he would be even tougher than he had been in the race last weekend. Robert always had him in tremendous shape for his races. I did not feel that Smoky had really had the time to get as fit as I would have liked for this distance. I hoped that I was being fair to Smoky with the decision that I had made.

Race day came. I found myself anxious and concerned once again. I wondered if I would ever feel easy about Smoky racing any more. There was so much more to worry about when everything on one whole side of his body was invisible to his view. So many more things could happen, either unintentionally or not—a misplaced or wild whip action by another jockey, a bolting horse, or just a horse cutting across to the rail a little too quickly, things that Smoky could not see. I had to trust his jockey to see these things for him. Thank goodness Frank Quesada continued to pilot Smoky. He knew Smoky well, and Smoky knew Frank. There was a mutual respect and a mutual trust between them.

Race day came quickly. Bryan and I watched the TV monitor intently as Smoky broke from the gates. As the starting gates were positioned on the far side of the race oval, it was much easier to see the break on the monitor than to see it live at such a long distance away. Once again, I said my little prayer for Smoky to have a safe and uneventful trip, and once again, I included Grandpapa in my heartfelt words. I wondered if my jittery nerves and fears of something going wrong would ever go away. Then the gate snapped open, and the field of horses was off.

"Thank god!" I sighed in relief. "He's out of the gates."

Smoky had once again left the gates with his newly acquired relaxed, easy style and settled into sixth place. This time, my pride had been mixed with equal parts of anticipation. Now that the break from the gate was over, I breathed a little easier and even ventured to watch Czub, who was impatient to get on with it, race for the lead.

Bryan left to watch the rest of the race live. I stayed at the monitor. I could see a lot more there. Later, when Smoky came around the turn, I too would go outside to watch him race pass the grandstands for the first time. As the field settled in, I saw that Frank had Smoky galloping easily and, at the same time, passing the slower horses in the race. Frank had his eyes focused on the front-runner. He knew that if Czub got a free run at the front of the pack without any challenge, his heart would soar, and he would be literally impossible to beat. Frank let his hold on Smoky out another notch, and very quickly, Smoky was close on Czubuthan's heels. The rest of the field fell farther and farther behind.

I raced outside to stand beside Bryan.

"This is going to be a good practice. Smoky has already cleared all the other horses, and he can see Czub in front of him!" I happily exclaimed.

"Piece of cake," Bryan added. "But . . . I don't think Czub will be caught today though."

Bryan was right, as usual. Smoky chased Czub completely around the oval again. The times were fast, as shown as they flashed up on the infield tote board. Smoky ran his heart out but could not cut the two-length distance that separated them. Czubuthan was the victor. Smoky ran second. He had been beaten. I was sad for Smoky, but I could not have been more proud or happy that the race had been such a success. I knew that Smoky had not been properly conditioned for the distance. Czub had been. Still, Smoky gave it everything he had. He never gave up, and he had another great experience racing with one eye under his belt. I just wished that I had been able to tell Smoky that. It meant so much to him to win. Maybe extra pats, hugs, and carrots would somehow convey the message that he had done wonderfully and that we were very, very proud of him.

Races were becoming fewer and further between now. Most of the Arabian trainers had elected to leave Los Al for the summer months to race on the California Fair Circuit. Most of these trainers loved the fair circuit and supported it wholeheartedly. Several trainers and many owners actually owned a home in one of the towns offering a fair meet, and they enjoyed the special perks of having their horses race in front of their friends and families right in their own backyard. There were a total of eight different California fair meets ranging from those offered in Sacramento and Ferndale in the north to Fresno and Pleasanton in the south.

So it was that I decided to travel north to Ferndale for our next race. Ferndale was offering a nice little stakes race that I thought would fit us perfectly. I had made the trip to Ferndale the year before with Smoky and Indy, and both the horses and I had loved the change of pace and the clean air, and both horses had absolutely relished the lush green grass that was everywhere. I figured the competition would not be as tough at Ferndale, and I thought that Smoky would relish the change of pace and relaxed atmosphere. I knew that I definitely would.

For company, I decided to take along Koshada Star, a new mare that Bryan had liked and I had bought in 1991. Although she had set a track record at Los Al for six and a half furlongs in 1991, she hadn't really raced well since. I felt that she too could well use the change of pace and that she could run in any mare race that was offered. It was a long haul to Ferndale, but I felt that it might be what all three of us needed.

And enjoy the Ferndale atmosphere, we did. For me, it was fresh and low-key, *and* it was fun, and to tell the truth, it had me reminiscing about the good old days at Holly. I wondered if Smoky ever thought back to those good old days.

Koshada raced first. It was a colt race, but I hadn't been able to enter Smoky as he had his stakes race the very next day. Whether it was the grass, the atmosphere, or the fact that Koshada was in top shape, she ended up running the race of her life, romping home all alone, defeating a field of extremely talented *colts*. She even thoroughly tromped a big gray horse named FS Orion. Even Smoky had had his work cut out for him when facing FS Orion. She was awesome, and I was absolutely thrilled. The race was sponsored by Peggy and Ed Gibson, who owned Baywood Builders, and Koshada won a beautiful blanket as well as a nice purse. Several years later, I would meet Peggy and Ed again. They would approach me about training a very talented but very sore mare named Cash on the Spot for them. This exceptional mare would overcome almost insurmountable problems and win thirteen races in a row, including several big stakes races, when we finally teamed up. She would prove to be a story of her own.

Smoky ran next. It was a small stakes race, and Smoky was reunited with our favorite Ferndale jockey, Victor Miranda. However, even before the race, Smoky didn't seem quite right. I was perplexed and dismayed. What was going on? Leading him over to the saddling paddock, I kept watching him. He wasn't moving quite right.

"Are you all right, Smoke?"

It wasn't that Smoky was sick or lame. It was just that old feeling that I had had back in Colorado when Bryan and I had left Smoky behind at Pikes Peak Meadows when we trailered to Holly for two stakes races. There was something amiss. Was he trying to tie up? It was so slight that I questioned myself and my eyesight. I continued to watch him closely as we made our way to the paddock area.

Am I imagining this? I wondered. *Am I just looking for things to go wrong now?*

Smoky seemed alert and excited for his race. I kept walking him toward the paddock area. Saddling went well, but just the same, I mentioned my concern to Victor.

"If he doesn't seem to be moving quite right to you, Victor, I'd like you to tell the state veterinarian. We may have to scratch him at the gate."

Victor nodded. "I'll check him out, Barb. Don't want anything to go wrong for Smoky now, what with all he's been through."

I gave Victor a leg up and wished him a safe trip.

As Victor headed Smoky out onto the racetrack, I felt a wave of relief. Smoky seemed to be traveling just fine. Victor must have felt the same way as shortly after, they were being loaded into the starting gate.

The race was seven furlongs, a distance that Smoky loved. The break went smoothly, and as usual, Smoky broke slowly and easily. Victor eased him toward the outside, and I knew that Smoky would have a good trip. I was relieved to see Smoky traveling fluidly as he gained on the leaders and took the lead into the turn.

This is going to be an easy win for him, I thought. *Just what he needs.*

However, as Smoky came into the stretch, I detected a change. He was lumbering, I thought. *He isn't right.* Rey Romer, a major player on the fair circuit, was moving up on Smoky now.

He's going to catch you, Smoky, and you can't get those legs moving like you want to, can you?

It was heart-wrenching to watch. Smoky was by far the better horse, but I feared Rey Romer was going to be the winner. I put my hands to my face and cringed. *How much pain was Smoky in?* I wondered. *How much damage are you doing to yourself, Smoky?*

I wondered if Victor could detect the change in stride. Did he just think that Smoky was tiring? I kept watching as Smoky kept churning those mighty legs of his. I watched as he struggled for every yard. *He's not going to give up*, I thought. He's fighting with everything that he has in him. But Rey Romer kept coming.

I knew that there was no way to stop Smoky or even slow him down even if Victor had wanted to. Smoky was racing to win. Rey Romer was at his heels now. Smoky could see him coming up on the inside of him. Victor had intentionally kept Smoky off the rail for exactly this reason.

The wire was just ahead. I was yelling and screaming. I wanted this race for Smoky. I just hoped that we weren't paying too high a price.

Romer was at Smoky's side.

Oh no, Smoky, you've tried so hard. Please, dear Lord, help Smoky across that finish line. I tried to mentally push Romer back and, at the same time, nudge Smoky forward. It was agonizing.

"Only a few more strides. Hang on, Smoky!"

Then miraculously, the wire was there. And so was Smoky. He had won.

I raced down to greet him.

We were lucky. Smoky had won, and he appeared fine in the winner's circle. It was a gratifying win for the both of us both emotionally and financially. Smoky had needed this win to boost his confidence and morale. Ferndale had been a clean sweep. I just wished I didn't have that eerie and disturbing gut feeling that something was amiss. Although Smoky didn't have any postrace problems, I couldn't wait to return to Los Al now and seek out Dr. Moak's expert opinion and advice.

When we returned to our home base at Los Al, Dr. Moak gave Smoky a thorough going-over. But the symptoms were long gone now, and so the whole incident left us both baffled.

"The only things different were the traveling and the grass that both horses got to eat. Think the grass did it, Doc? I didn't really let them graze that much, but maybe that's the culprit. You know, Smoky had more grass to eat in Colorado also, and I saw the same thing happen to him there."

"Could be the problem, Barb. There aren't but a few blades of grass around here, so let's see what happens."

"Only problem with that idea is that Smoky was practically raised on grass. I never encountered a problem at all until Colorado last year and now Ferndale."

We left it at that. I had to accept that perhaps time and the absence of grass would tell.

There wasn't much time left for us at Los Al, however. A harness meet was scheduled for the next several months, and there wasn't room for us as well as the trotters and pacers. Fortunately, Hollywood Park, a thoroughbred track to the northwest of us in

Hawthorn, California, had agreed to accommodate the Arabians in the interim. This marked quite a milestone for us as it would be the first time in the history of this very famous and prestigious track that Arabians would be racing there. I looked forward to the new adventure but was also a little nervous. Bryan had warned me of the less-than-desirable neighborhood surrounding Hollywood Park. Although at one time, this area had been the home of the rich and famous, it had deteriorated badly in recent years and was now a high crime area with many slum-like areas. He warned that we would have to be careful and watch our horses and tack carefully.

When the time came for our move, however, I found that although we traveled past some very questionable dwellings, Hollywood Park itself proved to be a beautiful facility with huge gorgeous lawns and trees. The track was immense after Los Al's five-eighth-mile oval. I found myself thinking, *Wow, this is the* true *big league. It is absolutely and amazingly beautiful.*

We were not quite awarded big-league status, however. As we were a temporary commodity, the Arabians were stabled in temporary portable stalls behind the main barns. It was fine with us though as Hollywood Park even had a swimming pool for horses and a training track should we wish to gallop there instead of on the main racecourse. Although we had to use one stall as our tack room, it was a much safer environment than I had been led to believe. Very quickly, I found how much some of my horses loved to swim. CJ Steed would almost drag me to the pool once he knew where we were going. Smoky wasn't too keen on swimming though, so I decided not to push it with him.

Although the track and the facilities were wonderful, Smoky had a terrible meet at Hollywood Park. He ran five times and never won a race. Was there something going on within Smoky that was escaping all of us? I hadn't seen any signs of tying up if that was indeed what the problem had been at Ferndale. I hated this time of *"never-never* land," never knowing what was going on with Smoky. I wished that something would just blatantly surface so that Dr. Moak and I could at least deal with something tangible. Not knowing what was wrong yet knowing that something was indeed not right was driving me crazy.

One terrifically good thing did happen while we were at Hollywood Park, however. Because Hollywood Park was such a state-of-the-art facility in the thoroughbred horse-racing world, it had available to all attending veterinarians exceptional resources, including a vet clinic that included the latest and the best in X-ray machines. So it came to be that Dr. Moak approached me about taking some X-rays of Smoky's stifles.

"Barb, I can't think of a better opportunity to see what is going on in those stifles of his. I have always been intrigued by what we might see there, and now we have that opportunity. Want to give it a go?"

"Wow, would I? You bet!"

I thanked Doc for thinking of doing this. I knew that the both of us were eager to see if any significant changes had occurred since Smoky's surgery back in 1988. And although he didn't say as much, I felt Dr. Moak was also looking for reasons for Smoky's lackluster performances.

When the X-rays were taken and Doc had time to develop them, he swung by the barn.

"You've got to see the X-rays, babe. I have a couple of horses to check on. Then I'll be back. Would that work for you?"

"You bet, Doc. I'll be here and waiting."

Doc had the endearing habit of calling many of his female clients "babe." It was not done in a sexual or derogatory way. It simply was his way of greeting you, and it implied that he cared for you. When I had taught school, I found myself calling students "hon." It didn't matter if they were male or female. I used the term the same way that Doc used "babe." These days, I don't think it would be a good idea to use either term with students or clients. Times have certainly changed.

About forty-five minutes later, Doc swung by the barn. I hopped in my little Datsun and followed him to the building where he had developed the X-rays.

"Can't wait for you to see this, babe!"

I wondered what he had seen. Anxiously, I followed him to a room with a large empty wall where he hung the X-rays.

"Take a look here. Can you see the calcification in Smoky's stifle, right here?"

"Yes, I see it."

"Well, that is all 'old' calcification. It happened before you had the surgery done on Smoky's stifles. You can tell that it is old by the shading. Newer calcification would be lighter. There isn't any new calcification. What is really interesting here is that with the way the calcification was progressing, it is safe to bet that without the surgery as a two-year-old, you would not be racing Smoky today. You probably would not have even made it to the races with him at all."

"Oh my lord, I can't believe it, Doc!"

I truly couldn't believe it! I had Smoky's stifle surgery done against the advice of many very good veterinarians. I had had it done on "gut feelings" alone, what had gone through my mind that I felt so strongly that it needed to be done and done then. I couldn't believe just how fortunate I had been. How wonderful is "gut feeling"! It was one more time that Smoky made me think about the timing and sequence of events that had brought us to this point.

"Man, this is great to see, Doc. What wonderful news. You are great to be doing this for us."

I thanked Doc profusely, wondering at the same time how many racehorse track vets would have taken the time and had the foresight to do something as time-consuming as this for a client. It meant the world to me.

"Well, guess we can rule Smoky's stifles out as far as causing him any problem," Doc laughingly responded.

"Guess we can. And that is a huge relief." Now I wished it could be as easy to find out what Smoky's current problem was.

As I looked back, I thought, *What a year this had been*, from the lowest of lows, when I questioned Smoky's very survival, to the fantastic high of winning his first race back after eye surgery. However, other than his first race back after losing his eye, our racing success had been very frustrating and disappointing. It was, by far, the worse racing year of his career. Even with Dr. Moak's observant eye and Bryan's helpful suggestions, we had not really gotten Smoky back on track. He just didn't seem quite right. I didn't think it was time to retire Smoky, but maybe I was wrong. Maybe the stress that he had undergone during his stay at Chino Vet Clinic had altered something within him. Maybe it had triggered the same response that I saw overcome Smoky when he first came to stay at Dick's place in Fort Collins. Was it a physical thing or a chemical problem, or was it a mind issue? I was really at a loss as what to think.

Even so, Smoky's terrible year of racing—12(2-6-2)6, which meant he had raced twelve times with two firsts, six seconds, and two thirds, with six of his races being stakes races—had still been good enough to earn him not only ARAC (California) Top-Aged Horse but also ARAC Horse of the Year honors. When they announced this at the ARAC year-end awards banquet, I was taken by *total* surprise. As I accepted the award, I couldn't hold back the tears. They were tears of joy, tears of utter amazement and surprise, and tears of hope. I was so proud of Smoky. He had endured a terrible year and still had been the best of the best on the West Coast. It was his third straight year to win this award. Even with a subpar performance, he had been the best. What might he be able to do if I could get ever him totally right again?

Robert W. Moak, DVM

25 A "New" Year... A Gentler Wind?

1993

It was a fresh, new year. I hoped that it would also be a fresh new start. Smoky's first race of the new season was to be a race on January 15. The distance would be a mile and a sixteenth. It always amazed me how Smoky could run every distance they had to offer and race extremely well at all of them. It was an exceptional feat. Most racehorses had the talent or ability to race either short (four and a half furlongs to six furlongs) or long (seven furlongs to one and one quarter miles). It was a rarity to find a horse that could run both long and short races and win.

Smoky had just run a four-and-a-half-furlong race on December 26. He had placed second but was only beaten by a head. The race had gone in a very fast 57.4 seconds, and he had closed from seventh to *almost* first in a tremendous stretch drive. As he approached the turn into the stretch, he had had to angle very wide to circle the field of horses in front of him. It was a beautiful thing to watch him pick off his rivals one by one and then thunder down the stretch, closing the distance on the leader by leaps and bounds. I yelled and screamed and urged Smoky on, but it was not to be. If Frank Quesada (his jockey) had just moved him just a tad earlier or if Smoky hadn't needed to go quite so wide, it would have been a victory for Smoky to savor. Either slight difference would have been enough for the win. I felt Smoky had been cheated on this one. He had been the best horse I felt, but unfortunately, fickle luck had not been on his side. I was crushed as I knew that a win would have done so much for his confidence and demeanor—and mine too!

Today he would be racing one and one sixteenth miles. He only had twenty-one days to make the necessary adjustments. You are probably thinking that I'm crazy doing this to Smoky and that Smoky would have had a better chance of winning if I had stuck to either short or long races. But Smoky thrived on exercise and racing. He was a racehorse through and through. It was what he lived for, and if horses dream, it was, I'm sure, what he dreamed about. Over the months and years, he really had learned to adjust well. Since he had learned to break from the gates in a slower and more relaxed manner, it was easier for his jockey to rate him. It wasn't a tug-of-war battle anymore to get him to relax and go easy for the first part of the race. The lactic acid that built up from early exertion in the first half mile of a race never affected Smoky anymore, and he had a fantastic and crowd-pleasing late run that the fans learned to love and expect. In addition, he was willing to listen if the jockey indicated he had to go past the finish line twice, as was the case in all long races at Los Al. With Los Al being such a small track (five-eighth miles), horses often used themselves up racing for that first finish line the first time it came into view.

Although today's race was an open allowance, the purse was only $4,000. This meant that it would pay $2,200 (minus 10 percent to the jockey) to the winner. Our purses couldn't hold a candle to thoroughbred purses. Because of the low purses, all of us Arabian trainers had to race more often just to survive financially. Twenty-two hundred dollars did not go far. Even with Smoky's consistent style of placing in the money, it was a struggle to keep financially ahead of this game. Expenses were huge. There were always vet bills to deal with as well as feed and bedding, gallops and ponies, necessary supplements, shoeing, and the expensive workman's comp insurance that all trainers had to carry.

Sadly, the race today proved to be even more of a heartbreak than Smoky's four-and-a-half-furlong race. Frank had opted to ride Minos, a good-looking and talented gray who was owned by Sheik Tahnoon Bin Zayed and trained by Yancy Carter, in this race instead of Smoky. There was a full field of twelve horses in the race. I had put Severiano Martinez up on Smoky. Smoky ran a beautiful race, but perhaps Sevi moved him a little too soon. Smoky made his late running move around the bend into the stretch and led down the stretch. However, Frank, who knew Smoky well, had Smoky's late move well calculated, and he waited patiently and then urged Minos on to follow Smoky down the lane, catching Smoky on his blind side right at the wire. It was another heartbreaking, gut-wrenching loss. Smoky had again run his eyeballs out—or, should I say, eyeball out—and had again just missed. I wondered what it would take for him to win a race once again.

Smoky had now raced in a total of sixty races. He had won an amazing twenty-three of them and had placed second twenty times and third nine times. He had earned $139,727. It was a phenomenal achievement. Alice had to be quite pleased with her 3 percent investment.

We now had a short break from racing. I hoped the break might be good for all the horses, including Smoky. Bryan and I once again rented stalls and pastures at A-Bar Ranch in Norco so that all our horses could have a well-deserved period of rest and relaxation. It did my heart so much good just to see the horses out in the fresh air, contently grazing on the acres of green grass and basking in the warm California sun. As I really couldn't see that green grass was the cause of any of Smoky's problems and because I couldn't really bring myself to deprive Smoky of something that was so natural to him, he too was turned out to just be a horse.

It was a nice break for all of us, but all too soon, Los Al was ready to start up again. The first race for Smoky was the Sierra Knights Stakes Race run at six furlongs. I had elected to try a new rider up who was mainly a quarter-horse rider. It was a lackluster performance by Smoky; he just ran in fourth or fifth place the whole race and ended up finishing fifth. However, we managed to get Frank Quesada for Smoky's next race, and Smoky put in a strong finish down the lane to win easily. Our spirits were rejuvenated, and Smoky literally dragged me to the test barn. I was very happy to be dragged.

However, two weeks later, Smoky's half brother, Broyuri (also out of Smoky's sire, SW David), showed a good turn of foot to defeat Smoky in a four-and-a-half furlong race. Then in another turnabout, Smoky raced a superb six-furlong race in the fantastic time of one minute and 18.3 seconds and won easily again. It was rather an inconsistent period. I was either ecstatic or disappointed. I felt like we were on a never-ending roller-coaster ride.

During this time, Ona Natural High (Murphy) offered a nice diversion as he had actually matured enough to win several races. And hard-knocking little Aurzel, who always tried so hard, broke his maiden. What a success story he had been! I ordered an extra copy of his win photo and sent it to Dr. Stashak back at CSU. I wondered what he would think of his little cancer patient now.

The first week in September, I decided to again trailer up to Ferndale for the Ferndale Arabian Stakes. Smoky had enjoyed it so much the year before that I felt the change of environment and the change of pace might be good for him. However, TC Tomtyr proved to be a new rival on the scene as he won the race, defeating Smoky for the second time in as many races.

Smoky was racing well and seemed to be in top form now, but we couldn't seem to put two wins together in a row. Then whether it was luck or fate, Frank Quesada failed to show up at the racetrack to ride Smoky in his next race. When we were told that Frank had failed to show and that I would have to choose another jockey, I was totally blindsided. What a terrible situation to find yourself in! Here we were, in the saddling paddock, ready to race—and no jockey. I was livid. I felt that Smoky was almost being sabotaged. How could Frank do this to us? I hoped that he had one hell of a good excuse for not being here. How could I choose another jockey? All the others already had a mount in the race, and besides that, I couldn't just put any rider up on Smoky. Smoky's jockey needed to know Smoky to understand his style of racing and to accommodate for his missing eye.

My initial reaction was to scratch Smoky from the race. I couldn't risk using a rider that we didn't know. However, for whatever reason, I decided to glance over the list of jockeys who were left and noticed a new talent who had just arrived at Los Alamitos Race Course named Jerry Parenti. Jerry had been riding the Texas circuit, and I knew that Robert Knight, trainer of KA Czubuthan, had used him regularly when in Texas. I thought if Robert liked him that well, maybe I should give Jerry a shot. So I did just that.

It was to be a great decision. Jerry proved to be just what Smoky needed. In this, their first race together, Jerry followed directions to a T and used all his expertise in saving Smoky for an utterly phenomenal stretch drive. Smoky reeled in the field, flying from the back of the pack in seventh place to win by almost two lengths. It was a *huge* finish. The crowd went crazy, and I did too. It was the kind of race every trainer dreams of. This Jerry Parenti was for real, and I dared to dream that we had our new lease on life and racing.

Two weeks later, Jerry and Smoky teamed up again for a seven-furlong invitational handicap race at nearby Pomona. Smoky drew post position 1, not my favorite post position for a horse with a missing right eye. As the horses broke from the gate, they almost immediately had to cross over the main track. Sun Phlare, who was in post position 2, ducked in. Smoky never saw it coming, but thank the lord Jerry did. Jerry gently and expertly eased Smoky back and behind Sun Phlare. Smoky not only went on to win the race by a sensational seven lengths but also set a new track record of one minute and 33.6 seconds for the distance. We had finally done it; we had put two wins together in a winning streak, and to add icing to the cake, we earned a new track record to boot. Smoky was almost as excited as I was. He dragged me around the oval in the test barn. He knew exactly what he had done. Whoever says animals are dumb doesn't know animals—especially this animal!

Jerry had turned out to be the perfect fit for Smoky. I was so glad he had decided to leave Texas and come to Los Al. It was ironical that the person who influenced this decision was none other than KA Czubuthan's trainer, Robert Knight. Jerry had ridden for Robert when they were both in Texas, and Robert convinced Jerry that he could ride more horses and make more money by coming to California. Sadly for Robert but happily for me, KA Czub was on the injured list, which meant Jerry was available to ride Smoky. What a difference having the right jockey can make! Jerry didn't fight Smoky. He had a natural way with horses, and Smoky responded.

Exactly six days after his sensational win at Pomona, Smoky ran in the Silk Designs Sprint. It was a race sponsored by Bob Rudolph and was four and a half furlongs in distance. The fog threatened to cancel our sprint race.

All of a sudden, a voice was heard in the stands: "Run the race. The fog won't bother Smoky. He can't see anyway." The crowd laughed.

The stewards must have agreed with him, for they went on with the race. It would be the last race of the evening, however, as the stewards canceled the rest of the race card after Smoky's race. Eddie Burghart resigned himself to having little commentary on the race. He simply announced, "When I can see something, I'll let you know!"

It wasn't until the horses were closing down the stretch that Eddie or any of us could see the horses at all. And what we did see delighted us all. It was the gray ghost, Magna Terra Smoky, racing for the finish line. I was so glad they hadn't canceled our race. Smoky not only won the race easily but also won in 57.4 seconds, the fastest clocking of the meet. An old familiar figure, Broyuri, owned by Rudolph, ran second.

Smoky now had three wins in a row. We were on a roll! The newspapers went wild with articles about Smoky and his winning race in the fog. It was an exciting and rewarding time for us. John Petti, publicity person and main writer for the racetrack, loved Smoky and the excitement he brought to the racing public, and he wrote numerous articles for the *Los Al Racing Program* giving tribute to Smoky. During this time, it was the rule rather than the exception to have Smoky featured in the main article written inside the cover of the program. I saved every article and sent extras that I found and collected from around the stands to friends and family. It was again the best of times.

The press coverage that Smoky was receiving was so invigorating and encouraging that I felt a new lease on life, and I felt that Smoky did also. The year 1992 had been such a roller-coaster ride that by the end of the year, I feared that many fans and trainers felt that Smoky was about finished. But Smoky had proven them all wrong. What an awesome comeback he had made! The press began tagging him with a new nickname: "The One-Eyed Wonder." It was interesting to read the various accounts of how Smoky had lost his eye, but most of all, it was an honor to have so many articles written about him. Seldom did sports writers write about an Arabian racehorse. Smoky was catching the eye of a whole new audience.

And Smoky wasn't even finished with his comeback. Three weeks after his spectacular Silk Design Stakes win, Smoky proved that he was indeed here to stay by not only winning the six-furlong California Gold Cup stakes race in Fresno but also setting a new track record. Smoky now had won his third stakes race in a period of less than two months. What's more, he had won them at three different tracks, and he had set track records in two of them. In all my wildest dreams, I could not have asked for a more sensational return to top form. He had shown his fans what he was truly made of. He became the number-one drawing card at the races. People came just to see him run. I was so happy for Smoky, and Smoky was happy with himself.

Then the bad news came. Jerry could not make a decent living at Los Al. Even though he won his share of races, there just weren't enough Arabian and thoroughbred races at Los Al. Most of the races were shorter quarter-horse races, and Jerry did not ride quarter horses. I would have loved for him to stay, but Jerry was going broke. He felt he had to leave. He would go back to Texas. I was devastated. Smoky and Jerry had become such a good fit. What would become of Smoky now? I hoped it did not mean the end of Smoky's winning streak and his fabulous comeback.

The upside to all this was that when your horse was running like no other around, it made your jockey selection much larger. Everyone wanted to ride Smoky, and I had my pick of jockeys. I chose a talented, conscientious, very likable jockey named Richard Pfau. Richard was winning at a high percentage and was aiming for the top jockey award. Richard did not disappoint us. His first race up on Smoky was a seven-furlong open-allowance race. The two of them put away their competition in almost track-record time. Chalk up five wins in a row. Three weeks later, Richard and Smoky teamed up for another seven-furlong open-allowance race. This time, they did one better and tied the existing track record, held by none other than Rio Hondo. It was *so* sweet! We were finally on a roll, and I was loving it.

What was really enjoyable about this period was that Rudolph had little to tease me about. In fact, he was downright quiet. Rio Hondo had aggravated an old bow and was still on the mend. Bryan had advised me that Rio would bow again even before it happened.

"Garland has no idea how to shoe a horse that has bowed," he would repeatedly tell me. "Next time you see Rio Hondo up at the track, check out his feet. They have his hooves way out in front of him. There's no way Rio's tendons can take that."

I agreed. "Why was it so difficult to get a horseshoer to back a horse's foot up? They all seem to want a long toe on a horse."

Most horse owners trusted their farrier to shoe their horses correctly. It was no different at the racetrack. If a horseshoer did a bad job, most owners and many trainers were unaware of the fact. It was a sad but true fact that the most important part of a racehorse was so badly taken care of. Even a well-conformed horse could only survive so long on a badly shod undercarriage.

Bryan was annoyed. "They do it because it is easier than trying to set a horse up correctly. It takes less time and a whole lot less work. They all seem to want to get as many horses shod in a short period as they can."

I totally agreed with Bryan. It was ridiculous. Horseshoers at the racetrack had it made. They didn't have to travel far to shoe any of their horses; they were able to shoe a lot of horses each day, and they charged an arm and a leg to do it. Almost every shoer went along with the old philosophy that a long toe increased the stride of a horse. It made no sense as with longer toes, dynamics dictated that correspondingly, more pressure and tension would be placed on the vulnerable tendons and ligaments running up along the back of a horse's lower leg. As the long toe hit the hard surface of the racetrack bottom, the lower leg would absorb the shock of the impact, with the toe floating on out in front. The impact would be borne by the tendons and ligaments, which would be unduly stretched the longer the toe was. It was only a matter of time before the tendon fibers would be stretched to capacity and start to fray like the strings in a rope.

"I'm sure glad that Tom listens to us and doesn't shoe our horses that way."

Bryan grinned. I could tell that Bryan was a little smug in his knowledge. "Rio would never have bowed again if he were still in my barn."

"I know that. For Rio's sake, I wish you still had him. On the other hand, it has been a wonderful heyday for Smoky, with Rio in Garland's barn."

I could tell that Bryan felt that justice had been served to Rudolph, but Bryan missed having that "special champion" horse in his stable. He liked seeing Smoky win because he felt that Smoky was really his creation. He had created the match between Smoky's dam and daddy, and he had believed from the beginning that it would create a good racehorse. Smoky was his prodigy. But Smoky wasn't his. Although there was pride in Smoky's accomplishments, there was also a little jealousy, a little resentment. Bryan loved both Smoky and me, but he had a hard time dealing with my success with Smoky sometimes. I thought, *It's a male thing. He has a hard time with a woman beating him.* But then I wondered if I wouldn't feel the same way if I were in his shoes. I wished that Bryan could find a new champion but not too soon. I enjoyed basking in Smoky's success too much. I didn't want it to end—at least just yet.

From Bryan, I learned that Rudolph was not happy about Smoky's success and that he was causing a lot of disruption in Garland's barn. He accused Garland of treating him and his horses unfairly.

"Garland is having a hell of a time," Bryan would relate to me. "Now he's accusing Garland of using feed that Rudolph bought and paid for to feed other client's horses."

"How does he think that is happening?" I asked.

"Rudolph has Garland on a special deal," he responded. "Rudolph buys all the feed for his horses and pays Garland a fixed amount for training each month. He's not paying the daily rate that most trainers charge. Rudolph knows that Garland is down on his luck and needs the horses, so he is setting his own rules and conditions. Garland either has to accept it or go under."

"Trust Rudolph," I sarcastically added. "I'm sure glad that you are done with him. You'll get your barn built back up again. Just don't get sucked into any of Rudolph's deals."

"You don't have to worry about that! Rudolph is the last person I want around."

"I'm glad to hear you say that. He is nothing but bad news. He thinks his money can buy anything he wants. He's just, plain and simple, bad news."

The final race of the meet was coming up next for Smoky. It was the California Heritage Stakes, to be contested at seven furlongs. TC Tomtyr, trained by Yancy Carter and owned by Sheik Tahnon Bin Zayed, was the top competition. Tomtyr, like Smoky, was coming into this race with a string of wins to his credit. In fact, he was gunning for Horse of the Year. We were now gunning for it also. What an exciting end of the year race this was going to be for racing fans—the two top Arabian horses on the West Coast meeting in the last stakes race of the year—knowing that the winner of this race would surely earn Horse of the Year!

Richard Pfau was as determined as I was to have Smoky outrace TC Tomtyr and, unknown to me, had developed his own strategy for this race. Richard realized that both Smoky and Tomtyr liked to sit off the pace and make a huge three-quarter-to-half-mile all-out dash at the finish. Richard decided that to beat Tomtyr, he would never let Tomtyr head Smoky. That meant that he would set Smoky up so that he always raced just a little in front of Tomtyr. Whatever Tomtyr did, Richard would ask Smoky to do a little more.

So it was that I watched as Smoky and Tomtyr raced this way all the length of the backside to the half-mile pole, and then before Tomtyr had a chance to set down for his run to the wire, Richard already had Smoky in high gear. Smoky never relinquished his lead, and a surprised and defeated Tomtyr finished in the dust two lengths behind. It was a totally awesome finish to an absolutely awesome year. How could anyone have predicted such a tremendous turnaround in Smoky? It locked up Horse of the Year honors for him. It couldn't have been a better finale to the year. He had now won seven races in a row, and he had defeated his toughest rival, TC Tomtyr, in the final race of the year.

What a year it had been! Smoky had raced and won at distances of four and a half furlongs, five and a half furlongs, six furlongs, seven furlongs, one and one sixteenth miles, and one and one eighth miles. He had now raced a total of seventy-one times in his lifetime, with thirty-two wins, twenty-two seconds, and nine thirds. Now we had another record well within our sights, and that was most wins by an Arabian racehorse. Both Smoky and Smoky's old rival, News Release, currently had thirty-two wins to their credit. The Arabian world record of thirty-three race wins, held by a horse named Sam's Count, was definitely in jeopardy.

During 1993, Smoky had raced thirteen times, with nine wins and three seconds. Six of his races had been stakes races, of which he won four. He had earned $39,902 for his year's work. His lifetime earnings now stood at $179,453. Only a handful of Arabian racehorses had ever earned over $150,000. Smoky was now one of them.

Smoky had not only earned ARAC Horse of the Year for the third straight year but also won national honors by earning a Darley Award for Older Horse of the Year. It was the third Darley Award he now had to his credit. Although I did not attend the awards ceremony and still did not have much respect for the Darleys myself, I was glad that Smoky was justly recognized at a national level.

All in all, Smoky had now raced across the continent, from California to Delaware, with Wyoming, Colorado, Arizona, Montana, and Kentucky in between. He had set sixteen different track records. At Los Al, he had set records at six furlongs, seven furlongs (twice), one and one sixteenth miles, and one and one eighth miles (twice). He had also set track records at Bay Meadows, Fresno, Pomona, Pleasanton, Kentucky, Holly, Turf Paradise, and Wyoming.

It was unbelievable, as I look back, that Alice, Dick, and I had laughed about Alice ever being able to earn the $300 stud fee that she had traded for 3 percent of Smoky's race earnings. She had certainly earned quite a return on a trade that I had suggested just to keep her involved in Smoky's career, for she now had earnings totaling almost $5,000.

To add to all this, Aurzel, ever cheerful and totally huggable, even with his own set of problems, had earned the ARAC Four-Year-Old of the Year Award. He had beaten all the odds. Yes, *what a year it had been indeed!*

Article from "Race Arabian" magazine
Oct. 1993

Smoky emerges from the fog

Not even the fog could beat Magna Terra Smoky in late September.

In two stakes races, the 7-year-old gelding devastated his competition, winning the $7,500 Pomona Invitational Handicap by seven lengths at Fairplex Park on Sept. 19 and the $5,900 Silk Design Sprint by four lengths at Los Alamitos six days later.

The two victories pushed his earnings to $156,697, giving Magna Terra Smoky the distinction of being the seventh Arabian to pass the $150,000 earnings mark. The Silk Design Sprint was also his fourth victory in eight 1993 starts.

"He's just been training so good," said owner-trainer Barbara Jagoda. "He's just a real happy horse. You can see it in the saddling paddock. I think he's going to fall asleep."

In the Pomona Invitational Handicap, Magna Terra Smoky set a seven-furlong track record of 1:33 3/5. The race wasn't without its scary moment, however. Magna Terra Smoky started from the rail with Sun Phlare in the two post. As the field approached the main track from the chute, Sun Phlare ducked in, but Magna Terra Smoky, who lost his right eye to disease in 1992, never saw Sun Phlare. Instead, jockey Jerry Parenti, Jr., who was aboard for both stakes wins, eased Magna Terra Smoky back and around Sun Phlare.

On the clubhouse turn, Parenti took Magna Terra Smoky to the lead and never looked back. Sun Phlare, a 4-year-old gelding by Sun Dancer, was second a length in front of 4-5 favorite PL Cavalier.

Sun Phlare is owned by James Zoller and trained by Bobbie McAlister. John Tatro was aboard. PL Cavalier, a 4-year-old colt by Mokasz, is owned by Tahnoon Bin Zayed and trained by Yancey Carter, Jr. PL Cavalier, who was ridden by Ken Blackstun, was also second in the $30,000 California Derby at Los Alamitos in early September.

Six days later, a new cast was assembled to challenge Magna Terra Smoky for the Silk Design, which was the fifth Arabian race run at Los Alamitos on Sept. 25. Didn't matter.

Magna Terra Smoky's stakes wins in late September pushed him over $150,000 in earnings.

Parenti came from off-the-pace again, taking the lead entering the stretch of the 1/2- furlong race and winning by four lengths over Broyuri. The time of 57 2/5 seconds was the fastest clocking at the distance for the Los Alamitos season, but it was lowered a week later by the maiden winner Taf.

Broyuri, a 6-year-old gelding by SW Dawid, is owned by Bob Rudolph and trained by Danny Garrett. Christine Davenport was aboard. Broyuri was also second to Magna Terra Smoky in an early September allowance at Los Alamitos.

FF Stryker, who is owned by Claudette Mironuck, finished third, a nose behind Broyuri. Trained by John Burger, the 6-year-old gelding by Triple A Halarr

Credit: Steve Anderson

Magna Terra Smoky Upsets T C Tomtyr

By John Petti

California Heritage Handicap

Article from "Arabian Finish Line" magazine
Jan. 1994
written by John Petti

The California Heritage Handicap is a race that T C TOMTYR and trainer Yancey Carter would like to forget. Last year, T C TOMTYR got bounced all over the track and was eventually moved up to second as the 3-5 favorite through a disqualification. In 1993 T C TOMTYR was the 4-5 favorite and was outrun by the seven-year-old gelding MAGNA TERRA SMOKY who was picking up his seventh straight victory. The win was also the 32nd for the Barbara Jagoda-owned and trained MAGNA TERRA SMOKY, leaving him tied with NEWS RELEASE just 5 victories shy of the all-time Arabian mark of 37 held by MOHAK. MAGNA TERRA SMOKY, who is known as the one-eyed wonder due to the fact he lost his right eye due to a fungus last year, earned $11,000 for his efforts to move his lifetime bankroll to $179,197.

The $20,000 California Heritage was contested over seven furlongs and turned into a cat and mouse game between the two favorites. While FLAMING TIKI was carving out the fractions for the first half-mile, jockey Bruce Pilkenton kept T C TOMTYR well off the pace in seventh, right behind MAGNA TERRA SMOKY. "I was surprised TOMTYR didn't go to the front," MAGNA TERRA SMOKY's rider Richard Pfau said. "I just wanted to stay with him. I knew if he got the jump on me, he would be very tough to catch."

MAGNA TERRA SMOKY circled the field on the turn for home with T C TOMTYR following behind. As the field raced into the stretch, it became apparent the race was down to these two horses. "I swung wide on the turn because I wanted Bruce (Pilkenton) to go inside with TOMTYR. I thought that if SMOKY could see him he would run better," Pfau said. "He stayed outside of me, but I had plenty of horse left." MAGNA TERRA SMOKY covered the seven furlongs over a tiring track that was labeled as good in 1:36.4, more than four seconds slower than the track record 1.32.2 he had posted on December 3.

"This feels so good," Jagoda said. "This is the first time we have ever been able to beat TOMTYR in four or five tries. This win and the one right after he had the surgery are the most gratifying. Right now he's going to the ranch in Norco. He'll be back here next year to break the record. We want him to do it at Los Alamitos because Dr. Allred (track owner) has been so good to the Arabians." The victory, the seventh this meet at Los Alamitos, also wrapped up the Horse of the Meet title for MAGNA TERRA SMOKY.

Runner-up T C TOMTYR appeared to be making up ground on MAGNA TERRA SMOKY in mid-stretch, but never could get to the winner. The Yancey Carter-trained five-year-old was packing high weight of 130 pounds, spotting MAGNA TERRA SMOKY seven points, and that may have cost him over the tiring track. T C TOMTYR brought a six race win streak into the Heritage after his seventh length triumph in the Korona Open at Bandera Downs in Texas on November 20. In those six wins, no horse had finished within five lengths of the SAMTYR stallion. He defeated MAGNA TERRA SMOKY by 10 lengths in the Ferndale Arabian Handicap back in August. T C TOMTYR earned $4000 for his second place effort for owner Tahnoon Bin Zayed and now has career earnings of $140,893.

KD KALIBOR, who held the lead briefly at the top of the stretch, was 2-1/2 lengths behind T C TOMTYR in third. Apprentice Wayne Howard was aboard for trainer Diane Hansen. Ken Danyluk earned $2400 for KD KALIBOR's third place finish. Following the top three across the wire were FLAMING TIKI, TAK (a three-year-old that was undefeated in three lifetime starts including the California Arabian Futurity), BC RABI SAM, VALS STARBURST, and AWE SHUCKS.

the "California Hertiage" race where Smoky finally beats TC Tomtyr and also nails "Older Horse of the Year" and "ARAC Horse of the Year"
photo credit – Los Alamitos Race course

Jockey-Richard Pfau
Owner-Barbara Jagoda
T C Tomtyr (2nd)

* MAGNA TERRA SMOKY *
Winner Twelfth Race
Purse $20,000
7 Furlongs-1:36.4 December 11, 1993
CALIFORNIA HERITAGE

Tr -Barbara Jagoda
Los Alamitos Race Course
KD Kalibor (3rd)

Accepting Smoky's award from David Wright (ARAC chairman) for "1993 Arabian Racing Association California Horse of the Year"

Magna Terra Smoky is California Horse of the Year

Article from "Arabian Finish Line" magazine
June 1994
written by John Petti

By John Petti

For the fourth straight year, the Barbara Jagoda-owned and trained MAGNA TERRA SMOKY earned the California Arabian Horse of the Year Award. The award, covering the 1993 racing season, was announced at the Arabian Racing Association of California Awards Banquet held at Los Alamitos on May 14, 1994.

MAGNA TERRA SMOKY won nine of thirteen starts in 1993 and finished worse than second only once. He never started outside of California during 1993 and won four stakes races at three different tracks. his biggest victory came in the $20,000 California Heritage at Los Alamitos on December 11 when he defeated arch-rival T C TOMTYR by 1-3/4 lengths.

"What more can I say about this horse," a tearful Jagoda said as she picked up the award. "Smoky means so much to me." MAGNA TERRA SMOKY, who also picked up the award for Top Older Stallion/Gelding, has now earned the California Horse of the Year title the last four years.

FRYGA, the Darley Award winner as the nation's Top Older Mare, earned top honors as California's Top Mare and Top Aged mare. FRYGA is trained by John Burger, who was named Top Trainer, and is owned and bred by Helen Elizabeth Burger who was named Breeder of the Year.

Robert J. Rudolph was Owner of the Year and campaigned Sprinter of the Year BROYURI.

The complete list of winners are as follows:

Horse of the Year	MAGNA TERRA SMOKY
Mare of the Year	FRYGA
Sprinter of the Year	BROYURI
Claiming Horse of the Year	FS ORION
Cal-Bred of the Year	BATAL SMT
Aged Horse/Gelding of the Year	MAGNA TERRA SMOKY
Aged mare of the Year	FRYGA
4-Year-Old Filly of the Year	FMR HADASSAH
4-Year-Old Colt/Geld of the Year	AURZEL
3-Year-Old Filly of the Year	HF ORZONNA
3-Year-Old Colt/Gelding	SEEKING AH
Owner of the Year	ROBERT J. RUDOLPH
Breeder of the Year	HELEN BURGER
Trainer of the Year	JOHN BURGER

Article from "Race Arabian" Magazine
July, 1993
written by Steve Anderson

Magna Terra Smoky's most recent victory was an allowance race at Los Alamitos in early June.

A Hollywood ending

BY STEVE ANDERSEN

In the last three years, Magna Terra Smoky's racing career has come of age racing in Southern California, which might be the most appropriate circuit for him to be based.

If the suits in Hollywood sat down and pondered a movie about Magna Terra Smoky's life, it might go something like this:

Small-town kid from the West moves to California, finds fame and fortune, falls on hard times, makes successful comeback, gets the girl, rides off into sunset.

Okay, he's a gelding and he won't wind up with the girl and he's not yet ready to ride off into the sunset, but the 7-year-old Magna Terra Smoky does have Barbara Jagoda for an owner and trainer. Plus, he's still a factor on the Southern California circuit despite losing an eye to disease last year.

This year, Magna Terra Smoky has started four times, including a victory in a six-furlong allowance race at Los Alamitos on June 12 by 2 1/2 lengths, his 24th victory in 62 starts.

He's lost a few steps since he was named the 1990 champion 4-year-old and the 1991 champion older horses, but Jagoda feels Magna Terra Smoky will be a factor later this year when Los Alamitos runs longer, and more significant, races.

But even if he doesn't win another stakes, or even another race, he's proven to Jagoda that courage isn't something limited to the silver screen.

In May of 1992, Magna Terra Smoky was coming off one of his best year's. He's won six of 22 starts in 1991 and been second or third in 13 other races. As Jagoda was preparing Magna Terra Smoky for the Los Alamitos summer meeting, she noticed problems developing with his right eye.

"It started like a weepy eye," she said. "It seemed like it would clear up and then it wouldn't. He had a bump on his eye and I suggested (to the veterinarians) that it might be a spider bite."

Jagoda and the vets monitored the eye closely, but the situation worsened. The early diagnoses was a scratched cornea. He was still racing and ran second in two races in May, but since it didn't heal immediately, Jagoda and the veterinarians decided that more drastic measures were needed. They sent Magna Terra Smoky to a clinic in Chino, Calif., an hour's drive from Los Alamitos.

"They didn't know what it was either," Jagoda said. "They put him on all kinds of medications. Once he got to Chino, his condition worsened fast."

Jagoda feared the worse and talked vets into stitching the eye shut in an effort to save it. When it was reopened, it looked awful. Jagoda was forced to make a difficult decision.

"That was the saddest thing I'd ever gone

Please turn to page 32

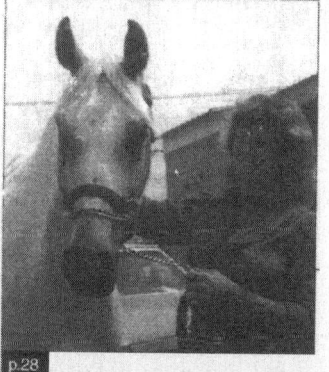

Despite losing an eye to disease in 1992, the 7-year-old gelding Magna Terra Smoky is still racing, and winning, in Southern California.

> 'I didn't know how (the surgery) would effect him. That race was one of the highlights of my life and it was so soon after the surgery.'
>
> - Owner-trainer Barbara Jagoda

Continued from page 28

through with a horse," she said. "The fungus had worked through two layers of the cornea and there's only three layers. I didn't see how they could save it.

"One day, I went and saw him and I realized he isn't going to come out of this unless I do something. It just wasn't working. We opened the eye and it looked terrible. They said there was no way, he'll every be able to see."

The right eye was removed on a June morning and the improvement was immediate. Three days after surgery, Jagoda pulled a van up to the clinic and took him back to the track.

By then, Magna Terra Smoky's situation was common knowledge on the backstretch. Those who hadn't heard about him, soon saw him. Jagoda spent considerable time walking the horse around the backstretch and gray, one-eyed geldings aren't soon forgotten on a backstretch full of sorrel quarter horse geldings.

After a few weeks, Jagoda was stunned at his improvement and began entertaining the thought of racing Magna Terra Smoky before the end of the summer. The chances of his racing increased after an exercise rider reported the gelding showed no fear or hesitation when he was ponied in company with other horses in the mornings.

The final endorsement came from jockey Frank Quesada.

One month after surgery and two months after his last start, Magna Terra Smoky was entered for the Samtyr Sprint Handicap over 4 1/2 furlongs. He broke in the middle of the eight-horse field, but was sixth on the backstretch. When the field hit the top of the short Los Alamitos stretch, Magna Terra Smoky was third, a half a length behind the leaders. Racing on the outside, he closed furiously in the final 100 yards and caught KA Czubuthan in the final strides to win by a neck.

"I didn't know how (the surgery) would effect him," Jagoda said. "That race was one of the highlights of my life and it was so soon after the surgery."

Magna Terra Smoky was back. A week later, KA Czubuthan returned the favor, beating Magna Terra Smoky by 3 1/2 lengths in a 1 1/16-mile allowance. At the end of August, in the northern California town of Ferndale, Magna Terra Smoky won a seven-furlong stakes by a neck.

He made four more starts before the end of the year with two wins, a third and a dismal performance in the Abu Dhabi Handicap at Hollywood Park. The seconds and thirds came in seven furlongs allowances races, while the Abu Dhabi Handicap was over 1 5/8 miles. By the end of the year, he'd earned over $20,000, but his record after the surgery was as consistent as his 1990 and 1991 form. In seven starts, his only bad effort was the Abu Dhabi Handicap.

"When they get five, six and seven, they run out of conditions so I have to run him in what's offered," she said. "I'd like to see if I can get him good for distances."

One disadvantage of not having a right eye is he can't see the opposition that close on his outside, which may have cost him in a few races last year when horses passed him late in races.

This year, his four starts have all come at Los Alamitos. He ran second to Minos in a 1 1/16-mile allowance last January, beaten a head. His only bad race was a well-beaten fifth behind TC Tomtyr in the Sierra Knights Handicap in early May, his first start in four months. He followed that with the allowance win. The program comment summed up the six-furlong race quite well - "confidently ridden".

In his last start on June 27, he finished second to Broyuri, who ran 4 1/2 furlongs in :57 2/5 seconds, the fastest clocking of meeting at that distance.

Jagoda nominated Magna Terra Smoky for the Silk Designs Handicap in early July, but the race never materialized.

"He always tries," she said. "Even in this last race he was coming at the end. He didn't have enough time to catch Broyuri. He's 7, but he's probably got the best legs."

Jagoda was teaching high school science in Colorado Springs in the late 1980s when she first came upon Magna Terra Smoky. A friend was caring for Magna Terra Smoky, but he wasn't working out as a racehorse, so Jagoda took him on.

"I started working with him every day and darnit if he didn't start to follow me around like I was his security blanket," Jagoda said.

After stifle surgery, which a veterinarian later said was the difference in him becoming a racehorse, Magna Terra Smoky raced in Colorado, Wyoming and Montana.

At 3, he was never worse than third, winning five of nine starts. In 1990, as a 4-year-old, he won an astonishing ten of 15 starts. The last few years, have been much of the same. He won six of 22 starts in 1991 and two of 12 starts last year. This year, he'll continue to be a face in California racing.

"It seems like we've been through so much," Jagoda said. "You can't put a price on something like him. It's important for me to keep him. I just look at him and get happy."

26 More Problems Than the Wind

1994

During the off season, Bryan and I again stabled our horses at A-Bar Ranch in Norco. It was a very pleasant change from the cement roadways and tight, crowded spaces of Los Al. Doc Allred tried to make the track facilities as pleasing as possible, but there was just so much space. The track was, after all, plumb in the middle of a hugely populated area, and real estate was at a premium. One of the biggest drawbacks of residing in Norco was the long and challenging commute to Los Al when we were racing. The traffic was always horrendous, even though we would leave A-Bar Ranch before 5:00 a.m. The thirty-plus-mile commute would take an hour even when all went well.

Bryan was always very gracious about doing the driving. He never complained about it even when I slept for most of the trip, waking up just as he pulled onto the racetrack grounds. He'd just give me a soulful look every time I would say, "Wow, that was a quick trip!"

It was while we were at Norco that one day, while I was tending to the horses in their pastured pens, Bryan called to me from the door of the main office. He had been working on some paperwork and visiting with the manager. I was loath to leave my work, but Bryan indicated that it was important.

"Can't this wait, babe? I'm just in the middle of treating some scratches on Kaleidoscope."

We were in the middle of a very wet season, and some of the horses had developed a fungal and/or bacterial infection on their pasterns. Kaleidoscope had four white pasterns, which made her more susceptible to the infection than most horses. A thick crust would form over the infection, allowing the fungus or bacteria (or sometimes both) to flourish underneath. The resulting damage could become very painful for the horse if not treated. As store-bought remedies were not very successful at treating and curing the infection, I had, by trial and error, developed an ointment recipe that was very successful at both softening the scabs and treating the infection. Even Dr. Moak referred other trainers to me to treat their cases of scratches.

Bryan, as was often the case, was holding a phone to his ear. I would often kid him that I couldn't recognize him without a phone in his ear. This time, however, he was motioning that this call was for me.

"Think you're going to want to take this call. It's Guy Neivens."

"Guy Neivens? Are you sure he wants to talk to me?"

I knew Guy Neivens as he had been to the racetrack at Los Alamitos on several occasions. He represented Sheikh Tahnoon Bin Zayed and bought numerous racehorses for him, including track-record holder Minos and Vanessa Du Loop, a good-looking French-bred mare, and, of course, the brilliant TC Tomtyr. I wondered what he wanted with me.

I took the phone from Bryan. "Hello, Mr. Neivens, this is Barbara."

I listened to Guy as he congratulated me on an extremely successful year with Magna Terra Smoky. And then I listened as he announced, "We have admired Smoky for a long time, Barbara. Bryan tells us that he is currently the fastest and best Arabian to race at the distance of four and a half furlongs. Sheikh Tahnoon Bin Zayed, whom I represent, wants to buy the best four-and-a-half-furlong Arabian racehorse, and we agree that would be Smoky. The reason for my call is to buy Smoky."

I felt my heart almost skip a beat. This was Guy Neivens, and he wanted to buy Smoky. I hadn't anticipated this. I was caught completely off guard. Tears started to swell up in my eyes. I knew my voice was breaking, but my response was all reflex.

"Smoky isn't for sale, Mr. Neivens. I'm sorry, but he is not for sale. I thank you for your call, but I cannot sell him. I'll let you talk more with Bryan if you like."

I didn't know what else to say. I wasn't very diplomatic, I knew. I handed the phone to Bryan, who stood there in shock. Bryan talked on with Guy, but I really didn't hear much of what was said. I went and sat on the leather couch across the room while he and Guy finished their conversation. After a while, Bryan set the phone down and came over to where I was sitting.

"Why didn't you at least listen to Guy? You could have at least entertained an offer. I think they were willing to offer you whatever you asked. You would have been very well off, even bought that ranch you've been dreaming of."

"Don't get after me, babe. You, of all people, know what Smoky means to me. Maybe I'm disillusioned, but I don't think he could understand or cope with traditional training methods. He has so many quirks, and I've gone along with all of them. Who else would take the time and effort to deal with all those idiosyncrasies? And how would I deal with the fact that I deserted Smoky after all the trust he has put in me? I wouldn't be able to live with myself. And you wouldn't be able to live with me. He's like the son I never had."

"I know. I know! It just would have been nice to know the price they would pay. Guy said he stopped talking when you started crying."

"I didn't think he could tell I cried, but I knew I had to wipe my eyes several times. We'll just have to admit we'll never be rich, at least at Smoky's expense."

I stood up and let Bryan hug me. I knew I had done the only thing I could have done.

It was still a frustrating time. Smoky was again exhibiting problems with tying up—if that indeed was the whole problem. Whether or not this had been his problem all along was questionable. I asked Dr. Moak to test Smoky for the HYPP gene (tying-up gene), but Smoky tested negative for it. This gene (for tying up) was first discovered in the quarter horse Impressive. Impressive was a huge athletic, handsome horse, but he passed several undesirable genes onto many of his offspring. Dr. Moak and I talked frequently about Smoky's diet and level of activity, and neither of us could fathom any reason for this annoying and troublesome problem.

Although Smoky was fed vitamin E/selenium (the main product used to combat tying up) daily in his evening dinner of grain, it was not always successfully combating his tying up. Dr. Moak even sometimes supplemented his oral dose of this with shots of the same. Smoky always had adequate electrolytes and certainly enough exercise. It was hard to figure out what caused Smoky's problem. He was not getting excessive grain, and he was in a turnout pasture where he could move around as much as he liked. The grass was not lush or that abundant as our horses had grazed it down. When I attempted to ride him, some days, he was fine; other days, he exhibited a shortened stride, He never did exhibit tying up to the extent that he didn't want to move, but I saw or felt a change in his stride that I did not like. I always stopped what we were doing and dismounted when this occurred. Although I knew that you shouldn't walk or move a horse that was tying up, it happened with Smoky so often and so slightly that I felt a need just to get him back to the barn. He did not resist moving as a horse that is badly tying up would do, so I hoped I was making the right decision. Sometimes he was short-stepping; sometimes he just wasn't moving equally on both sides of his body. I would rub warm alcohol over his large hindquarter muscles and blanket him. Before the morning was over, he was again fine and eager for lunch and/or turnout.

Ever since I began seriously training Smoky for racing, he had required a lot of consistent exercise. If this was neglected, I knew I would pay the price. The Scottsdale Cup race in Phoenix was coming up, and I was loath to nominate Smoky. He was not 100 percent, and therefore, I had not been able to gallop him as much or as often as I would have liked to. Now the constant heavy rains had interrupted his conditioning as well. However, in the back of my mind lurked the temptation to earn Smoky's thirty-third race win. That win would tie him with Sam's Count for most wins by an Arabian racehorse. Smoky's main rival for this record, News Release, had not won any more races of late, and he still remained with thirty-two wins. To further complicate the issue, I debated racing in Phoenix as I really wanted Smoky to break the record for most wins at Los Al. That track had always been good to Smoky. He loved that oval, the crowds at Los Al adored Smoky, and he had run so many races there and earned the bulk of his earnings there. However, after talking things over with Bryan, we decided that the competition would not be as tough at Turf Paradise as it was in California. We decided to nominate Smoky and make the trip to Phoenix. I knew I could always choose not to run him once we got there.

Once we had arrived at Turf Paradise, Smoky didn't exhibit any more problems, so after talking it over with Bryan, I decided to race him. It was not a good decision, for Smoky didn't perform well and ran fourth. Jane Teutsch's gelding, Soaring Big Red, pulled off a big upset. Jane was absolutely thrilled. Her little red homegrown gelding has just beaten the best horse in the western states. It was quite a disappointment to Bryan and me, but I knew I should have expected it. Smoky's winning streak had just been broken, and I felt that my bad judgment and greed had caused it to happen. Smoky came back from the race in great shape, so I was grateful for that. I just had to swallow my pride, accept the defeat, and resign myself to the fact that this race might have set him up to run a big race at Los Al when we returned there. Maybe he could earn his thirty-third win at Los Al Race Course after all.

It wasn't long before it was time to pack up and go back to our old stomping grounds. I was hoping Smoky would be able to pick up where he had left off last year. His first race was to be the Sierra Knight Handicap Sprint. The distance of the race was six furlongs, and I was very happy to have Richard Pfau back in the saddle. Having a good jockey in the saddle was *so* important!

Smoky did not disappoint his fans. Richard placed Smoky so that he stalked the leaders down the backside and into the final turn. When he turned Smoky loose, he flew by the pace setters, and he won the race easily to record his thirty-third win. He has just added another milestone to his incredible career. He had now tied the record for the most victories ever by an Arabian racehorse. To add to the achievement, he now had the honor of having the most Arabian wins at Los Alamitos (seventeen) and also the most Arabian stakes wins at Los Al (seven). Because of these achievements, Smoky made the covers of the *Race Arabian* and *Finish Line* magazines. Articles were written about him in the *Orange County Register*, the *Los Al Racing Program*, and the *Daily Racing Form*. Smoky had become "star" quality, and his fan base increased even more. I wondered if Smoky had any inclination of the sensation he had become and the records that he was demolishing.

Smoky's record did not last very long, however. News Release and Judy Rutten wanted the record also, and News proved that he was up to the challenge by recording his thirty-third victory on May 11 at Bandera Downs in Texas. Smoky and News Release were tied again.

In the meantime, Bryan had been nurturing and fine-tuning a new horse in his barn. His name was Styxx, and he was a well-built Samtyr son bred by Sam Harrison and now owned by Roger Lang. He was to be in Smoky's next race, and Bryan relentlessly teased me with the distinct probability of being beaten by Styxx. Bryan knew how badly I wanted the win. It would put Smoky back in the lead with the most Arabian wins. Bryan wanted the win too. He had done a remarkable job of repairing the damaged suspensories that Styxx had come to his barn with. Roger, who now owned Smoky's sire, SW David, would be equally thrilled if he owned a horse that could beat Smoky.

The competition between our two barns was on again. Neither of us was willing to go down to the defeat of the other. This rivalry between Bryan and me always amazed me as Bryan, who was Smoky's biggest fan, was also the very trainer who spoiled the most victories for Smoky. I could reel off the dates of numerous more wins for us if Bryan hadn't had a horse in the race. Bryan, who had helped me win so many races, including the first stakes races we had won at Los Al when Smoky was just a four-year-old, reveled just as much in handing us defeat. It was quite unreal when you thought about it. Yet this rivalry kept us both going throughout the years, and it definitely kept us both on our toes. At times, there wasn't a person I liked more, and at other times, there wasn't a person that frustrated and angered me more. Bryan was still drinking heavily and loved spending most of his free time with his drinking buddies. It was useless to try to get him to quit drinking, and it was just as useless trying to discuss anything with him when he had been drinking. I found myself constantly upset and realized I didn't like being with Bryan anymore. During this time, after one of our heated arguments, I moved out of his fifth wheel and into a small twelve-by-twelve-foot tack room at the front of my shed row. I set about cleaning it, painting it, and adding carpet to the floor. I bought a bed and a table (to use as a desk) and a rod to hang my clothes from. It worked perfectly. It was all I needed. I could see my whole barn of horses right from my doorway, and I felt totally at peace with my new world.

Race day came, and the showdown between Smoky and Styxx was on both our minds. I knew that one of us had to lose this race. I was just hoping and praying that it wouldn't be Smoky and me. Unfortunately, this time, it was. Styxx was for real. I wondered how many more losses we would suffer to him. Bryan was once again in his heyday. I was glad for Bryan as he had needed this win. He hadn't had a top contender in his barn since he lost Rio Hondo to Garland McAlaster. He needed this comeback. I also felt it was sad that Bryan might be the one who would prevent Smoky from reaching some of the goals that were now so close yet so far. None of this stopped Bryan from teasing me at every opportunity.

We didn't win our next race either. We were getting a lot of press but couldn't seem to put two wins together again. On June 3, Richard would guide Smoky to a third-place finish in the Markel Classic Stakes. It would be Richard's last race on Smoky. Richard had been one of the most honest, reliable, and dedicated jockeys I had ever known. Smoky and I would dearly miss him.

I worried about what we would do for a jockey now. We had had such a good run with Richard. Then as if by providence, a big opportunity came our way. For some time, Bryan and I had been watching and commenting on a new jockey on the scene named Jerry Lambert. We were both very impressed with Jerry's quiet manner on a horse and his ability to read a race and make good tactical moves. He made his wins look so easy. It was the way it was with superb athletes. It may have looked easy, but it took a lot of talent, thought, strategy, and dedication to the sport. I wondered how I could ever get Jerry Lambert up on Smoky. The problem was that Yancy Carter, who trained TC Tomtyr, had first call with Jerry. Yancy was the reason that Jerry had come to Los Al. He had talked Jerry into coming out of retirement just to ride his Arabian racehorses. Yancy had a good stable of horses, and with Jerry up on them, Yancy's win percentage skyrocketed. They made a fantastic team that the rest of us had a hard time beating.

Jerry had ridden for many years at Hollywood Park and was famous for guiding a very difficult horse named Native Diver to a record three straight Hollywood Gold Cup victories back in the middle 1960s. Sometime later, I was to learn more about Native Diver from Jerry and was surprised to learn that the Diver, as Jerry affectionately called him, always raced with his head held very high to alleviate a back injury he had suffered as a yearling. He also had sickle hocks and was slightly over at the knee. He had such a fiery high-strung disposition that he had to be gelded, but even that did not moderate his racing behavior greatly. I wondered who would have ever bought this racehorse prospect at a yearling auction. Yet here, he overcame all these issues and went on to win three consecutive Hollywood Gold Cups with none other than Jerry Lambert aboard. Jerry said he just let the Diver be himself and tried not to interfere with his style of racing. Jerry never was one to brag himself. He always gave the credit for the win to the Diver.

The Diver raced for seven years and was the first California-bred racehorse to earn over $1,000,000. Few horses ever appealed to California racing fans like this dark rambunctious speed demon. He won the hearts of fans and broke the hearts of horses foolish enough to go head to head with him. He won so many races at Hollywood Park that when he passed away, he was honored by being buried beneath a huge beautiful memorial located in the walking ring of the racetrack. Native Diver never won a national championship, and he lost more races than he won. He also never won a race outside the state of California. But the fans loved him. He beat the odds, he wasn't perfect, and he rebelled against authority, but he loved to win and tried his darnedest, and they loved him for that.

Jerry had understood the Diver. He had a natural gift for reading a horse and figuring out how to ride it most effectively. He studied his racing form and went into each race well prepared. He did not need to even ride a horse before a race to figure his mounts out. He used the post parade and the *Daily Racing Form* to tell him what he needed to know. His gentle hands and brilliant ability enhanced the talent of every horse he rode. He would literally outsmart the other riders. It was beautiful to watch him ride. He hardly moved on a horse. With Jerry aboard, every horse he rode moved up several notches in ability. Yancy had been smart enough to realize that bringing Jerry out of retirement to ride at Los Al would be a very rewarding move—and indeed, it was.

Bryan and I watched Jerry ride with admiration and sometimes envy. Then to my surprise and delight, a race came up for Smoky that Yancy did not have an entry for. Smoky was definitely entered, and he needed a rider. I was still hesitant to attempt to try to get Jerry Lambert's services, so I talked it over with Bryan. I didn't know whether it was ethical or not to approach Jerry with my request. Bryan gave me some very good advice.

"Why don't you go to Yancy and ask him if he would object to you asking Jerry to ride Smoky? That way, there won't be any hard feelings. If Yancy doesn't have a horse in the race, I can't see that he would mind."

I was a little intimidated to approach Yancy, but with Smoky's future on the line, I resolved to do it. It turned out perfect. Yancy was very gracious and said he didn't own Jerry, and if Jerry wanted to ride Smoky, that was fine with him. It was to be the beginning of a partnership and a friendship that I cherished, and it definitely proved to be the rebirth of Smoky's racing career.

Smoky is Jagoda's Knight in shining a[rmor]

Magna Terra Smoky scores his 33rd victory in the Sierra Knights Handicap on April 22 at Los Alamitos Race Course.

BY STACY PIGOTT

Five years ago, nobody thought Magna Terra Smoky would make it as a racehorse. Nobody, that is, until Barbara Jagoda acquired the grey gelding.

Two years ago, Jagoda thought Magna Terra Smoky would never race again when he had to have an eye removed due to a fungus that infected the eye.

But Magna Terra Smoky is a special horse. He raced, and won, before and after the loss of his eye. On April 22, 1994, Magna Terra Smoky once again proved how special he is when he became the Arabian racehorse with the most all-time wins after a victory in the Sierra Knights Handicap at Los Alamitos.

Magna Terra Smoky, dubbed the "One Eyed Wonder", has chalked up an impressive record in his five years of racing. He is a multiple stakes winner who has hit the board in 64 of 73 lifetime starts, including 33 wins and earnings of more than $185,000.

Magna Terra Smoky ended 1993 with a victory in the California Heritage Handicap before taking a few months off. He started 1994 at Turf Paradise, in Phoenix, Arizona.

Looking back, owner-trainer Barbara Jagoda says she should not have entered Smoky in the Scottsdale Arabian Cup. The weather in California was rainy, interrupting Smoky's training schedule. When he traveled to Phoenix, he was greeted by more rain and more missed works.

Magna Terra Smoky ended his seven-race winning streak with a fourth-place finish in the Scottsdale Arabian Cup.

"I had mixed emotions about Turf Paradise anyway, because I wanted him to break (the record) at Los Alamitos," Jagoda said. "(Los Alamitos) is his favorite track anyway, it's kind of like his security blanket track."

The grey gelding returned to California, where he was entered in the Sierra Knights Handicap, a race he lost last year to TC Tomtyr. This time, Magna Terra Smoky was ready.

As the starter released the five-horse field, Magna Terra Smoky settled just off the pace, in the middle of the pack. In his usual come-from-behind style, Magna Terra Smoky quickly advanced and stole the lead from the pacesetter, Ona Natural High.

Jockey Richard Pfau, who had ridden Magna Terra Smoky in his previous four starts, took Smoky wide to give the gelding a better chance to see any challengers that may try to sneak up on his blind side. Only one horse tried - Murkana Mike.

Advancing from last, Murkana Mike made a late bid for the lead, but came up short. At the wire, it was Magna Terra Smoky by 2 1/4 lengths. Murkana Mike finished second, 2 1/4 lengths in front of Vals BL Striker.

With this victory, Magna Terra Smoky passed News Release as the Arabian racehorse with the most wins, according to the official standings of the Arabian Jockey Club.

Magna Terra Smoky, the horse who was hard to train as a young gelding and overcame adversity later in life, had just earned the greatest honor of his career.

"This horse just amazes me that he keeps going and going," said Jagoda. "The horse always tries, so there's no sense in being nervous. If he doesn't win it, I know the horse did his best."

Jagoda should know. She and Smoky have the kind of relationship that young

Owner-trainer Barbara Jagoda and jockey Richard Pfau after Magna Terra Smoky's victory in the California Heritage Handicap last year.

horse-crazy girls dream about. When Jagoda took on the young Magna Terra Smoky, she had been told he was "impossible" to train. But all Smoky needed was a friend.

"Once he developed confidence in me, we really developed a bond. That's all he really needed was someone to have confidence in," Jagoda said.

It also seems the public has formed a special bond with Smoky. Jagoda laughingly says that most people don't even know her name, they just call her "Smoky's owner." Jagoda recalls a couple who approached her just to tell her how much they liked Smoky. They had just bought a white dog, and named him "Smoky" in Magna Terra Smoky's honor. Smoky seems to be as much the public's horse as he is Jagoda's.

Magna Terra Smoky will try to win his 34th race in the Equest International Stakes on May 13 at Los Alamitos.

Runnerup Murkana Mike, a 4-year-old colt by Wiking and out of Murkana, was making his first start of 1994 in the Sierra Knights Handicap. Robert Rudolph owns the colt who is trained by Danny Garrett.

Christine Davenport rode Murkana Mike.

With only six career starts to his credit, Murkana Mike has never finished off the board. His last start of 1993 was a victory in a six-furlong allowance race.

Murkana Mike will face Magna Terra Smoky again in the Equest Stakes.

Jockey Steve Treasure rode Vals BL Striker to a third-place finish for owner-trainer Bryan Braithwaite. Vals BL Striker, a 4-year-old gelding by Nehalems Muhuli, finished third in the Scottsdale Arabian Cup on Feb. 19 and won an allowance race on April 17, five days before the Sierra Knights Handicap.

Last year, Vals BL Striker finished fourth in the Drinkers Of The Wind Futurity and second in the California Arabian Cup Juvenile, both times behind Tomanchie.

No matter what the future may hold, Magna Terra Smoky will always have the respect of the racing community, the adoration of the public, and the friendship of Barbara Jagoda.

"I like watching him run," Jagoda said. "I enjoy watching him run. I really enjoy the public response to him.

"It's really nice for them to have a horse like him, and I think he's a good horse for them to like."

EDITOR'S NOTE-After Magna Terra Smoky's April 22 victory, News Release won an allowance race at Bandera Downs on May 7. Therefore, News Release and Magna Terra Smoky are once again tied for the most wins. Each have 33 wins.

Sierra Knights Handicap
April 22
Los Alamitos, Cypress, Calif.
$9,100, 6 furlongs, 1:21
Owner & Trainer-Barbara Jagoda
Breeder-Magna Terra Arabians (Colo.)
Jockey-Richard Pfau

1-**Magna Terra Smoky**, 8-g $5,005
(SW Dawid-Cyroga)
2-**Murkana Mike**, 4-c $1,820
(Wiking-Murkana PASB)
Owner-Robert Rudolph
Trainer-Danny Garrett
Jockey-Chris Davenport
3-**Vals BL Striker**, 4-g $1,092
(Nehalems Muhuli-Valentine Dream)
Owner & Trainer-Bryan Braithwaite
Jockey-Steve Treasure
4-**Ona Natural High**, 7-g $637
(Magna Terra Rajah-Jamitas Bethany)
5-**Anwarr El Balad**, 8-g $364
(Ibn El Balad-Love An Warr)

27 THINGS ARE GOOD

We would be going into the Charles O. Pollard Stakes Race as the oldest race team around. Smoky was the oldest horse at eight years of age, Jerry was the oldest jockey at fifty-three, and I was fifty-one. Jerry's comeback had been amazing. He continued to smoke heavily and was often short of breath after a race. Even so, he proved he was still the best. Many people thought Smoky should be retired now before his downward decline spiraled out of control. I wondered—prayed, actually—that he could prove the public wrong as Jerry had.

The race was a long one, especially for Los Al, as it was one and one eighth miles. Horses would have to cross the finish line three times in the course of the race. I felt Smoky was fit and ready to tackle the long distance as I had been galloping him two to three miles most mornings. He had been assigned high weight of 121 pounds, spotting the rest of the field at least five pounds. However, because this was a quarter-horse track, most of the jockeys couldn't make weight under 120 pounds (unlike most thoroughbred jockeys), so the real weights his competition would carry weren't really much different from Smoky's. Bryan had Styxx in this race also. However, with Jerry riding, I felt a whole lot more confidence in our ability to beat Styxx.

The horses were at post. I watched intently as Jerry let Smoky break from the gates nice and easy and was immediately pleased to see that Smoky seemed content to set behind the early leaders. A good-looking gray named Tak and his stablemate, Luebeck, were the early pacesetters. The field of horses were racing easily, content with the soft pace. Then midway through the race, I watched as Jerry let Smoky out a notch, and Smoky immediately swept by the leaders, opening up a one-length lead over the rest of the field. Styxx was left in his dust. As they rounded the final turn for home, no real threat materialized, and Smoky poured it on and extended his lead to four lengths. As they approached the wire, Eddie couldn't help himself; he had to announce the winners as the senior citizens of the field. Smoky had won by a convincing two and a half lengths over a second-best Deste Onismus. Styxx ran a badly beaten fifth. There wouldn't be much teasing from the Braithwaite barn tonight.

Yancy's wife, Ruthie, came over to congratulate Jerry. Jerry smiled and replied, "That's how you're supposed to ride good horses, isn't it?"

It was Smoky's eighth stakes victory at Los Al. I thought we were again tied with News Release as News had won another race in Texas; however, News had actually won two more races, including the Independence Handicap at Bandera Downs. The tally was now an amazing thirty-five wins for News Release and thirty-four wins for Smoky. Smoky had to get smokin' again!

It was during this time that another major player joined our barn. I had been looking for a good groom for some time now, and Dr. Moak, ever on the lookout for me, told me of a black groom named Antoine that he thought would be the ideal fit. He thought Antoine was very good with horses and genuinely cared for them. That was my number-one criteria for hiring a groom, so I was very interested. Dr. Moak also went on to say that Antoine had a reputation of being a little lazy and unreliable if not closely monitored. After having taught junior-high students for twenty-three years, I thought I could handle that. The main problem appeared to be that Antoine was currently working for another trainer, and I didn't want to backstab anyone by stealing a groom away from them. However, Dr. Moak assured me that Antoine was on the verge of being fired.

"Just talk to his trainer, Barb," Doc advised.

So I did. Antoine joined my barn that same day.

I came to greatly appreciate and genuinely like Antoine. He really did love his horses, especially Smoky and Aurzel. Both horses were put in his care. I felt so good knowing that my favorite two horses had a groom who really looked after them. On the other hand, Antoine was exactly what Dr. Moak had told me he was. He needed a lot of supervision and reminders. So each morning, I took to writing down the day's agenda and posting it on the tack-room door. It would include the names of horses that needed to be galloped or ponied and leg care that needed to be done afterward etc. As I galloped many of the horses, I also assumed the role of groom for the horses that I felt I wanted to check and monitor. Antoine needed a firm mother figure, so I became his mother. Bryan made it quite clear that in no way would he be called Antoine's father. I loved teasing Bryan about that as I knew it really got to him.

Bryan did love to tattle on Antoine. He would tell me how Antoine would disappear from the barn the moment that I was out of sight. I think Antoine thought I never knew he did this. I rationalized that if Antoine got his work done and the horses were well cared for, I could forgive him this. We did have our encounters, however. Antoine could be very frustrating. He sometimes pushed his limits. He could also be very charming and likable. I now had a stable of eighteen horses, and I tried very hard to lighten the load of all my grooms, including Antoine. I wanted them to be happy at their jobs. I made sure they all got a day off each week and also worked it so that each Monday (the dark day at the racetrack), they would have an easy day as I would haul four horses up to the end of Katella Avenue (a forty-five-minute drive), where I had discovered two arenas belonging to a riding club that were open for public use. I would arrive with my horses at an early hour (usually before 6:00 a.m.) when no one was yet up or using the arenas and turn two horses out in each arena to run, play, roll, and afterward graze on the grass surrounding the arenas. There was even a water hydrant that I could attach a hose to so that I could give each horse a shower before returning to the track. The horses loved it and looked forward to each Monday when they would get to go on vacation. And I absolutely loved watching them have so much fun.

Doc was not oblivious to the interactions between Antoine and myself. He began calling me Ms. Daisy after the movie *Driving Miss Daisy*. Bryan thought this was too funny and teased me about it all the time. Doc still called me Ms. Daisy years later.

It was during this period that I acquired a new horse that Bryan and I both liked and felt sorry for. His name was BJ (my initials), and he was an eleven-year-old gray gelding. We had watched him being saddled for many races and often commented on BJ's fantastic conformation and great bone. BJ was a well-built horse with a gigantic and powerful-looking rear end. We always felt so sorry for him as he was never cleaned up very well for a race and often had huge green manure stains on his neck and sides. I told Bryan that I liked him when I first saw him. It was then that Bryan told me that he had always liked BJ also and that he had seen BJ run his first race at Delaware Park way back in the early 1980s.

He told me that BJ had run away from the field and won the race easily. He said he also saw the trainer throw BJ in a pen and then proceed to get drunk. For several days, all BJ got to eat or drink was what sympathetic bystanders threw into his pen. BJ never really had a chance after that to show how good he could have been. He was never given a chance to show what he was capable of. We both wished we could have owned BJ back then.

So when Bryan told me that BJ was for sale for $1,000 and that his owner/trainer was in the track kitchen (the backside cafeteria), I immediately got my checkbook and ran to the kitchen to write Charles Tolbert, the owner and trainer, a check. However, when I approached Chuck, he said he was only teasing and BJ was not for sale. I immediately realized that Chuck thought BJ was much more valuable if I was interested in him. After that, Chuck raced BJ though the winter and early spring without any success. Then Bryan heard once again that BJ was for sale and told me that the price was now $500. I was angry at Chuck for retracting his offer the previous year when he realized I was interested in BJ and thought he would probably do the same thing again if I was interested, so when Bryan brought BJ to my barn, I told Bryan to take him back to Chuck. I didn't want to deal with the likes of Chuck Tolbert. Bryan knew I was just angry at the way Chuck had handled this, so he put BJ in his barn and took five $100 bills over to Chuck. Later, when I got over being angry, I went over and gave Bryan $500 and brought BJ over to my barn.

Once I had BJ under my care, I realized just how much abuse or misunderstanding he had endured. He acted as if he was scared he would be hit for every little thing he did wrong, and he really didn't know what was right or wrong anymore. My first surprise was when I tried to lead him into his new stall. He hesitated and then ran in so fast, he almost bowled me over. *Something we need to work on*, I thought, but right now, I'd let BJ get used to his new surroundings and stablemates.

That afternoon, when my other horses were on the walker while their stalls were being cleaned, I decided I would bring BJ out of his stall and practice going in and out. I had a pocket full of carrots. Antoine was there to help if needed. I knew BJ would probably try to run over me again, so I haltered him, brought him to the front of his stall, and just petted him and offered carrots. He knew he was supposed to go out and got nervous having to stand back of his stall webbing. I tried to be ready for his bolt when the webbing was unsnapped and, at the same time, try to get him to exit slowly. As Antoine quietly unsnapped the webbing for me, I talked to BJ and lightly asked him to move forward. He bolted out, hitting his right hip on the stall wall. I realized BJ was not above hurting himself to get out of his stall.

What was it that he was so afraid of? I wondered. So just as I had done with Smoky when he lost his right eye, as we went back in the stall, I made sure BJ had a nice direct approach to his stall. He bolted in again but missed both me and the sides of the stall. I petted him, offered him a carrot, and kept reminding him that he was "a good boy."

For all the years I had BJ, we never stopped practicing his stall entry and exit. However, he never got over his anxiousness. Granted, his behavior did improve a great deal, but he would still bolt occasionally and sometimes miss the opening, grazing his hip or shoulder, and each time, I would flinch, hoping he hadn't caused himself any permanent damage.

Once BJ had a good bath, his bridle path clipped, and a new set of shoes, he looked a great deal better. In my eyes, he was a gorgeous-looking horse. It would take a couple of shoeings to get his feet right. His toes had been allowed to travel out in front of him, putting a lot of stress on his tendons and ligaments, and he had pieces of hoof missing and lots of cracks. It was amazing that his legs were so good; I didn't detect any fill or heat or problem anywhere on his legs. He had such great bone and conformation to him. None of this fine, elegant stuff for BJ.

Whatever all BJ's problems were, he oozed personality. I couldn't help hugging him. He seemed so vulnerable and unsure of everything. My next surprise was his reaction to being saddled. As soon as he felt any tightness of the girth, he would rear up, often almost falling over backward. For days, we just worked on saddling, breaking the session with practice at stall entry and exit.

I didn't relish getting on BJ for the first time as I knew it would probably bring on the rearing habit again. Sure enough, it did. But by now, I felt BJ was starting to realize that I wasn't going to hit or whip him or punish him for anything he did. Finally, after many aborted attempts, I was able to get on him. His back dropped as if I had dropped a ton of weight on him. I had landed very lightly in the saddle, so there wasn't reason for him to drop like that. BJ must have had a lot of riders land pretty darn hard on his back. BJ took a few steps in his crouched position and then must have realized his back was all right and straightened up.

Although nervous at first, BJ became one of my favorite horses to gallop. He learned to tuck nicely and use that massive rear end of his, and he was easy to rate.

What a great year this was turning out to be! We had acquired the best jockey ever for Smoky, we had a new groom who loved the horses and the horses loved in return, and we had rescued a wonderful old racehorse that literally made my heart smile. Life was indeed very good.

As time went on and I worked more with BJ, I began to realize just how tough he really was. He was definitely a survivor. Although he was eleven years old, he was tough enough that I began to think that he might still have it in him to win a few more races. I didn't make my thoughts known except to Bryan. He and Dr. Moak were probably the only people who would even entertain the notion that BJ might have a chance at such a ripe old age. Quietly and patiently, I began conditioning him for his possible return to racing. He seemed very happy with himself and enjoyed getting back in shape, and he definitely ate up all the attention. He was proving to have quite a personality. You couldn't help but like him.

I enlisted a jockey named Polo Sanchez, and together, we put two works in on BJ. Both of us were very impressed. I decided I would wait for a $4,000 or $5,000 claiming race for BJ's debut. However, just before I was to enter BJ, Antoine didn't take quite enough time to line BJ up before entering his stall, and BJ hit his right hip charging into the stall. It broke my heart. BJ favored his right hind. I had worked so hard on BJ, and he looked and acted so good. Now it would take time to make sure his hip was okay, and we would miss the race I had planned for his debut.

Fortunately, BJ recovered, but it took several weeks. I wanted to be convinced that he was sound and his hip didn't bother him. My biggest concern now was getting BJ saddled in the saddling paddock without him rearing up. At night, when there were Arabian races that we didn't have horses entered in, Antoine and I would walk BJ up to the saddling paddock, and I would practice saddling him while Antoine held him. Bryan would stand on the other side of BJ to pass me the overgirth. BJ did not like having people on both sides of him as he was saddled and would revert to his old behavior of rearing up. However, with lots of pats and words of encouragement, I finally felt he was as ready as I could get him. I entered him in a four-and-a-half-furlong $4,000-claiming race, Polo Sanchez up.

I was really nervous the night of BJ's first race. I knew that one little thing done too fast or carelessly could set BJ off. I prayed we could pull it off. Because BJ knew me the best, I played groom and led him up to the receiving barn, where his tattoo was checked, and we awaited our call to the saddling paddock. Everything had gone well so far. Michelle, who worked in the receiving barn checking tattoos, told me that she was delighted to see BJ in my barn. It made me feel happy as Michelle cared deeply for all animals.

Now, I thought, *if we can just make it through the saddling paddock!*

BJ was getting a little wound up, so I didn't go into his stall right away but took him on several trips around the enclosure. Finally, I took him into his stall and tried to settle him. I let Antoine hold BJ now as I had to do the saddling. I asked Polo's valet, who worked on the right side of BJ during the saddling, to be extra slow and quiet as BJ was pretty light on those front legs. BJ thought about rearing straight up, and I thought he would, but he listened to me, and we got the job done. I made a fuss over him and took him for a loop around the enclosure. We were almost to his first race back!

We had also practiced legging Polo up onto BJ. Although Polo landed as lightly and quietly as he could into his tiny racing saddle, BJ crouched down through habit. It took several steps for BJ to straighten up. Polo had instructions to just to make sure BJ had a good experience and to make sure the gate crew handler loaded him straight into the gate. I hoped BJ wouldn't bang his hip on the sides of the gate.

I watched the load on the TV monitor, and it seemed to go well. Then they were off. BJ didn't break well, and he never got into the race. Polo just let him idle and have a good trip. He finished fourth, but he had a good trip, and everything had gone well. It would definitely boost BJ's confidence. Indeed, it did, for BJ turned out to be a tiger on the track, and when Jerry Lambert eventually rode him, he was almost unbeatable. The racing public loved him. He went on to win fourteen races for me over the next three years. He had only won five races from the ages of three to eleven. Who would have thought, with all he had been through, that BJ could make a comeback at age eleven?

Then the unthinkable happened. When BJ was at the ripe old age of fourteen, Bob Rudolph claimed him from me. It was done totally out of spite. Bryan had claimed a cute little bay named Hardmoney Basque from Rudolph several weeks earlier, and Rudolph was trying to avenge Bryan's claim. He knew that this would hurt both Bryan and me. It did. Jerry Lambert kept riding BJ, so he won a couple more races. However, after a year, Rudolph offered BJ back to me, and I readily accepted his offer. I did not try to race BJ again as he was much more arthritic now, and I decided he had definitely earned his retirement.

Not to be left out, Aurzel was making his own history. In spite of recent seizures that I thought were epileptic fits, he had just won his seventh lifetime race, defeating the likes of stakes horses FMR Tikis Shadow, Keen Edge, and even Bryan's champion racehorse, Styxx. He now had earnings in excess of $23,000. What an amazing animal he had turned out to be! Along with Smoky and BJ, Aurzel now joined an awesome array of horses that had made remarkable comebacks for our barn. During this time, Doc finally witnessed one of Aurzel's seizures and diagnosed it as anxiety attacks that resulted in Aurzel raising his head so high that he cut off his air supply. This, in turn, resulted in Aurzel flipping over and/or falling to the ground. Doc gave him cobalt shots every so often, and it took care of the problem. I have no idea why it worked, but it did.

In the meantime, Smoky was putting on his own show. Two weeks after winning the Charles Pollard Handicap Race at a distance of one and one eighth miles, Smoky demonstrated his amazing versatility by winning the Silk Design Sprint Handicap at four and a half furlongs in a blazing time of 57.4 seconds. How he could adjust to such extreme changes in the distances he raced and won at never ceased to amaze me. He had only had two weeks to make the adjustment this time, and he had won both races. The public went wild over his gutsy and astounding victories, as did the writers that wrote about Smoky. To add to his accomplishments, it was the second consecutive year Smoky had won this race, and it was all the more satisfying because Rudolph sponsored the blanket awarded for the victory. Rudolph's entry, Broyuri, finished a tired eighth. And the Smoky and News Release battle continued. Once again, they tied for the most lifetime wins. The record now stood at thirty-five, and once again, Smoky was seldom out of the news.

Two more champions —- BJ (gray) and AURZEL (bay)

Stakes

Score One For The Oldtimers

Charles O. Pollard Memorial Handicap

At age 53 most jockeys have long since retired and an eight-year-old gelding is likely doing his running in the pasture. However, 53-year-old jockey Jerry Lambert and the eight-year-old gelding MAGNA TERRA SMOKY combined to capture the $10,000 Charles O. Pollard Handicap on July 1 at Los Alamitos.

Jockey Lambert has won more than 1100 races in his career, including a record setting three wins in the Hollywood Gold Cup with Native Diver back in the 1960's. Lambert resumed his riding career aboard Arabians this year at Los Alamitos after being sidelined for over a year after a serious spill on a Thoroughbred in Northern California. Lambert's win aboard MAGNA TERRA SMOKY was his first Arabian stakes victory while MAGNA TERRA SMOKY was picking up his eighth stakes victory over the Los Alamitos oval.

TAK—under jockey Richard Pfau who is the usual rider aboard MAGNA TERRA SMOKY, went right to the front in the 1-1/8 mile stake. Not content to let TAK rest on an easy lead, Lambert hustled MAGNA TERRA SMOKY to challenge TAK going into the Clubhouse turn. MAGNA TERRA SMOKY then put away that rival going up the backstretch and opened up a four length lead turning for home.

At the top of the stretch the only question became, whether the oldtimers would hold up through the stretch. That question was quickly answered as PESTE ONISM made a late run but was never a serious threat while finishing 2-1/2 lengths behind the winner. TAK was another seven lengths back in third.

MAGNA TERRA SMOKY covered the distance in 2:04.4 while earning his 34th lifetime win, tying him with NEWS RELEASE for the most career wins for an Arabian. He earned $5500 for his effort for owner/trainer Barbara Jagoda. His career earnings now stand at $195,400.

Credit: John Petti

The "2 OLD TIMERS" ---Smoky and Jerry Lambert
article by Stacy Pigott in "RACE ARABIAN July, 1994

Not too old for Smokin'

BY STACY PIGOTT

Magna Terra Smoky returns after winning the Charles O. Pollard Memorial Handicap.

If you're a country music fan, you've probably heard George Jones sing a song about getting older in which he says "I don't need your rockin' chair." Well, Magna Terra Smoky and jockey Jerry Lambert could easily be singing that same song, as the duo recently won the Charles O. Pollard Memorial Handicap at Los Alamitos.

At 8-years-old, Magna Terra Smoky was the oldest horse in the field. Jerry Lambert, at 53, was the oldest jockey. When the two teamed up in the Pollard Memorial Handicap, the results were quite impressive.

Breaking from the seven post in the nine-horse field, Magna Terra Smoky was content to sit behind the early leaders in the 1 1/8-mile contest. Tak and Luebeck were the pacesetters early on, until Magna Terra Smoky made his move.

Carrying highweight of 121 pounds and spotting the rest of the field at least five pounds, Magna Terra Smoky opened a one-length lead midway through the race. Rounding the final turn for home, Magna Terra Smoky had a four-length advantage, with Deste Onismus making a late bid.

But Magna Terra Smoky and Lambert refused to yield. As the pair raced down the stretch, announcer Ed Burgart made a classic call about the winners, calling them the "senior citizens of the field."

Lambert and Magna Terra Smoky crossed the wire 2 1/2 lengths in front of Deste Onismus, who was seven lengths ahead of third-place Tak. Winning his eighth Los Alamitos stakes race, Magna Terra Smoky posted a winning time of 2:04 4/5. The victory was worth $5,500 of the $10,000 purse for owner-trainer Barbara Jagoda.

Jagoda gives much of the credit to Magna Terra Smoky and Lambert.

Charles O. Pollard Memorial Handicap

July 1
Los Alamitos, Cypress, Calif.
$10,000, 1 1/8 mile, 2:04 4/5
Owner & Trainer-Barbara Jagoda
Breeder-Magna Terra Arabians (Colo.)
Jockey-Jerry Lambert

1-Magna Terra Smoky, 8-g $5,500
  (SW Dawid-Cyroga)
2-Deste Onismus, 6-h $2,000
  (Brusally Zbruenu-Deste Sanenasong)
  Owner-James & Marjorie Estes
  Trainer-Bill Nelson
  Jockey-Wayne Howard
3-Tak, 4-g $1,200
  (Pyat Gorsk-Resza)
  Owner-Khaled Albadi
  Trainer-John Burger
  Jockey-Richard Pfau
4-Naibara Ben, 4-c $700
  (Skamper-Natalyx)
5-Styyx, 6-h $400
  (Samtyr-HCC Moloska)
6-Murkana Mike, 4-c $200
  (Wiking-Murkana PASB)
7-Time For Victory, 5-h
  (Tiki Tessar-LN Kabrus Shatim)
8-BC Bukler Streak, 4-g
  (Edenstreak-Bukler Rose)
9-Luebeck, 5-g
  (Pierrot PASB-Lukrecja Ka)

(past races) and I said 'You ride him like the race develops.' And he did," Jagoda said

"This is Jerry's story. I owe it all to (Yancey and Ruthie Carter). They lent us Jerry for this ride."

Lambert generally rides for the Carters, who were on hand to watch the race. The win was Lambert's first Arabian stakes race. The veteran jockey is no stranger to stakes wins, however, as he scored a record-setting three Hollywood Gold Cup wins with the thoroughbred Native Diver in the 1960s.

"This is a good horse," Lambert said of Magna Terra Smoky. "I like to ride good horses. He's an old campaigner. He knows what he's doing out there."

Deste Onismus finished second under jockey Wayne Howard. Bill Nelson trains the 6-year-old horse for owner-breeders James and Marjorie Estes.

Deste Onismus, by Brusally Zbruenu and out of Deste Sanenasong, won the Markel California Classic on June 3, defeating Tak and Magna Terra Smoky. Favored Tak finished third for owner Khaled Albadi. John Burger trains the gelding who was ridden by Richard Pfau.

Tak finished second in the Markel Classic earlier this year and won the California Futurity at Los Alamitos last year.

The Pollard Handicap was Magna Terra Smoky's 34th career win, leaving him one win behind News Release, who recently won the Independence Handicap at Bandera Downs. Magna Terra Smoky has earned the respect and devotion of many in California, not only the public, but also the horsemen. As Lambert returned to the jockey's room after the race, Ruthie Carter stopped to congratulate him. Lambert had one thing to say.

"That's how you're supposed to ride good horses, isn't it?" he asked with a

Smoky (with Brian Green in the saddle) winning the "Silk Design Sprint" handicap, July 15, 1994, Los Alamitos Race Course
article by John Petti in the September issue of Arabian Finish Line magazine

Stakes

Magna Terra Smoky Wins Again
By John Petti

Silk Design Sprint Handicap

Distance does not matter to the eight-year-old MAGNA TERRA SMOKY. Two weeks after winning the 1-1/8 mile Charles O. Pollard Handicap, the Barbara Jagoda owned and trained gelding was back in the winner's circle after the 4-1/2 furlong $9450 Silk Design Sprint Handicap on July 15 at Los Alamitos.

MAGNA TERRA SMOKY has now won 35 races in his career, trying him with NEWS RELEASE who is currently racing in Texas, for the most lifetime wins for an Arabian. MAGNA TERRA SMOKY earned $5198 for the win to move his career earnings past the $200,000 mark to $200,660. The winner's circle at Los Alamitos is becoming a second home for MAGNA TERRA SMOKY as his Silk Design win was his record ninth stakes victory at the California track. It was also the second consecutive year that he won the Silk Design Sprint.

Under jockey Brian Green, who was riding MAGNA TERRA SMOKY for the first time, he trailed the field early then unleased a strong rally to get the win by 1-1/2 lengths. TAK finished second with LF ALLJAYS finishing third in the field of eight older horses.

28 Records Are There to Be Broken

On Sunday, September 25, 1994, I was delighted to read a write-up in the *Los Alamitos Racing Program* stating that Magna Terra Smoky had moved to within a few thousand dollars of the all-time Arabian racehorse earnings record held by Monarch AH. The article concluded with the statement "The One-Eyed Wonder is truly one of the great stories in racing." I cried when I read it. My little unwanted country bumpkin was on the verge of breaking unimaginable records in the Arabian record books. He had come from out of nowhere, out of basically unproven racing stock, with a novice racehorse trainer (who learned the ropes alongside her horse) to becoming a record-breaking phenomenon. I felt no horse deserved it more. Smoky had overcome so many obstacles, and like the Duracell battery, he just kept going and going. He wasn't always the fastest, and he sure wasn't unbeatable, and some horses, he never did outrace, but in the final analysis, he had outlasted them all. He lived for his races. Every day he went to the track, he was ready to take off at a dead run given half a chance. He loved running. As the Bedouins would say, "He ran as the wind," and he never seemed to tire of it; he never lost the desire for it. How fortunate I had been to be a part of it!

Then on October 14, 1994, upon winning a seven-furlong open-allowance race, Jose Fuentes up, Smoky actually became the *"richest racing Arabian of all time."* Robert Strauss leaped off his pony horse to be in the win photo with us. Smoky had done it. We all had smiles on our faces stretching from ear to ear. He had now earned $214,206, breaking Monarch AH's old record of $213,646. He had raced a total of eighty-two races with thirty-six wins, twenty-six second places, and eleven thirds. When AJC sent me an official letter, I was also to learn that Sam's Count, whom I thought we were battling for most wins at thirty-three, only had twenty-three official career wins to his credit. However, I also discovered that News Release had won again and currently held that lead with thirty-eight wins. I told Smoky we weren't finished yet!

A month later, on Sunday, October 23, the Los Alamitos publicity team would write another tribute to Smoky in the *Los Al Racing Program*. This article was extra special for me and has remained a treasured souvenir to this day. For Smoky to be compared to Refrigerator was a tremendous honor, and I marveled at the nature and content of the article as it was so well researched and written. What a fantastic tribute to Smoky! Thank you, Los Alamitos Race Course publicity!

But one day's glory is another day's woe. Who could have ever imagined what would happen only five days after this article was written?

article in the LOS AL race program 10/23/1994
Credits: Los Alamitos Race Course Publicity

Sunday, October 23, 1994   111th Racing Program   Post Time 4:00 p.m.

SMOKE & ICE, THEY MAY BE OPPOSITE BUT THEY ARE A LOT ALIKE

The quarter horse Refrigerator and the Arabian Magna Terra Smoky are about as different as two horses can be. Refrigerator is a bay quarter horse gelding that can cover a quarter mile in 21 seconds and change while the gray Arabian Magna Terra Smoky would barely cover an eighth of a mile from a dead start in the same time. Refrigerator has always raced at the premier quarter horse tracks and won the richest race for his breed, the All American Futurity where he earned $1 million. Magna Terra Smoky has raced at such tracks as Adams County Fair and Gateway Downs in Colorado, Energy Downs, The Western Montana Fair, Bluegrass Downs and even Ferndale. His biggest paycheck was $13,816 earned while winning a stakes race at Bay Meadows in 1990. Yet with all their differences, Refrigerator and Magna Terra Smoky have a lot in common.

Both are the richest horses of their respective breeds. Both are owned by the nicest people you would ever want to meet that have never missed seeing their horse race live once. Both horses are crowd favorites here at Los Alamitos and both set earnings records here last Saturday night. Both have been California's Horse Of The Year for their breed the last two years (four for Smoky) and both are multiple stakes winners here as Refrigerator has six stakes wins at Los Alamitos and Smoky nine.

Refrigerator, owned by James Helzer, became quarter horse racing's first $2 million winner while finishing second to Brotherly in the Los Alamitos Championship. Less than one hour later, Magna Terra Smoky became the all-time leading Arabian earner when he posted an easy allowance win. The victory moved his earnings to $215,523 for owner trainer Barbara Jagoda. Ask Jagoda about Smoky and it's 3-5 she'll get tears of joy in her eyes and I swear I saw Helzer and trainer Blane Schvaneveldt with tears of joy in their eyes after Refrigerator won last year's Champion Of Champions, making him quarter horse racing's all-time leading money winner.

Did you know that 23 minutes after Refrigerator won last year's Champion Of Champions, wrapping up his second straight World Champion title, Magna Terra Smoky won the California Heritage Handicap and wrapped up the California Horse Of The Year title? Did you know that the pair will likely race again on the same night, December 17? The Fridge will be in the Champion Of Champions and one race later we'll see Smoky in the California Heritage. Once again, they will both set earnings records for their breed.

Right now Refrigerator has lost his last four starts and, before his win Friday night, Smoky had lost his last four starts before his allowance victory.

I have this funny feeling on December 17, Refrigerator is going to win his third Champion Of Champions and 23 minutes later, I bet we'll see Smoky in the winner's circle after the California Heritage. Now we are not rooting against anyone, but it sure would make a storybook ending to see the six-year-old Refrigerator and the eight-year-old Smoky start and win on the final night of the meet in perhaps their final career start.

Ask any casual race fan at Los Alamitos to name their favorite quarter horse, they will likely answer Refrigerator. Ask the same question about Arabians and they will likely answer Magna Terra Smoky. Ask me what horses I like to see run. You'll get the same answer.

We sure are lucky to see the all-time greats from two breeds here on the same night.

Photo Credits: "Los Alamitos Race course Photography"

Magna Terra Smoky—
The Richest Arabian Racehorse in History

By Stacy Pigott

It has been said that once in a lifetime, if you're lucky, that special horse will come along. Barbara Jagoda has found her once-in-a-lifetime horse, and his name is Magna Terra Smoky. Only Magna Terra Smoky isn't just a special horse for Jagoda, he is very special to the whole Arabian racing community, and to fans of Arabian racing everywhere.

Magna Terra Smoky (SW Dawid x Cyroga) has accomplished more than any other Arabian racehorse in history. The 10-year-old gelding is a multiple Darley Award winner, the highest accolade available in Arabian racing, as well as having won numerous California racing awards. He is the all-time leading Arabian racehorse by number of wins and money earned. In short, Magna Terra Smoky is the epitome of Arabian racing.

"He's definitely one of the favorites of the racing fans," said Vandi Boag, of the Arabian Racing Association of California. "They come out just to watch him."

And fans have had a lot of opportunities to watch Magna Terra Smoky, as the gelding has raced 101 times during his career, which started in 1989. Even more amazing than his high number of starts is his penchant for winning. Magna Terra Smoky has won 44 races, finished second 29 times, and third 15 times. That's 88 times in the top three, and only 13 times lower than third. Throughout his career, Magna Terra Smoky has won $288,413 for owner Jagoda, making him the *richest Arabian racehorse in history.*

In addition to his stellar race career, something else sets Magna Terra Smoky apart from other top racehorses. Magna Terra Smoky continues to race, and win, with only one eye.

Jagoda first met "Smoky" as a two-year-old in Colorado. She was training competitive trail and endurance horses when Smoky's owner asked her for help breaking the unruly gelding.

"We had to trap him with the older horses in a pen," Jagoda said, explaining how unmanageable Smoky was. "I would just go in his stall and pet him for a long time."

Eventually, Jagoda introduced Smoky to the saddle and got him to the point where he could be galloped when another problem surfaced.

"When we got him to the point where he could gallop, he started catching in his back stifles," said Jagoda.

Smoky's owner didn't want to spend any more money on him and made a deal with Jagoda. In exchange for training services for three other horses, Jagoda would get to keep Smoky as her own. Jagoda took the deal and soon afterwards Smoky underwent stifle surgery to correct the problems he was having.

Meanwhile, Jagoda made the decision to start training racehorses, and worked as an exercise rider in Colorado to learn the trade. The next year, with Magna Terra Smoky and a few of her own home-bred horses, Jagoda started her racehorse training career.

"His first race was at Adams County (in Colorado). He won his first out," Jagoda said of Smoky. That first win was only a foreshadowing of the great

Magna Terra Smoky, with Jerry Lambert aboard, after capturing the ARAC Directors Sprint.

things that were waiting in the future.

Despite the potential Smoky had shown on the racetrack, he was, by no means, a horse that would be considered easy to train.

"He wouldn't do it when we were galloping, but when I would go to take him back, and a horse would work by him, he would whirl and twist around so fast. I knew it was coming, and I still couldn't stay on him."

With Jagoda's unending patience and guidance, Smoky's racing career took off. As a 3-year-old, Smoky was never worse than third. As a 4-year-old he won ten of 15 starts, and was the named the Darley 4-Year-Old of the Year. In 1991, as a 5-year-old, he won six of 22 starts, finishing in the top three in 13 other races, and was crowned Darley Older Horse of the Year, joining an elite group of horses to have earned two Darley titles.

But in 1992 disaster struck again. Smoky's right eye became infected with a fungus. Despite veterinary treatments, there was little chance that Smoky would ever see out of his eye again. Jagoda was left with the hard decision of removing the eye.

"That was one of the saddest things I've ever gone through with a horse," Jagoda said. "The fungus had worked through two layers of the cornea and there's only three layers. I didn't see how they could save it," Jagoda said in a 1993 interview with RaceArabian. "I said, I'm going to lose this horse if I don't take his eye out."

For most horses, that would have spelled the end of their racing career. But Magna Terra Smoky is not any horse, and Barbara Jagoda is not any owner.

"I never thought that he, of all horses, would adapt to it," Jagoda said. "He was always such a spooky horse anyway."

Determined to work through this obstacle in their path, Jagoda started Smoky on a type of rehabilitation program, to teach him to function without his right eye.

For weeks, Jagoda could be seen leading Smoky around the barn area at Los Alamitos. Even the simplest task of walking into a stall could cause problems, as Smoky was unable to see any obstacles on his right side, and was therefore wary of anything on that side.

As his confidence in Jagoda grew, so did his ability to function on his own. The bond between Smoky and Jagoda became so strong that many mornings Smoky could be found leading Jagoda around the barn area as she held on to his tail, allowing him to learn his own limitations.

"Once he developed confidence in me, we really developed a bond," Jagoda said. "That's all he really needed was someone to have confidence in."

A short month after the surgery, Smoky returned to racing at Los Alamitos, winning his first race back, the Samtyr Sprint Handicap, by a neck.

"The biggest (race) had to be the one after he lost his eye," Jagoda said, recalling that race. "That was such a big change. He amazed me. I couldn't have been happier."

Later, Smoky would go on to beat legends in the world of Arabian racing, such as TC Tomtyr in the 1994 Sierra Knights Handicap, and earn the nickname "The One-Eyed Wonder."

"I put him in almost every race he fits," Jagoda said of Smoky.

"The thing about Smoky is he just keeps going and going. It's just that he's a durable horse. He hasn't gotten sour and he stays sound.

"Still today, when he goes out to the track he's always jumping and leaping. And he kicks and bucks all the way back from the track. I've never had a horse that enjoys it and feels so good every time he comes up to the track. I think that's important with a horse, whatever they're doing."

While Jagoda is generally credited for Smoky's success, she refuses to take all of the credit.

"There's a lot of horses that would probably make good racehorses if they just had the chance," Jagoda said. "I was really lucky. I just walked into it."

Magna Terra Smoky celebrated his tenth birthday in 1996, and spent the first few months of the year at Turf Paradise in Phoenix, Arizona. While there, he entered the Scottsdale Arabian Cup race and finished fourth, showing he is still a top contender in the stakes ranks.

According to Jagoda, Smoky is taking it easy for a few months after sustaining a minor leg injury during the Scottsdale Arabian Cup. But Jagoda has her sights set on bringing him back during the 1996 racing season at Los Alamitos, where the fans seem to think of Smoky as part of their family (one adoring patron even named her dog after Smoky).

While Magna Terra Smoky doesn't win every race (although admittedly he wins quite a few), he always tries his hardest, and shows the true Arabian heart and courage that has allowed him to overcome such adversity and become one of the most beloved Arabian racehorses in recent history. ❑

Barbara Jagoda receives the trophy awarded to "Smoky" as 1993 California Arabian Horse Of The Year.

29) OH, FICKLE WIND!

Neither the Los Al Publicity team nor I could ever have ever foreseen what would happen in the Pioneer Stakes Race to be run on October 28. Smoky was fit, happy, and ready to run. Jose Fuentes was in the saddle. Smoky was the odds-on favorite, and I didn't think any horse in the race could beat him.

I had my eyes fixed on the starting gate, and I watched with excitement and wonderment as Smoky broke from his slot in the gates with his now typical easy style and settled into fourth place. He looked so remarkably fit and toned yet also so entirely relaxed as he passed the finish line for the first time. As he came into the first turn, I watched as Jose eased Smoky down to the rail. Smoky was now in third place. Bryan's horse, Vals BL Stryker, was advancing up on Smoky's outside. I was a little concerned that Smoky might get boxed in, but I also figured that there was a lot of race left. As I continued watching Smoky, I also noticed that Stryker was being strongly urged on. In less than an instant, Stryker was up alongside Smoky. It was then that I observed Stryker's jockey look over his left shoulder and, at almost the same instant, drop Stryker down to the rail. I gasped. What was the jockey thinking? Stryker was coming down on Smoky, and Smoky hadn't even seen it coming. I gasped again. Oh my lord, Smoky was going down.

I felt a sickening wave sweep my body. *This can't be happening!* In less time than a heartbeat, Smoky was down on his knees, and Jose was up on Smoky's ears. There were horses diving everywhere to avoid running over Smoky. I saw that Smoky was literally running on his knees.

"Oh my god!" I yelled to myself. "Oh my god!"

My worst nightmare was happening right in front of my eyes, and there was nothing I could do! *Oh god, please . . . Don't let this be happening! Please, please, please!* I knew that I was going to be sick, but I had to get out there, out to the racetrack. I had to help Smoky.

I forced my legs into a run. But just then, to everyone's total amazement, especially mine, Smoky was struggling to his feet. I watched dumbfoundedly as Smoky literally threw Jose back in the saddle in a tremendous effort to regain his feet. Smoky was up! He has done the impossible. How he had regained his feet, I could not fathom. I couldn't imagine how he had done it, but he had! What an amazing feat! What an amazing horse! And not only that, but also, he was up and racing! However, I found myself cringing with every step Smoky took. Could he possibly be uninjured? Could he possibly have survived this terrible fall without having hurt himself? He obviously did not want to be pulled up; he was fighting Jose to finish this race!

Eddie Burghart gasped with the rest of us, and now he was just as amazed. I heard him announce that unbelievably, Magna Terra Smoky had regained his balance. And then he was telling the crowd, "He looks to be all right. What an amazing recovery! Smoky has literally lifted himself back up and thrown Jose Fuentes back into the saddle. He has lost about seven lengths. What a remarkable feat if Smoky could regroup and go on to win this race!"

I did not care about winning anymore. I was just concerned that Smoky was all right and not running on adrenaline, which could cause him to injure himself more. Surely, Jose would pull him up if he felt anything wrong. But would Smoky allow Jose to pull him up? I strained to see but could not detect any unevenness in Smoky's stride. I was beside myself with worry for the rest of the race. Smoky had been blindsided. Even if he was all right physically, I wondered what this race would do to him mentally.

I could do nothing but watch as Smoky gallantly chased the field, and with the true heart of a champion, he actually passed three horses and finished fifth. What a remarkable effort! I felt unbelievable admiration—and worry.

Immediately, there was a steward's inquiry. The red light indicating an inquiry into the race events seemed to flash incessantly in my head. But I could not wait to see what the stewards saw and ruled on. I ran down to meet Smoky and Jose, who were backtracking to the finish line where all the horses would be unsaddled.

"Smoky! Jose! Are you both all right?"

Jose nodded. "That was *too* close. We were very lucky . . . Smoky is quite the athlete!"

"Yes, he is, and so are you, Jose. Thank god you both look all right."

I was hugging and petting Smoky and looking him over for any sign of possible injury. His knees and nose were scraped, and he was covered with dirt from the track, but he was all in one piece. I ran my hands down each of his legs, looking for possible ligament or tendon damage. I couldn't detect any unusual fill or heat. *A wonderful sign*, I thought. Hugging him again, I held him to be unsaddled. All the while, I looked around for Stryker and his jockey, but they were nowhere to be seen. Didn't want to face me, that was for sure!

Bryan came up after he had evidently handed Stryker off to his groom. "Is Smoky okay, babe?"

I nodded. "He seems to be, but I want to have a better look back at the barn."

Antoine took hold of Smoky, and the two of us walked Smoky off the track and down the backside. I knew Bryan would watch the replay and report the steward's ruling to me later.

While Antoine gave him his bath, I held Smoky and fed him carrots. He was hungry enough—a wonderful sign, I thought. I had run my hands all over Smoky's body and legs more thoroughly once we arrived back at the barn. He hadn't flinched or shown any discomfort and still no unusual heat or fill. I felt a little more relieved, but I also knew we weren't out of the woods yet. What might show up later was often an indicator of the bigger picture. Even so, Smoky was in one piece. He hadn't had to be brought back to his stall in the horse ambulance. He had walked off the track on his own. Once again, I felt that someone had been looking out for us and had protected Smoky and Jose. I believed that with all my heart. *Thank you, dear Lord, and thank you, Grampa and everyone up there who might have helped! Thank you! Thank you! Thank you!*

Bryan came down to the barn while Smoky was still cooling out on the walker. He had watched the replay. He had heard the steward's ruling. I know he felt badly. It had been his horse. I asked what the stewards had ruled.

"Stryker was disqualified and placed fifth behind Smoky. Smoky was moved up to fourth. They'll rule on my jockey tomorrow. He knew what he was doing for sure. You can see him look back at Smoky and then drop Stryker down to the rail."

"Look at who won the race, babe." I looked at Bryan and nodded. I wanted to see the replay but knew I would have to wait until the following day.

I couldn't get over being upset and angry. I wanted to confront the jockey face to face, eyeball to eyeball. But the next morning, it was still not to be. He totally avoided showing up at the track. I knew he knew how angry and upset I was.

The next day, I finally got to see the replay for myself and was even more convinced that it had not been an accident; it had definitely been deliberate. I requested a meeting with the stewards. I knew they had to have seen what I saw.

As Monday was a dark day, the stewards scheduled a meeting with me for Tuesday. George Slender, Merlin Volzke, and John Herbuveaux were the stewards. I liked all three of them and thought they were fair in their judgment calls. Therefore, it really surprised me then when they advised me to accept the fact that Stryker's jockey had been justly punished by being fined and given suspension days for interfering with Smoky's race. They had no proof that anything more was involved. I asked if they had seen the jockey look over his shoulder and then promptly drop down on Smoky.

"He could have killed both Jose and Smoky," I pleaded.

"Barbara, we've done all we can do. Let's move on. It was an unfortunate mishap, and we understand your concern. We have to leave it as just that!" George was indicating our meeting was over.

If the stewards wouldn't do more, I decided I would. When Smoky's nemesis returned to the racetrack after his suspension, I actively sought him out. Passing him while galloping a horse, I yelled at him, "How much did they have to pay you to try to drop Smoky?"

When I saw him walking to someone's barn, I fired spiteful comments at him. I even went up to the rail at the track entrance, and as he entered or exited the track, I was there to accuse him. The stewards called me in. They heard of my comments and of my anger. They cautioned me that what I was doing was unacceptable. The racetrack did not need or condone this kind of behavior. They played on my self-esteem, saying they felt that I was a classier person than to do what I was doing.

When I tried to argue, George said, "Barb, If you don't stop this behavior, I assure you that you will be ruled off the track." It was as simple as that. The choice was up to me.

As it turned out, I think I was fortunate. I found I had no one on whom to vent my anger and frustration. My adversary had opted to flee not only the racetrack but also the state of California. He was long gone. I delighted in the fact that the heat and pressure had been too much for him. I felt, at least, that a little justice had been served!

30 Perhaps the Time Has Come

Smoky wouldn't win another race in '94. I couldn't help but wonder if he had suffered repercussions from his knockdown in the Pioneer Stakes. Had he sustained injuries that I hadn't detected, or had he suffered emotional damage that might not be reparable? Before the unfortunate and traumatic fall, I had hoped Smoky would be able to at least tie News Release's record of thirty-eight wins. Now I was wondering if Smoky had another year of racing left in him. I didn't want to keep racing Smoky if he wasn't up to it or if he didn't enjoy it, and I really didn't want to see Smoky go out in a downhill slide. It was hard to know if the time was right to retire him or not.

Just as I was debating this issue in my mind, I learned that in spite of a less-than-spectacular finale to the year, Smoky earned not only earned the ARAC Older Horse of the Year but also the ARAC Horse of the Year Award. He had even edged out TC Tomtyr. He did it again on sheer endurance. He had raced an amazing fourteen times as an eight-year-old with four wins, five seconds, and two thirds. He had earned over $39,000. TC Tomtyr, although very good, had raced only seven times, and he had shipped to Texas for two of his races, so they did not count for ARAC (California) awards.

I was to be even more proud as Aurzel and BJ had also been nominated for Aged Horse of the Year (that meant that out of five horses nominated for Aged Horse, three were from my barn), and Aurzel was also nominated for Horse of the Year. BJ and Aurzel had also been nominated for Sprinter of the Year, and Aurzel ended up winning top honor in this category! To top it off, BJ had also been nominated for Claimer of the Year at a remarkable eleven years of age.

Needless to say, it was an amazing and very fulfilling awards night for me. I was so proud of what all three of these horses had accomplished. I thought of all the obstacles that they had overcome. It was absolutely amazing. I wondered how many other horses had their own personal story to tell. I wondered also how many horses never had the opportunity to show their greatness. How many could have been great but had suffered an unfortunate injury? How many were never fortunate enough to team up with the right owner or trainer? How many had been tossed aside because of financial, location, or time restraints? There were probably as many reasons as there were horses. Thank goodness timing and luck had been so good to us.

To his credit, TC Tomtyr would earn his dues at the Darleys, where all his races counted. He would win the Darley for Older Horse, defeating both Smoky and News Release.

Smoky's last race of 1994 had been the California Heritage Stakes Race held on December 17. It was the race that John Petti had predicted Smoky would win when he wrote the article comparing Smoky and the Fridge. Smoky not only didn't win the race but also never was even in the hunt. He had finished a dismal fifth.

Thank goodness we would now have a break from racing because of a harness meet being held at Los Al. Bryan and I planned to travel to Turf Paradise again, but races would not start there until February. So I had time to think about Smoky's future and also to see how he felt and acted after a vacation and some turnout time.

Smoky loved his time off. The grass was good at A-Bar Ranch, and he was turned out with his race buddies. I loved these vacation times in my horses' lives. It rejuvenated all of us, whether horse or human. A little time off, and I was ready to race again. I wondered if Smoky would feel the same way this time around.

As much as I enjoyed vacation time, I soon began to really look forward to Turf Paradise. Phoenix offered such a nice change of pace and scenery. Antoine would be going with us, and Jane Teutsch would be sending me some of her horses to train once again, including Strawberry Fields, Soaring Big Red, and Soaring Fastneasy. Soaring Big Red had developed quite a sour attitude recently, and Jane was hoping that I could figure out the cause and turn him around. Soaring Fastneasy was a three-year-old filly by SW David (Smoky's daddy), and Jane was hoping that she would show some of the talent that Smoky had.

Four years earlier, Jane had called Bryan, asking him if she should buy a mare named Dachshina from ARA (the same group from California that I had trained for in my novice year of racing). ARA was asking $1,000 for the mare, and she was in foal to SW

David. It was interesting how Bryan always seemed to be in the picture when SW David was involved. He couldn't believe that Jane wouldn't jump at this opportunity and told her so. He did warn her, however, that "Dachshina" bloodlines could produce difficult horses to work with. With Bryan's good analysis and advice, Jane went ahead and bought the mare. Now the foal that she had been carrying was three years old and ready to start racing.

We would be leaving A-Bar early to have the horses ready to race at the beginning of February. I decided to take Smoky, Aurzel, Koshada Star, and BJ. I couldn't stand to leave Smoky behind even if I didn't plan to race him. If he wasn't up to racing, I would just let him have fun there. As a precaution, I had called the race office at Turf Paradise to make sure that BJ, at age twelve, was still eligible to race at their track.

We settled into our portable stalls, and Jane's horse arrived several days later. Bryan and I were both anxious to see Soaring Fastneasy. When she arrived, everyone thought the mare was a big disappointment—everyone, that is, except for Bryan and me. We both saw beyond her rough coat and her lack of strong muscle. We both really liked her.

"You know, Bryan, Jane has this mare for sale for $5,000 in the *Finish Line* racing magazine." I knew as soon as the words left my mouth that I had said the wrong thing. Bryan was off like a shot, and I knew it was to see if he could get someone to buy Fastneasy. I did my own motoring out of there. I called Jane.

"Jane!" I almost yelled into the phone. "Your horses have arrived safe and sound, and whatever you do, don't sell Fastneasy if Bryan calls. She's a good one! Keep her."

Soon, Bryan came walking back. "You know, that darn Jane changed her mind. She said that Fastneasy was really Ray's horse and Ray had decided not to sell her now."

Jane hadn't said a word about my call to her. I never said a word either. Bryan would later suspect that I had called Jane, but I didn't admit to it until months later, after Fastneasy had proven herself. Jane let it slip out during one of her visits.

"I knew it!" Bryan would declare. He was livid that I had nixed the sale. I laughed as I seldom got the upper hand on Bryan.

In the meantime, I had lined up a new rider named Rico Flores as our jockey. Rico had a friend named Duane who galloped for me.

He was really a good hand with the horses, and I decided to have him give Smoky a whirl. Smoky was so happy to be back on the track that I started to entertain racing him after all. A very beautiful and fast work later confirmed my belief. I decided to enter Smoky in an open-allowance race going six furlongs on February 4. If I was ever grateful that I had decided to race Smoky, it had to be this time. Smoky not only won but also set a new track record of 1:18-1 for the six-furlong race. What an unimaginable high I felt!

What an amazing horse you are, Smoky, I thought for probably the hundredth time since I had known Smoky. *You little devil, here, you almost had me convinced it was retirement time, and you do this! How am I ever going to know when the right time has come?*

Thinking back on it later, I think that a change of scenery (and, of course, his time off) was really beneficial to Smoky. It was like he had never associated his accident at Los Al with racing at Turf. Rico had kept him safe and to the outside, and Smoky had responded with confidence and power. I guessed it wasn't over 'til the fat lady sang. I hoped the fat lady decided not to sing for some time now.

31 A Decision, A Lesson

1995

BJ was the next to race. I had entered him in a $5,000 claimer, and I was anxious to see how he would fare at a new track. He ran an okay race, nothing spectacular, and finished third. However, later that day, I was called in by the stewards. They had not noticed BJ's age in the program and told me that he was too old to be racing in Arizona; their laws cut the age limit at eleven. I would have to forfeit the purse and the placing. I mentioned that I had called before I left California to make sure BJ could run, but my mistake had been to call the racing office, not the stewards. Poor BJ. Here he was in the prime of his racing life, and he had no races available for him. The stewards did feel badly enough that they did not fine me.

The next race for Smoky was the Scottsdale Cup. I felt Smoky was set up nicely to win himself another race. He was feeling very good and had already completed his prep two-minute clip. He would basically take it easy until the race now. The race was an ARC race (the kind Bryan would get a check for). Smoky wasn't an ARC horse, but he was out of an ARC nominated sire. As such, it had cost us $1,200 to be in this race. The purse was $20,000.

It was a nice morning, so I decided to take Smoky for a walk and tour of the grounds. He never lost his passion for his walks, and today was no exception. It was two days before his big race. Today Smoky decided that he wanted to go along the sandy edge of a dirt road that meandered through the barn area. He was very opinionated and always knew the exact route he wanted to take on his walks. Every so often, he stopped for a bite of grass. Ahead was one of Smoky's favorite rolling areas. I knew in advance that he would head for this irresistible big pit of sand to roll. Today, however, I would wish that I had not allowed him to roll or that we had taken an alternate route.

As predicted, Smoky fell to his knees and began his roll. Nearby were several outdoor pens that housed pony horses. They all knew Smoky well and often watched him roll here. Today, however, Smoky startled the gelding in the nearest pen as he was caught in a deep dream, perhaps in the thralls of running the race of his life. The gelding leaped to his feet, crashing into the welded wire sides of his pen. Smoky, who was caught in the process of dropping to the ground, stumbled forward awkwardly and fell to the ground. I helplessly watched while trying not to further hinder Smoky's attempts to regain his balance.

For a moment, while Smoky was still regaining his composure, I heard myself exclaim, "Oh no!"

Smoky was holding up his right front leg. I stroked Smoky on the neck, trying to reassure him that everything was all right now. Then I leaned down to run my hand down his leg. There was not much to detect. I knew that the heat and fill that would probably occur had not yet had time to show their ugly heads. I checked that the pony horses were all okay and made my apologies to them. Although Smoky favored his right front leg, he was able to walk on it, so we slowly made our way back to the barn.

Bryan was there. He saw immediately that something was wrong and just shook his head. For years, he had put up with all the little things that Smoky and I just had to do. He asked, rather impatiently, what had happened this time, and I reluctantly told him. In spite of being dismayed, he agreed with me on the plan of action. So I put Smoky in his stall and went to get a bucket of ice.

Ice is a wonderful substance. We used it a lot. Smoky was very agreeable to having his injured leg cooled down, and for the next half hour, Smoky and I visited while his leg literally froze in the bucket of ice water. I often wondered how horses tolerated cold icing for so long. I have tried icing my pained feet and legs sometimes, and after forty-five seconds, I have had plenty. My feet usually felt much relieved even after such a short period.

When I felt we had cooled the leg enough, I slowly removed Smoky's leg from the bucket of ice. I didn't want to tip the bucket over and have a wet stall to clean up. His leg was nice and cool, and Smoky placed it squarely on the ground and rested on both front feet. It was a good sign, and I was somewhat relieved as it confirmed that the injury was not too serious. At the same time, however, I felt we had just eliminated ourselves from the Scottsdale Cup race.

As I continued to ice Smoky's leg that afternoon and the next morning, it wasn't long before I realized that most of our opposition in the stakes race had caught wind that Smoky was injured. I felt sad knowing that they felt happy that their biggest competition might be out of the hunt. I guess it's a pretty natural reaction though. I remember just last year being rather relieved when our main opposition, TC Tomtyr, was injured and scratched from our big race.

Although Smoky's leg was responding well, there was still a little bit of fill and heat in the ankle. I sure didn't want to injure it further by running in a race before the ankle was 100 percent. I sought the advice of both Bryan and our veterinarian, Dr. Looper. Although Smoky continued to improve and they both thought he would be fine, we decided to wait until the last minute to decide whether or not to scratch him from the race.

As this was a stakes race, I had the privilege of scratching up to the last moment if necessary. I was really torn. I knew I would never forgive myself if I raced Smoky and he hurt himself more. On the other hand, I was broke. I needed the money, and I had already invested $1,200 in entry fees. I knew the money should not matter, but it did. When you raced so many of your own horses, it could get to be very expensive. Horses like Aurzel had to be cared for and brought along for years before they were even raced, and unexpected surprises like Aurzel's cancer drained the finances even more. Smoky had been my major breadwinner from the start. I was well aware I wouldn't be here at all without his help. He had supported me in being able to buy Koshada Star, BJ, LD Alexander, Ona Natural High, and CJ Steed, to name a few. And he had financially supported the cost of their training and care before they started racing for our barn. *He sure had a lot of weight on his shoulders*, I thought. Actually, I had also taken on outside horses such as Jane's to boost my income. I was particular in whom I trained for, and I knew and liked Jane and her husband, Ray. They had raised some very good racehorses, and they loved their horses. I liked people who genuinely liked their horses.

I fluctuated and worried more about Smoky's injury. I guessed if I was so worried, I should scratch him. Instead, I trotted him out for Bryan and Dr. Looper one more time. In the end, with their approval, I decided to race him.

Rico was already aware of Smoky's situation. We decided that he should feel Smoky out in the post parade. If he felt anything wrong, we would have Smoky scratched. Apparently, everything felt fine to Rico as all the horses, including Smoky, were loaded into the gate.

Then they were off and running. From my distant view, Smoky looked good. As usual these days, Smoky broke slow and easy. I was once again so glad he had learned to save himself from the powerful fast breaks he thought he had to make when he was younger. It placed much less stress on his legs.

It was a mile-and-one-sixteenth race, so Smoky had lots of time to catch the front-runners. On the backside, Smoky inched up, and it looked as if he would make a nice big sweeping move. Then he seemed to stabilize and appeared content to maintain. I knew Smoky would not win a race this day. He was not 100 percent. Rico did not pressure him for more.

Smoky galloped in. He had run fourth, a very decent effort. I ran to the track to greet my horse. It had been a terrible race to watch. It was not worth the price I might have had to pay. I watched Smoky gallop back to be unsaddled. I did not see any evidence of lameness. Thank goodness! Rico apologized, saying he had been afraid to ask Smoky for more. I thanked him. He did exactly what he should have done. Antoine, Smoky, and I headed back to the barn, happy that Smoky looked to have suffered no harm.

Smoky continued to look good. It appeared that the race didn't hurt him any. I was so relieved. I vowed I would never do something like this again. It could have turned out very badly. I wondered how many trainers had been in similar situations and if some of the wrong decisions resulted in their horse being severely injured. Did Barbaros or Eight Bells show any prerace signs that everything wasn't 100 percent? How many horses went into races each day not at 100 percent? Then there were so many signs that we could not even detect. I guessed we just had to do our best. I did not do my best today, and I did not like the feeling. For years afterward, the decision to run this race would haunt me. Even though Smoky came back fine, I knew I had risked *too* much. It could have been a very *dear* lesson. Could I have lived with it if I had run Smoky and crippled him? It was a terrifying thought.

Luckily, with several weeks' rest, Smoky's leg made a full recovery. I entered him in an open-allowance race and found that he would race against the same horses that he had faced in the Scottsdale Cup. This time, the outcome was much different. He soundly defeated Dae Gaa Zhay (who had won the cup race) by a convincing four lengths. It was a very sweet victory. The only thing that hurt was the purse for it was a mere $2,000 compared to the $20,000 for the cup race. Still, I had the satisfaction of knowing that Smoky had shown everyone that he could outrace Dae Gaa Zhay when he was 100 percent.

Two weeks later, to my utter delight, Aurzel flew around the racetrack, establishing a new track record for five and a half furlongs. He was absolutely awesome, winning the race by almost nine lengths. You could tell that he was really proud of himself by the way he stood up so smartly in the winner's circle. I couldn't help but smile. I was so proud of him. Antoine had really dressed up for the race. His timing was right on. Since coming to work for me, Antoine had really trimmed his waistline, and he enjoyed spending some of his hard-earned money on nice clothes. I had to admit that he looked mighty sharp. He had also jokingly taken to calling me Mom as I continued to try to guide his behaviors. Bryan still made it clear that Antoine was never to call him Dad!

Aurzel must have bragged to Smoky about his awesome performance, for the next day, Smoky turned it on to win the AHA Scottsdale Cup race run at a distance of seven and a half furlongs. It was one of the rare occasions that Arabian racehorses were allowed to race on the turf course. The win was extra sweet as Smoky beat Bryan's horse, Styxx, and it was also Smoky's thirty-ninth race win. He now held the record for most wins, and he held it all by himself. And to think I almost decided to retire him after last year's performance. How was one ever to know?

Not to be outdone and perhaps to quiet Aurzel's and Smoky's bragging, Strawberry Fields galloped home to victory in the Distaff Turf race. Score one for the girls. Jane and Ray were both there to enjoy the victory. Sadly, that was the last race of the meet. I would have liked to continue racing at Turf as my horses were loving it, and they had never collectively raced better. I hoped that we could continue the winning streaks back at Los Al.

32 THE DIRECTOR'S SPRINT

1995

When we returned to Los Al, I discovered that TC Tomtyr had been retired from horse racing. I never really confirmed my suspicions, but I believed he was injured the previous year, and rather than settle for subpar race performances or risk injuring such a good racehorse further, his connections retired him to stud. Although I sympathized with his owner and trainer, I cannot say that I did not have some degree of elation about hearing this, for it now meant that Jerry Lambert was now available to ride Smoky full time. I had the horse; now the horse had the best jockey I could ever hope for. The year had started out well, and now I really looked forward to what the rest of the year might bring.

Smoky's first race at Los Al was to be the ARAC Director's Sprint, going four and a half furlongs. It was extra special because the Darley Awards for 1994 were being held at Los Al, and all the "big wigs" of Arabian racing were here in attendance. Smoky would be on display for all to see. I hoped he would show all the Arabian owners, trainers, and spectators why he was such a crowd favorite and such a true champion.

It turned out to be *the most exciting* race I had ever watched! Smoky was unbelievable! The race was pegged correctly as a definite speed duel. The fastest of the fast were in the race, and the awesome speedsters, Fadwah Marchoy and King Shawn, literally flew out of the gate. Smoky, with his typical slow and easy break, was a dozen lengths off the pace almost immediately. He was in sixth place and seemed content to be there. John Petti would later write that Smoky was still fifth, going into the turn, and it appeared that the one-to-two favorite might have lost a step or two to his much younger rivals. He further wrote that Smoky started his run on the turn and was making up a little ground, but it seemed the front-runners weren't going to be caught today. He was still fifth entering the stretch (and mind you, the stretch is not very long at Los Al), and then the freight train came rolling. The old-timers, Lambert and Smoky, swung out around the field and charged up on the outside, blowing by the leaders in the last fifty yards. Magna Terra Smoky hit the wire half a length in front of long-shot TC Tomboy, who got the perfect trip along the rail.

I was in total awe. So was the crowd. Everyone was yelling and cheering as loud as they could. It was absolutely *wild!* I couldn't believe how much ground Smoky had made up in such a short distance. Nobody could.

Jane Teutsch ran up to me, saying, almost screaming, "Now I know why Smoky is such a fan favorite. That was absolutely unbelievable!" I knew that Smoky had just won the hearts and admiration of hundreds of new fans.

A whole lot of articles were written about Smoky after this huge effort. Rick Augustine would write about the Darley races in the *Finish Line* magazine. About Smoky, he would say, "My vote for best come-from-behind performance goes to the veteran runner Magna Terra Smoky, who literally flew past the pack in the stretch to earn his fortieth lifetime win and hold on to his position as all-time money winner, with career earnings that now totaled over $243,000. He was the heavy betting favorite and has become a real hero to many of the bettors at Los Alamitos. There were thousands of fans screaming and yelling as he flew past the field and showed that, at nine years of age and with ninety races under his saddle, Smoky still has what it takes to bring home the winner's share of the purse."

Smoky's win picture showed up everywhere. The Arabian Horse Registry even used it in a full-page colored ad to advertise Arabian racing and the Arabian Horse Registry. I was so tremendously proud of my one-eyed gelding. What an amazing racehorse he had turned out to be—year after year after year.

The weekend was not even over. The following evening, Strawberry Fields put the icing on the cake by winning the $35,000 ARAC/SamTiki Classic. I wouldn't be forgetting this weekend ever!

But alas, all good things had to come to an end, it seemed. Bryan had Styxx on the mend. He had been working diligently repairing the damage that had been done to Styxx's suspensories before he was given him to train. I really didn't think Bryan would be able to work his magic a second time, but he did. Bryan and Styxx once again proved to be my toughest competition as Smoky had to settle for second best, losing to Styxx in two consecutive races. Darn that Bryan! Here he is, my best friend and constant companion and my nemesis at the same time. He loves Smoky, and he loves me but loves to beat us more. What a relationship!

Roger Lang was ecstatic that he once again had a horse that could compete with and beat Smoky. Once again, he was making an appearance at the races every night that Bryan or I had a horse in a race. Bryan was again teasing and taunting me. I tried not to be bothered by it as I knew that I had had my share of glory. But I was anyway. I loved to win, especially with Smoky. I always had a hard time concealing my emotions, and Bryan knew that this upset me. He loved the torment it caused me. Looking back, I wonder how our friendship and committed relationship lasted through these years.

It was a long drought. Smoky did not win another race until August 4. It had been just over three months. Styxx was not in the race, so Smoky was able to fly down the stretch and remind himself what a victory felt like. He was always so cute after a race, and this time, he outdid himself. He was so excited and full of himself—and he was ravenous. I always went with Smoky to the test barn after a race as I liked to make sure everything was all right with him, and I especially liked to make a fuss over him. He loved the attention. Whoever says animals don't know when they have done a good job and don't love the attention doesn't know animals! Even when Smoky returned to the barn after winning a race, it was obvious to me that his nickers and mannerisms toward his stablemates were all part of letting them know what he had just done.

Photo Credit: Los Alamitos Race Course Photography

40th victory
article by John Petti in the "Arabian Finish Line" June, 1995

Magna Terra Smoky Earns 40th Victory
By John Petti

ARAC Directors Sprint

With Disneyland just seven miles down Katella Avenue from Los Alamitos Race Course, some of the magic from the "Magic Kingdom" is sure to rub off. For nine-year-old MAGNA TERRA SMOKY and 54-year-old jockey Jerry Lambert, Fantasyland returned for a visit to Los Alamitos, keeping Tomorrowland still a dream away as the pair combined to win the $30,000 ARAC Directors Sprint on April 28.

For MAGNA TERRA SMOKY it was his record 40th win from his 90th start and the $16,500 he earned pushed his career total to $233,278, the most ever for an Arabian. For jockey Jerry Lambert, who won three consecutive Hollywood Gold Cups in the early 1960's with Native Diver, it was his second stakes win of the evening and his fourth stakes win in his new career as an Arabian jockey. For the crowd of Arabian enthusiasts on hand for the Arabian Racing Association of California Awards, it was a trip to Disneyland, Fantasyland in particular.

In the 4-1/2 furlong Directors Sprint, things did not go MAGNA TERRA SMOKY's way early as the gelding was sixth, trailing the field by as many as a dozen lengths in the early stages of the race. FADWAH MARCHOY and KING SHAWN had popped the gate and opened a good lead on the rest of the field. MAGNA TERRA SMOKY was showing no signs of making any kind of move.

MAGNA TERRA SMOKY was still fifth

it appeared that the 1-2 favorite might have lost a step on his much younger rivals. The gelding then began his run on the turn and was making up some ground, but it seemed the front runners would not be caught. He was still fifth entering the stretch, but the oldtimers Lambert and MAGNA TERRA SMOKY were on a roll as they charged up on the outside through the lane and blew by the tiring leaders in the final 50 yards.

"Experience was on our side tonight," Lambert said. "This horse knows exactly what he has to do to win a race. He will do whatever he has to do to win and he showed tonight why he will go down as an all-time great Arabian."

MAGNA TERRA SMOKY hit the wire a half-length in front of the longshot TC TOMBOY who got a perfect trip along the rail. KING SHAWN tired to third, another 1-1/2 lengths back with AURZEL finishing fourth. FADWAH MARCHOY faded to fifth.

"Every time MAGNA TERRA SMOKY races he amazes me," Barbara Jagoda said. "He will never quit. That's the mark of a truly special horse."

Owned and trained by Barbara Jagoda, MAGNA TERRA SMOKY covered the 4-1/2 furlongs in :58.2 while earning his 10th stakes win at Los Alamitos.

AHA ad featured in the Arabian Horse World magazine (09/1995)
Photo shows Smoky winning the ARAC Directors Sprint

Photo Credit: Los Alamitos Race Course Photography

33 THE MARATHON

1995

Very seldom do I leave the barn and go up to the racetrack before Smoky on race day. I usually walk up with him and Antoine. But today, September 13, I wanted to watch a race running prior to ours. So I left Antoine to bring Smoky up by himself. It was the wrong thing to do. Antoine mistakenly brought Smoky up in the wrong bit. I had neglected to set Smoky's bridle out like I usually do, and somehow Antoine had not remembered which was Smoky's equipment. It was too late to race back to the barn to get the correct bridle, so we went with what we had. I should have told Jerry. I really thought Smoky would run well regardless of the bit we had on him. What a mistake I made. When I saw Smoky trying to run over the heels of the horses in front of him going into the first turn, I knew that Jerry could not control him. Even Eddie announced that Smoky was trying to run over his opposition. I started to worry that Smoky would cause a serious wreck. Finally, they made it through the turn, but Jerry had spent so much energy trying to contain Smoky, and Smoky had spent so much energy fighting Jerry that I knew it had cost us the race. We ran third, which was much better than we had deserved. Jerry came back very upset, and I didn't blame him. Very sheepishly and apologetically, I told him of our blunder.

In the meantime, I had been hard at work getting Soaring Fastneasy ready for her first race. We had nominated her for the three-year-old California Futurity later in the year, and I wanted her to have at least one race under her belt before that huge race. I entered her in a maiden race, and Jerry guided her to an easy win. My initial appraisal of Soaring Fastneasy had been right on; she was going to be a good one. Two days later, Li'l Smok, a gelding I had bred and raised by SW David and out of Aurzel's dam, Aura Maria, and named after his elder half brother Smoky, also won his first race.

He was a gorgeous steel-gray gelding that I had been very proud of since the day he was born. Richard Pfau was his jockey.

Smoky's next big stakes race in the book was to be the Los Alamitos Arabian Marathon, to be run September 29 at one and a half miles. Most trainers did not feel that Smoky would be in the race as they thought he was not as good at running distances as he was the shorter races. I knew both these things also. But Smoky was feeling awfully good, and the purse for the race was over $20,000. There were several horses at Los Al that really relished longer distances, so if Smoky were to race well in this race, he would really have to be well prepared.

. In addition, the track at Los Al was not conducive to long races. It was only a five-eighth-mile oval, so it meant that a horse had to cross the finish line a whopping three times to complete a race this long. It also meant galloping a horse a multitude of times around the track to get him in shape for a race like this. It made it hard on the horse and also hard on the rider, who had to contain his or her steed each time the pair entered the stretch where most horses habitually made their hard and fast drive for the finish line. Smoky was always hard to contain anywhere on the racetrack, and he was especially hard to hold once we reached the three-eighths pole, where he loved to start his stretch drive. I knew it would be hard getting him ready for this race.

I decided on a special strategy for this race. I woke up extra early and had Smoky up at the racetrack as soon as it opened at 6:00 a.m. We had several advantages. There were very few horses on the track at this time in the morning as it was still cold and dark (sometimes we were the only one on the track), and trainers were almost completely absent. Very few people would ever know that I was getting Smoky ready for the marathon. As there were very few horses up and about, Smoky was also much more relaxed and easier to gallop. With less stress on Smoky, there was also less chance that he would tie up. I could also two-minute clip Smoky right down on the rail if I needed to as the clocker was not up and about and there were almost no horses to worry about. Normally, you were not permitted to two-minute clip down at the rail as the rail was reserved for horses that were requesting timed works.

Our plan went very well. Smoky enjoyed his early-morning workouts and soon settled down nicely as he realized there would be a distance to go. On his easy days, Robert would pony him, or I would take him down to the receiving barn to roll. On his harder days, we would two-minute clip increasingly longer distances. Eventually, he was able to two-minute clip two miles with no undue effort, and I knew that he would be very tough in the marathon. It was not going to be a cheap race to enter, and I wanted to make sure we had a good chance of winning it.

It was fun to have this secret game. Each morning, I looked forward to our quiet gallops, knowing full well that Smoky was getting more fit with every lap around the track. I didn't think Smoky had been this fit since his days of long gallops at Stonewall Springs. Even Bryan was unaware of how extremely fit I had Smoky. I could hardly wait for the marathon.

In the meantime, Soaring Fastneasy had her futurity race. Unlike the quarter horses who ran their futurities as two-year-olds, Arabians waited until they were a more mature three years old. I still thought it was too early an age to be asking horses to run full out, but unfortunately, I was in the minority. Finances played too big a role, and most owners were unwilling to wait another year to have some income coming in. And after all, hadn't I started Smoky as a three-year-old? It sure hadn't hurt him. Guess my argument didn't hold too much water.

For her part, Fastneasy was in against a very talented mare named Cash on the Spot. Cash had won both her previous races and was the crowd and betting favorite. Fastneasy had only one race under her belt, and I was a little apprehensive as to how she might perform in a big and important stakes race. But Jerry Lambert, with his quiet manner and expert skill, brought Easy home to a three-length victory over Cash. Ray and Jane were besides themselves with joy and excitement. They were sure they had another "Magna Terra Smoky" in their barn!

The marathon sported a full field of ten horses. Smoky was in post position 10, and as Eddie commented, he could see 'em all from his starting post. Before the race, I had told Jerry that Smoky was exceptionally ready for this race and not to worry that Smoky would come up short in the stretch. Jerry knew how well I knew Smoky and took me for my word. After breaking sixth, he moved Smoky right up into the lead. It was obvious to me that Jerry intended to set the pace with Smoky and control the speed of the race. The other jockeys were content to let Jerry do this as none of them considered Smoky to be much of a threat. Styxx was the favorite. He loved these distance races and had won his last four races. He loved to rally in the later stages of a race, so he too was content to let Smoky control the early going. As a result, no one challenged Smoky, so he rolled along at an easy, unpressured clip. Eddie expressed surprise that Smoky was out front, and it was obvious that he too questioned that wisdom. Then with a whole lap yet to go, Jerry surprisingly let Smoky out a notch.

Eddie's whole announcing voice changed. He excitedly announced, "Magna Terra Smoky is loving this distance. With five eighths of a mile to go, he is showing no signs of slowing down and is pulling away from the field. He is literally widening the gap with every stride. Styxx is going to have to pick it up, as are all the others." And at the end, it was indeed a one-horse race. Eddie was working the crowd now, announcing, "Magna Terra Smoky is in a league of his own as the two old-timers, Jerry Lambert and Magna Terra Smoky, are destroying this field. They will win the race by seven lengths and have just set a new track record."

The crowd went wild, and so did I. I couldn't have been prouder of Smoky. Jerry had ridden an amazing race. He had surprised us all with his strategy. He knew what others didn't, and that was that Smoky was ready for this distance. Bryan was livid. Styxx had run a disappointing fourth. He had expected to win this race. He too had underestimated Smoky. Lacy, Jerry's daughter, ran over to me, and together, we held up the blanket that Smoky had won while we all posed for a winner's photo. It was such a sweet and rewarding victory.

Bryan was quite hard to live with after that race. He had been sure that he and Styxx would walk away with the race. He thought his jockey had lost the race for him, and he never did offer any congratulations to us. What a sore loser. I'm sure I never acted like that when we lost.

The next day, I decided to treat Bryan to dinner across the way at our favorite restaurant as a way of making him feel better. We often ate there as the food was good, and we like the owners, who both worked very hard, and often Don came over to watch our races. We were sitting at the bar, having a drink beforehand as we had run into some friends and wished to visit them. Bryan had tried one of the hors d'oeuvres sitting on the bar. I was tempted to have one also but was afraid they might be a little hot or spicy. I waited for Bryan to finish his to get his reaction. He said how good they were and that they were not hot at all, so believing him, I tried one. I think smoke must have come out of my ears and my eyeballs too. They were *hot!* I spit the rest out as quickly as I could and grabbed for my beer. Bryan broke into a belly laugh. I knew I had been had. He had held back his reaction so that I would be tricked into trying one.

He grabbed for his beer, still laughing wildly. "I didn't think I could hold out. It took everything I had to not give myself away," he was trying to say between laughs.

I couldn't believe he had gone to such extremes to trick me. It must have been his way of getting even with me for having been beaten him in a race. Why I kept falling for his little tricks always dismayed me, but this time, I too had to laugh.

A month later, Smoky would win another stakes race the ARAC Pioneer Stakes Race, at one and one eighth miles, and then I started having tying-up problems again. *Why now?* I thought. *What is different? What is going on?* I hadn't been letting anyone else gallop him, for if you held him too tight and tried to tuck his head, he would most certainly tie up on the way back to the barn. However, several times in the past few days, I had to stop Smoky on the way back to the barn and call for Dr. Moak. He was always very prompt and would come and give Smoky a shot. Smoky was tensing up and causing his own problems. But why? Why could he go long periods and be all right and then have periods of tying-up problems? I couldn't figure out the reason for the problem, and neither could Doc. I resorted to giving him tying-up pastes from a tube every morning as well as the usual vitamin E/selenium that he always got in his evening meal.

I was unable to condition Smoky as well as I wanted to because of this problem, so we didn't do well in the last two races of the year. We finished fifth and then fourth. I couldn't just rest Smoky and leave him in his stall either as he would tie up even more. It was a bad situation. I wished I understood this condition better. I tried to read up on everything I could but never found any advice different from what Doc and I were trying already. I wondered what Dwayne Lucas or Bob Baffert would do if they were training Smoky. I hated that my lack of experience and knowledge were affecting Smoky's career. I wondered how much better he could be if I could only get this persistent problem taken care of.

In spite of all this, Smoky had now run an amazing one hundred races. I reminisced back to his first race at Los Al, when he was almost scratched by the track veterinarian because of the way he moved in the hind end. Who would ever have believed that he would not only run one hundred races but also win forty-four of them. He kept breaking his own records, and I knew that records he would leave behind would be very hard to beat.

Once again, I was questioning if I would ever really know when it was time to retire Smoky. So far, he had bounced back from every setback that I felt he could not overcome. He had really proven me wrong this year as it had turned out to be his biggest "earning" year so far in his career. He had even broken his record for number of races run in a year. He certainly was a tough little rascal. He had raced fifteen times this past year with a record of 8-2-4 (meaning eight wins, two seconds, and three thirds), with earnings of $68,562 for the year. He earned ARAC Horse of the Year once again and even earned his third Darley Award, that being for Older Horse of the Year.

It was very hard to look at Smoky and realize that he had run in so many races. His legs were as clean and pretty as they had been the first day I saw him. By clean, I mean free of any lumps, swelling, or injuries of any kind. Most racehorses of any age did not have legs that could match up to Smoky's. The thing that was most important to me was that he was still happy to be racing. He had never been sour about going to the racetrack as horses will become if they are overworked or hurting somewhere. He loved to race. It was a huge part of him. It was, as they say, in his blood. I was so glad he was doing what he loved to do. Never had I run across a horse that loved his calling as much as Smoky did.

Winning the "Marathon" 9/29/1995
Jerry Lambert up, Robert Strauss to my left,
Antoine holding Smoky

Photo Credit: Los Alamitos Race Course Photography

Smoky loves Carrots

1. Clinton waits for the go-ahead to give Smoky a carrot

2. Getting the okay, he starts the process.

3. But he drops the carrot... they both look for it.

4. It's lost for good, so Clinton heads back to the carrot bucket for more.

5. Smoky graciously accepts the carrot, reminding Clinton to keep his hand flat.

6. By the last of the carrots in the bucket, Clinton had learned to feed carrots in the approved manner - hand flat

A cute sequence of photos:

Clinton, son of trainer Garland McAlester is shown feeding carrots to Smoky

photo credits: Author
Comments credit: Ruth Austin
published in "California and Southwest Arabians" 1995

34 1996 — A Tough Year

With Los Al over for the year, it was time to move back to Turf Paradise again. Even though these moves were tedious, we were very fortunate to have another place to race so that we could maintain some sort of income. Smoky was making good money for me, but horse racing is a very expensive proposition, and it never seemed that Bryan or I got very far ahead of the game. Along the way, I had bred a few good mares to Smoky's sire (SW David), perhaps hoping to breed another Magna Terra Smoky, and I had also bought an occasional horse that I liked. Although I never had a large stable of horses, perhaps I shouldn't have bought or bred quite so many. Not all my horses were success stories, and a few like Manteeya's Whisper (out of LL Manteeya by SW David) never even made it to the races.

A few new faces were added to my stable of horses at Turf Paradise. SE Ruby Tuesday came from Jane and Ray Teutsch and Magnifica MA from an endurance rider named Emmett Ross. Soaring Fastneasy, Strawberry Fields, Smoky, Aurzel, Li'l Smok, and Llightning Road (LL Manteeya and SW David) completed my barn. Smoky would only race once during the whole meet, and that was the Scottsdale Cup race on the turf. He would run fourth. He still wasn't right, and I knew it.

Thank goodness I had other horses and that they were good enough to hold things together financially for me. Magnifica MA would set a new track record for six furlongs, beating Li'l Smok in the process; then Li'l Smok showed how tough he was by bouncing right back to win another race at six furlongs just one fifth of a second off the track record set by Magnifica. Two weeks later, Li'l Smok again outdid himself, setting a new track record for seven furlongs in the Sahara Derby on the turf course. Tiyuri and LP Conquest would race second and third. Both these horses were also by SW David, so it was a huge sweep for Roger Lang's new stallion.

Both Bryan and Rudolph were a little miffed at being beaten by Li'l Smok. Rudolph, especially, had thought he had much the better horse. Sorry, boys!

Except for his one race, Smoky was basically on vacation. He loved being at the racetrack even so. I wanted to keep a close eye on him, so it worked out well, having him here, especially since there were places to graze. I had even weeded a grassy area between our barns and the racetrack and kept it watered just for my horses. Big eucalyptus trees afforded some shade, so I could just sit and relax while Smoky grazed. Some days, I would just ride him around the barns on the backside or take him for walks, which he always looked forward to.

One day, when I was returning from a ride on Smoky, I saw Chaser (Bryan's pony horse) tied to the side of my horse trailer. I thought that Smoky might like to say hi to Chaser, so we rode up to visit. What a mistake! Chaser was not in a good mood and did not want any company. He spun around and kicked Smoky so hard that the both of us were thrown under the front of the gooseneck part of the horse trailer. He had caught Smoky unawares on his blind side and surprised the both of us so much that Smoky completely lost his balance. I didn't have any time to bail off. The gooseneck part of the trailer was right there. We hit it dead on, and then Smoky fell down on top of me. He had flipped over, and now he had to scramble to regain his feet. It seemed forever, but finally, Smoky was able to get up and out of there. I felt dizzy and sick. I remember making it to a nearby log, and I sat there with my head between my knees.

Bryan rushed over when he saw—or rather heard—the commotion. He wanted to call for an ambulance, but I didn't want to go to the hospital again, so I vetoed the idea. However, I was unable to get up and felt as if I was going to throw up and pass out. I knew I was hurt worse than I had originally thought. When Bryan said he was taking me to the hospital, I didn't resist. This time, I was lucky; I had suffered a concussion, cracked ribs, and a bruised sternum, but it wasn't anything that would keep me away from the barn area. It had been another dumb accident. I wondered if I would ever learn.

Soon, it was again time to return to Los Al. On August 2, John Petti wrote in that night's daily racing program that Magna Terra Smoky had posted his first official workout since his return, covering five furlongs in a minute and nine seconds, the fastest time for an

Arabian at that distance for that day. He went on to say that I, as Smoky's trainer, was not yet sure when Smoky would make his 1996 local debut. It was obvious that John was anxious to see Smoky back racing.

One of the things that really saddened me was that Jerry Lambert had retired from racing during our absence from Los Al. We had been *so* very fortunate and privileged to have had his expertise and talent available to us for the time that we did. I knew that we would sorely miss him. Jerry and his daughter, Lacy, now lived at a rather nice thoroughbred training center in Riverside. The training center was up for sale and only had a few horses. Jerry and Lacy cared for the horses and the grounds. Later on, Magness Arabians would buy this facility and maintain Jerry as their trainer. As it wasn't too far from the racetrack and there were extra turnout pastures, I rotated some of my horses out there for a break.

I had a very hard time replacing Jerry. I knew that we would not win as many races without him in our corner. On August 16, Smoky raced in the California Heritage Stakes with Janine Painter up. Smoky ran evenly in sixth place and finished sixth. Janine had let Smoky dictate the pace, and when she had asked him to pick it up in the final furlongs, he had not responded, so she had not pushed him. I was grateful for that and was anxious to see how Smoky would look and feel a few days later. This had really been a trial run to determine my future plans for him.

Smoky seemed no worse, having run this race, but I still waited another month before racing him again. Richard Pfau rode him this time, and he ran third. He had improved but still lacked his usual late rally. Then on October 10, with Paulo Sanchez up, Smoky finally won a race. It had been an easier field, and the time of 1:21-1 was not that impressive, but Smoky had won. I was glad for it as I felt that it would be a good mental as well as physical fix for Smoky. It sure was for me!

It was to be Smoky's lone win in 1996. That wasn't by choice, however. A race came up—in the conditions that fit Smoky perfectly. I knew that it would be a sure win for him as the conditions were nonwinner of two races in 1996. It was late in the year, and most of the "really good" horses had already won two races for the year. Seldom did we get such a gift. When Paulo's agent, Rollie, came around, as jockey agents always did on race-entry days, I asked him to enter Smoky in that race. There was also a race for Aurzel, and he was to enter him also. Most of the time, I entered my horses myself, but sometimes, like today, I was too busy to walk all the way up to the racing office to enter. It was a huge mistake. When the overnight sheet came out, Smoky's race was there, but Smoky's name was not. I looked again. I was stunned. Here was one of the easiest races Smoky could ever have asked for, and his name was not on the card. What had happened? Of course, Rollie was long gone, and there was no way that I could contact him to find out what had happened. I looked at the race entries again. It made me sick. I couldn't wait to get my hands on Rollie. I knew that Smoky had been deliberately omitted.

It wasn't until the next day that I was able to run Rollie down, for he was clearly avoiding my barn area. He had entries to take though, so I knew that he would be canvassing the backside. When I finally spotted him across the way, I immediately raced over and, not very nicely, asked him what the *hell* had happened. I shouldn't have been surprised when Rollie just replied that he hadn't understood that he was supposed to enter Smoky. It was a blatant lie, and I accused him of it in no uncertain terms. I wondered how long he had practiced his excuse. It could not have been clearer that he was to enter both my horses. He had entered Aurzel but not Smoky. I could not help but feel that there was more to the story. Had he been paid off? I was sure he had. Jock agents were often just scraping by, so someone with a lot of cash could buy a lot of "luck." I told Rollie that he was despicable and that I never wanted to see him around my barn ever again, and that went double for Paulo and any other jockey that he managed. I made enough of a row that the whole backside was aware of what had transpired. I wanted it to cost Rollie. I hoped that Smoky would win so many races after this that Rollie would regret his actions for a long time.

I was not so naive that I failed to realize that shady things go on in all aspects of life and that the racetrack environment was probably more prone to shady deals than many walks of life. Still, I had never thought it would come down to this. It was now the second incident where Smoky had been deliberately singled out. Someone was sabotaging us, someone with a lot of money and power and who was perhaps very jealous of Smoky's accomplishments.

Financially, I was thankful that another horse stepped up to the plate in the meantime. That horse was Smoky's half sister, Soaring

Fastneasy. I was so glad that Jane had decided not to sell her when Bryan had inquired about her. She was amazing! In the Region Two Memorial Distaff held on July 6, with Janine Painter up, Fastneasy broke unbelievably slow from the gates. In fact, she spotted the leaders almost twelve lengths before she got her act together and was on her way. Ray and Jane had traveled from Colorado to watch their mare race, and all three of us gasped in disappointment as we were sure the race was over for her and us. We watched sadly as Janine and Fast trailed the field past the grandstand, around the turn, and down the backside. We just stood there, our dreams shattered.

Then just as we had resigned ourselves to a terrible outcome, Fast exploded on the final turn. We could hear the excitement in Eddie's voice as he announced that Soaring Fastneasy had come out of nowhere and was picking off her rivals one by one. Shivers ran down my back, and Jane, Ray, and I came to life, yelling and screaming at the top of our lungs. Fastneasy was literally flying. She flew by the leader, Cash on the Spot, in the final furlong to win the race by over three lengths. We were beside ourselves with the excitement of it all. What an absolutely thrilling race it had been to watch! We would talk about that race for a long time to come. Janine had ridden an absolutely perfect race. She had not panicked when Fast broke badly, and she had not tried to race Fast up to catch the rest of the field like many other jockeys might have done. She had saved her horse for a final dash to the wire. And Fastneasy had delivered in a huge way.

Fastneasy went on to prove her greatness that year by winning not only the California Oaks for four-year-olds but also the biggest filly/mare race of them all, the Gladys Brown Edwards Arabian Cup, with a purse of $50,000. Even Smoky, with all his many stakes races, had never raced for such a big purse. Daryl Montoya (a leading jockey from Colorado and a favorite of Ray and Jane's) had flown in from Colorado to ride Fast, and it proved to be a very good move. Jane and Ray were the happiest people I have ever seen. Winning this race had been Jane's number-one bucket-list goal for the past several years. She referred to this race as the "mother of all mare races." Now she had just won it with a mare that she had almost sold for $5,000 a year ago. To add icing to the cake, Fast would go on to win the Darley for four-year-old filly, upsetting the very talented mare Cash on the Spot for the honor.

Later that year, Guy Neivens, agent for Tahnoon Bin Zayed, would make an offer to buy Soaring Fastneasy from Ray and Jane. The offer was a tempting $100,000. It was to Ray and Jane's credit that they decided not to sell her. They reasoned that too many of the country's good Arabian racehorses were shipping oversees. We needed some good one to stay here. I was very impressed by their decision.

Sadly, Smoky could not even touch Fast's accomplishments. He would finish the year with a dismal record of 7(1-2-1), $11,165. I wondered if Smoky was telling me it was time to let the younger generation take hold of the reins.

35 So Close

1997

Bryan had a new horse ready to challenge Smoky this year. He was to be the first of many "Zell' horses that Bryan would do extremely well with. His name was RDZell, and he was sired by Brusally Orlen, the stallion we had unfortunately overlooked for way too long. Bryan would continue the practice of keeping the "Zell" in his horses' names to signify they had "Orzel" in their pedigree.

Sadly for us (that being Smoky and me) but for the extreme delight of Bryan, RDZell outran Smoky in all four of our races at Turf Paradise. It was getting harder to engage the top jockeys for Smoky these days. When your horse is running well, all the jockeys want to ride for you, but when you're on a losing streak, it's just the opposite.

With all these losses, I was anxious to again return to Los Al. Thank the lord it was a sweet reunion, for Smoky immediately found himself in the winner's circle after a seven-and-a-half-furlong race that RDZell did not qualify for. Smoky now had an amazing forty-six wins to his credit. It was such a great feeling to have Smoky win a race again. It was even more wonderful when two weeks later, Smoky won his second consecutive race, this one at four and a half furlongs. Gary Boag was up for both victories. RDZell was not in this race either. I knew that these were two victories where the condition book was our best friend.

Los Alamitos Race Course publicity, bless their hearts, again honored Smoky with a write-up in the *Los Alamitos Racing Program*. It was obvious that they had a soft spot for Smoky. I loved Los Al for that. The article was entitled "Smoky turns back time." It read, "Somewhere, sometime, I know I have written this story before. I just can't remember when it was . . . 1992 or 1993 or maybe 1994. The headline would read the same today as it did back then. 'After tough times, Magna Terra Smoky is once again the king of the older Arabians in California.'

"Last Saturday night, Magna Terra Smoky rallied from last to post his second consecutive win over the course this meet. This marked the forty-seventh lifetime win for the eleven-year-old—yes, that's right, eleven-year-old—gelding that is owned and trained by Barbara Jagoda. This marks the second, third, or maybe fourth time in his career that Magna Terra Smoky has been written off and then proved everyone wrong."

The article brought tears to my eyes, for they had followed Smoky throughout his career and knew him so very well. They also knew how to put very perceptive thoughts and observations down on a piece of paper. The result was that the reader felt a special bond and attachment to the horse or person being written about. Los Al's write-up on Smoky was extra special to me, and I treasured it.

Unfortunately, Smoky lost his next race. Even his half brother, Llightning Road, who was not at all in Smoky's league, beat him. It was a disheartening time once again. And once again, I pondered Smoky's future. Although Smoky looked extremely fit and he seemed very happy, he was not performing well. It was so very frustrating. As I couldn't just let Smoky rest without any exercise, I once again kept him in condition. Then a race came up for him that, again, excluded RDZell. With a new female rider, Daron Long, up in the stirrups, Smoky galloped home to a much-needed and rewarding victory. This was Smoky's forty-eighth victory as a racehorse.

Once again, Los Al paid a tribute to Smoky. And to top the cake with ice cream, BJ would also be honored. I was terribly proud of both horses. For these two aged horses to be racing at all was a phenomenon; to be written up as race winners extraordinaire was beyond remarkable. The article started with the following:

> BJ, at age fourteen, became the oldest Arabian to win a race at Los Alamitos when he scored an upset in the second race on Friday night. BJ covered four and a half furlongs in a quick 58.07 seconds.
>
> Magna Terra Smoky update: the old-timer did it again. At age eleven, this Arabian earned his forty-eighth lifetime win as he captured the ninth race

Sunday night. He added another $2,365 to his bankroll to move his lifetime earnings to more than $307,300 for owner/trainer Barbara Jagoda. How many winning old-timers does Jagoda have in that barn?

I sure got a kick out of John's last comment. I did tend to collect old-timers around my barn, and I realized that I wasn't any spring chicken either. Seemed to me that it was living proof that "old" didn't mean finished and a need to be put out to pasture. As if to clinch and emphasize that thought, just two weeks later, Smoky repeated his winning ways, and now he had two wins in a row. Not only that, but also, Smoky now had an amazing forty-nine wins to his credit.

Smoky was once again receiving a great deal of media coverage. With every race we won, he was setting another new Arabian racing record. On September 26, 1997, the Arabian Horse Trust rightfully inducted Magna Terra Smoky into the Hall of Fame for his exemplary nature and significant influence on the breed. I believe he was—and would remain for a long time—the *only gelding* to be inducted into the Hall of Fame. I was deeply honored by the award, even more so as Smoky was not yet retired. I'm not sure, to this day, if the registry believed that Smoky was retired or not.

Now the magical goal of fifty races was within the reach of our fingertips—or, should I say, "hoof tips"? I hoped we could get it this year. But as luck would have it, we ran into RDZell and Bryan again. I loathed and loved that man at the same time. He was both my most dreaded opposition and yet also my best friend. We remained at forty-nine wins.

Then on November 16, 1997, with a new rider named Twei Lian up, I entered Smoky in a six-furlong allowance race. I had been hard-pressed to find a good jockey for Smoky, especially after firing Paulo Sanchez and his agent. Even Daron Long had opted to ride another mount (Moment of Valor). I was concerned that Twei might not know Smoky well enough to pull off a win, but very wisely, she let Smoky dictate the game plan and pulled off this extra-special victory. He had done it. Never in my wildest dreams could I have thought that this would happen. What a remarkable horse Smoky had proven to be! What extraordinary endurance and talent he had shown the Arabian racing world! He had endured so many obstacles. He had raced at so many racetracks and raced against so many horses. He had not always won, but he had never given up the ship. He always bounced back somehow. He had an awesome heart, and he didn't know the word *quit*.

Los Alamitos Race Course publicity would write about Smoky again:

50

> No horse has received more "ink" in the front of the *Los Alamitos Racing Program* than the Arabian Magna Terra Smoky. Sure, quarter horses Refrigerator, Dashing Folly, Down with Debt, Corona Cash, My Debut, and a host of others have been written about time and time again, but compared to the Arabian Magna Terra Smoky, their time in the limelight has been brief. I guess every horse's share of the limelight is brief compared to a horse that has raced for nine years, started 119 times, and has now returned to the winner's circle following fifty of those races.

What a way to finish up 1997!

Featured write-up in Los Al race program 11/23/1997
Smoky's 50th win

Credit: Los Alamitos Race Course Publicity

Sunday, November 23, 1997   127th Racing Program   Post Time 5:10 p.m.

"50"

No horse has received more "ink" in the front of the Los Alamitos program than the Arabian Magna Terra Smoky. Sure, Refrigerator, Dashing Folly, Down With Debt, Corona Cash, My Debut and a host of others have been written about time and time again, but, compared to Magna Terra Smoky, their time in the limelight has been brief. I guess every horse's share of the limelight is brief compared to a horse that has raced for nine years, started 119 times and has now returned to the winner's circle following 50 of those races.

What makes the Magna Terra Smoky story so interesting *is* Magna Terra Smoky and owner-trainer Barbara Jagoda. You see, Magna Terra Smoky was not a $100,000 yearling purchase that was expected to win, he was an unruly colt that his former owner really didn't want.

Jagoda, a retired school teacher, picked up Magna Terra Smoky in exchange for training another horse in Colorado some 10 years ago. Jagoda knew that Magna Terra Smoky had plenty of talent, but no one, not even Jagoda, could have possibly imagined what would happen in Smoky's career.

Smoky began his racing career as a "good" horse in Colorado. He has outlived many of the tracks he won at in his early career.

Jagoda brought Magna Terra Smoky to California and he turned into a good solid stakes horse. He never would win a race worth $175,000 like the Drinkers of The Wind Futurity, that's because there weren't races like that when he was a 3-year-old in 1989. No, Magna Terra Smoky was winning races like the "Pioneer" Stakes, worth a lot less than $175,000

And a lot of those races he would win, so many as a matter of fact, he would be battling a horse named News Release for most lifetime wins by an Arabian.

Then fate would step in. After a few subpar races, Jagoda noticed something wasn't right with "Smoky". She took him to the vet and it was determined that a fungus had developed under one eye. Smoky's eye was surgically removed and, just like in the movies, he won his first race back. He picked up a new nickname, the One-Eyed Wonder. The wins just kept coming and Smoky would be voted California's Arabian Race Horse of the Year for four straight years.

As the years went on, Magna Terra Smoky, at age nine, would hook up with the oldest rider in the room, Jerry Lambert. The two were a perfect match in 1995..and of course the perfect story. The old horse with the old rider and all they would do is win.

The rider would retire, but the legend of Smoky would continue. However, in 1996 almost everyone had written the 10-year-old off as he won just one of eight starts, the worst year of his career. 1997 did not start out any better has he failed to win in his first four starts at Turf Paradise.

But, then it was time for the Los Alamitos meet to begin. If, at age 11, Smoky was still able to win, he would have to prove it now. In his first start this meet, he won an allowance race at 7 1/2 furlongs coming from well off the pace to win. Just nine days later he would win at 4 1/2 furlong, once again putting in his run through the stretch. After that his races would be spread out, and the victories much tougher, but he had four wins from six starts going into last Sunday's allowance feature.

Jockey Twe Lian perhaps has not won fifty races in her career, but the young rider put in a perfect "Smokyesque" trip on the old-timer and there he was....in the winner's circle for the 50th time.

Someday there will be a "Magna Terra Smoky" stakes run at Los Alamitos. But for now, let's not send Magna Terra Smoky to greener pastures just yet. He probably still has a few good years left in him. If you don't believe me, just ask Barbara Jagoda, she has believed in Smoky from day one.

ON THE COVER.... Dashing Folly and jockey Tami Purcell after winning the 1996 Champion of Champions. Dashing Folly was undefeated in 10 starts in 1996 and was voted World Champion Quarter Horse. This color pencil drawing

36   THE PROMISE

1998

> *For Allah took a handful of southerly wind, blew his*
> *breath over it, and created the horse. Thou shall fly without*
> *wings and conquer without any sword, O horse!*
> — Bedouin legend

Smoky's retirement had been on my mind for some time now. However, when I had been asked about it again and again at the end of the meet at Los Al last year, I could not give a definite yes or no. Three things really came into play now. The most important thing to me was that I felt that I owed Smoky the respectability of retiring on a good note. What constantly preyed on my mind was the age-old mistake that athletes often made of staying in the game one year too long. I didn't want Smoky to leave his game on a downhill slide. I wanted his fans and the public to have good final thoughts and remembrances of Smoky. Second, the people and fans at Los Al had been so very good to Smoky. I felt I needed to give them a "goodbye" race. The third thing that came into play was Smoky's record. Right now, it stood at 119(50-32-17). If he could race one more time and finish first, second, or third, his record would be evened out. He would have a very neat 120 races with a first, second, or third in one hundred of them, and he would have raced an even ten years. It just added a nice touch if we could pull it off.

So I made Smoky a deal. We would race one more time. If he finished third or better, it would be his retirement race. If he finished worse than third, it would be his retirement race also, but I didn't tell him that. I just hoped that wouldn't happen. So on May 22, 1998, I entered Smoky in his only race for the year, an open-allowance race at Los Alamitos Race Course. It was a six-furlong race, and Adolfo

Rodriguez would ride Smoky. It would be a tough race; he was in against the "hot" youngster Tiki Banderlera.

I felt as nervous about this race as I had Smoky's very first race in 1989. It had certainly been a great run. Smoky had given me more than I could ever have dreamed of. He had changed the whole course of my life. He had taken this little old retired schoolteacher on a whirlwind trip to the big time. He had given me thrills that were beyond any words I could find to describe them. He had done all this because he loved doing it. Somewhere, it had been instilled in his blood, way back in the time of the Bedouins and their beloved and magnificent horses.

I had hauled Smoky in from Roger Lang's ranch in Kingman, Arizona, for this race. Even though I had kept him fit, he had been enjoying his days in turnout pastures with some of his buddies. As was ever the case with Smoky, he was once again very happy to be back at the racetrack. He knew exactly where he was and why he was here. He had that special sparkle in his eye, and as he pranced onto the racetrack, he seemed to be showing off. Eddie was announcing each horse and rider as they stepped onto the track, and when Smoky's name was announced, the crowd let out a tremendous cheer. There was no doubt Smoky knew the cheers were for him. He pranced a little higher, arched his neck more proudly, and kicked out his left hind leg. The crowd laughed, and Smoky turned his head to them in acknowledgment.

I was happy that Smoky was retiring a happy horse. I was happy also that he was retiring a sound horse, both in body and mind. Over the years, he had withstood the beating on his hooves, legs, and body of 119 races and all the many miles of conditioning that it had taken to get to those 119 races. He was twelve years old now, and he was competing against a whole new generation of younger, ambitious, well-bred racehorses. He had never exhibited any of the habits of an unhappy or sour horse such as weaving, cribbing, wind sucking, biting, kicking, or pawing. He looked in incredible shape, and his legs were as clean and fine as the day I had first seen him. I was very proud of that. I could not have done all this any other way.

I realized that tears were running down my face. I had really become immersed in the emotion of it all. The decade of Magna Terra Smoky was coming to an end right here, right now. Nobody except me and maybe Smoky knew (I wondered how much he knew, how much he read my mind and thoughts). I knew already that I would miss the highs and the lows, the victories and the defeats that we had shared together. There might be other good racehorses, but there would never be another Magna Terra Smoky. He was the one in a lifetime, and I was so glad that it had been my lifetime.

The horses were loading now, and then I heard the old familiar call from Eddie: "They're all in the gates." Then they were off.

There were several grays in the race, but it was always easy to pick out Smoky. He had a special way of holding himself, a special way of running. He was a beautiful white color now, his coat having lightened a little more each passing year. So many past races came to mind as I watched him settle in behind the leaders. He had learned that over the years. He didn't get excited early and waste his energy trying to gain the lead. I wondered if the young horses teased him about being old and slow or if Smoky told them, "I'll see you in the winner's circle." At the same time, I wondered if any of the horses that had raced against him before were in awe of him. Horses communicated on a different level than we humans. They didn't need to open their mouths or even say a word to communicate with one another. How much did we humans miss by having lost that ability to perceive those subtle movements and gestures?

Smoky looked so fine, and I could tell he loved to be there, racing among the field of horses. *What went through his mind?* I wondered. *What did he see? What did he feel?* Was the wind and the breadth of the desert before him as they were his ancestors? Did he think about why he loved to race as he did? Or was it so deep inside him that it was a natural thing, unexplainable and all-consuming? Would he ever know? Would I ever know? Did we have to know? Or was it just something to enjoy, something that didn't need to be questioned, a gift to our genes?

I gazed now with pride and awe at this little champion of mine who had come so far. He had risen above all the odds, had battled all his adversities until they lay along the wayside. I watched in awe even as I could tell his step was a little too slow to win the race today. Tiki Banderlera was not to be caught. As the leaders made their way into the stretch, Smoky was picking off horses one by one. Smoky was third now, and I swore as I watched him that he knew he was third and he would race to stay there. He had earned his retirement. He had made his record book complete. With immense pride in my heart and tears in my eyes, I ran down to greet him.

Horse, O horse, what thou does for the heart and soul of a man! Words cannot describe.

37 Retirement

1998

The next day, Smoky and I made the trip back to Lang Park Ranch in Kingman, Arizona. As I drove along on the busy highway leading to the Arizona border, I found myself thinking back on the past ten years. What an amazing ten years it had been. I would miss those times, I knew. But I was happy for Smoky. He loved the racing, but he loved his turnout time too. He had certainly earned it, and I wanted to make it as enjoyable as I could for him. Roger Lang's ranch was a wonderful place for him to be.

That summer was wonderful for Smoky. He had a large ten-acre enclosure that he shared with Aurzel, Koshada Star, and LL Manteeya. Since we were located out in the country and there were very few homes near us, there were numerous days when I would simply open the gates and let Smoky and several of buddies loose to run and graze along the country roads or wherever they wished. They loved those hours of total freedom, and it was so enjoyable watching them head out for a special patch of grass and then come tearing back when they had enough to eat. Smoky was always in the lead. He was fit, full of himself, and still the champion.

As the blissful days of summer turned into the early days of fall, I received an unexpected phone call from Deanna Sparks at Los Alamitos Race Course. ARAC and Doc Allred wished to honor Smoky with an official retirement ceremony. Apparently, everyone at Los Al had finally become convinced that Smoky was really retired now. I was overwhelmed. What an honor this was! No Arabian horse had ever been so honored, and to have this happen at a predominantly quarter-horse racetrack was unbelievable.

The date was to be October 24, Super Saturday for Arabian racing. Four stakes races would be offered for Arabian horses. One of the stakes races would be the California Derby, which was the same race that Smoky had won when first arriving at Los Al. Deanna asked if Smoky could lead the post parade for that race. I told her Smoky would be delighted and that I would be even more delighted. She also said that a special dinner table of ten overlooking the finish line would be reserved for us. I could invite whomever I wished.

I busily started calling people I wished to be part of this special event. Of course, Bryan was my first priority. Then I called Robert Strauss to see if he would pony Smoky in the post parade and if he and his wife, Rozera, would also be part of the special table and dinner offered us. Then I called Jerry Lambert to see if he would ride Smoky in the post parade. The only person I could not find was Antoine. I would have loved for him to be there. However, Kelly was still at the track, and she was delighted to be able to lead Smoky into the awards ceremony.

It was the most wonderful evening. Smoky was so excited to be there. He was all spiffed up, and we were all dressed up to match. As Smoky was led into the winner's circle, Eddie began his announcement. A large TV screen in the center field began showing clips of Smoky's most exciting races as Eddie recounted the many achievements and awards that Smoky had racked up. As the film clips came to an end and Eddie summed up Smoky's awesome ten years of racing, the crowd let out a tumultuous ovation. Smoky's head went up, and he leaped into the air, kicking out that left hind leg. The crowd went wild with laughter and admiration for a lively old-timer. Thank goodness Kelly was alert. She kept hold of Smoky and circled him back to his place of honor.

Then Eddie was announcing that Smoky, with Jerry Lambert up and Robert Strauss as pony person, would be leading the post parade for the California Derby, a race that Smoky had won in track-record time almost ten years ago. Smoky looked like a young colt. He was sure he was going to the races. He pranced out onto the racetrack as Eddie announced him and the field to the crowd. A photo was taken of Smoky that day that will remain a favorite of mine forever. It graced the cover of the *Finish Line* magazine later that year, and I have chosen to incorporate it into my cover design for this book.

As I watched Smoky enjoying his day of glory, I thought about the records he had broken, the achievements he had accomplished, the awesome things he had overcome. He was twelve years old and had raced for ten of those years without missing a year. How many horses besides BJ could attest to that? He had raced clear across the country and set track record after track record. He had raced in twenty-five stakes races, had broken the record for most money ever earned by an Arabian racehorse as well as most races ever won. He had been California Horse of the Year an outstanding four times, had won three Darley Awards, and had been inducted into the Arabian racing Hall of Fame. He had run in a phenomenal 120 races, been first, second, or third in a hundred of them, and had won fifty of them. And last but not least, he was still *sound*! That was probably the most wonderful achievement of all. I delighted in the exquisite cleanliness and tightness of Smoky's legs. Even his stifles didn't show any issues. His back was strong, his lungs clean, and his mind and body sound.

What a remarkable athlete and representative of the Arabian breed Smoky had proved to be! Thank you, Doc Allred and all the people and fans at Los Alamitos Race Course for acknowledging this and making this day such a very special occasion. I will never forget this honor, and if Smoky could talk, I believe he would thank you too.

38 Home at Last

2004

The time had come, I realized. Smoky and I needed to find a home of our own. Bryan had been a wonderful friend and a true and faithful companion for many years. I knew that I would never have experienced the thrills and successes that Smoky and I so thoroughly enjoyed if it had not been for his encouragement and support. He had been there from the beginning, even the force behind the conception of Smoky, and he had been there for the voyage. I doubt that Bryan could have ever imagined or foreseen what he had started. I knew that I never could have. How much my life had changed! Even today, I am still amazed at how I ever became a part of this amazing puzzle.

When I look back, it was rather ironic that I was leaving now, for Bryan had even given up drinking, and what's more, he had also beaten the habit of chewing tobacco. It had been interesting the way that both these changes had come about. We had had so many bad times with his excessive drinking over the years, and then one day—it was New Year's Eve—I bet him $50 that he couldn't give up drinking for a year.

"Okay. You're on," he said.

It was a simple as that. He just gave it up. I was beyond aghast. Why hadn't I ever thought of that before? I would have paid him a whole lot more than $50! After that, I paid him $50 each New Year's Eve. He never took another drink all the years I was with him after that bet. In fact, he made a complete turnabout.

"You know," he would say, "I can't believe how much of life I missed just sitting in a bar. Everything is so much clearer now. I wasted so much time. Why did it take me so long to realize that? This might sound hypocritical, but I really can't stand to be around people that drink too much now. Did I really act as obnoxious and dumb as they do?"

I laughed. I never thought I would ever hear him say that.

Breaking the snuff habit came about almost as interestingly. It was another habit I didn't like, even though Bryan made a point of not spitting out his old chew in front of me.

For several days, Bryan had tossed around the idea of investing in a life-insurance policy. I thought that it was a very caring thing to do, for he wanted to be able to leave me with some cash to take care of things, especially the horses, if something happened to him. Even though I cautioned him that the premiums might be high at our age, he still made an appointment, and the agent he called came to the house to build a policy. It started with a lot of questions, and eventually, the agent asked if Bryan drank. I was tickled at how proud Bryan acted when he was able to answer.

"Nope, gave it up. Haven't had a drink in over a year."

However, when he was asked about smoking, although Bryan could say he gave that up years ago, he did admit that he chewed. The premiums for a life-insurance policy skyrocketed. Neither of us could believe the difference.

"All right, I'll give that up too."

"Just like that?" the agent jokingly responded.

"If he said he'd do it, he will," I added. Then I went on to explain about the drinking bet.

The agent was apprehensive, so he made Bryan a deal. He would be back in one month. If Bryan hadn't chewed tobacco during that time, he would write him a policy at the reduced premiums. One month later, Bryan got his policy. He never chewed again that I was aware of.

Even so, I still realized it was time for me to find a home of my own. I doubted that I would ever be able to maintain a long-term commitment with the opposite sex. Bryan and I were both strong-willed, and we were hard on each other. Our relationship had become more and more strained in recent months. We were arguing about more things, and each of us insisted on holding our ground.

Also, in the back of my mind was the fact that I missed Colorado. I missed the mountains and the prairie and all the grass. I wanted a place where Smoky could graze and race and play and enjoy the rest of his years. I wanted him to have the grassland home that I had promised him over fifteen years ago.

The year was 2004. I felt that I owed Bryan one last thing. He badly wanted to go back to Delaware. That was where buyers were buying and race purses were huge. He felt that the time was right and that he had the horse that could do it. His new superstar was Zachzell, a gorgeous chestnut stallion. He was convinced that Zach could compete with the Delaware horses and that his trip would also provide the opportunity to showcase "Zach" back east and let owners and trainers visually witness the quality of horse he was producing. Although I was leery of Delaware after my experience there, I felt Bryan was better prepared this time and that he did have an exceptional racehorse in Zach. I would stay in Kingman and care for his horses while he borrowed my truck and horse trailer to head back to our nemesis, Delaware Park. We both hoped he could sell some promising youngsters and also win some races with Zachzell.

However, once again, it was not to be. Although Zach turned heads, Delaware proved no easier this time around, and Bryan returned disheartened and no richer. Bryan did sell a few horses upon his return, so at least it was not a total loss.

Now it really was time to strike out on my own. Bryan lent me his Buick, and I drove to Colorado, hoping to find a place that had some grassy acreage for Smoky and for Aurzel too. I was not rich but felt I had enough money saved to put a down payment on something that was of a reasonable price. When, on one of my exploratory trips, I happened upon a modest dwelling with an oversized garage on forty acres southeast of Colorado Springs, I knew that I had found our new home. I did not need a fancy place to live in, and the land was rolling grassland with a large draw running down the center of it—just what I wanted for Smoky. Although there were weeds galore, there was also a lot of nice gramma grass. I saw the potential this acreage offered.

Weeks later, when the deal was done and Bryan had helped me move, I surveyed our new home. I thought back to the promise that I had made to Smoky those years ago and reminisced how there had been "something special" about Smoky that had captured my heart right from the day I first saw him. I thought back to the obstacles we had faced together even before Smoky made it to his first race and to the excitement he brought into my life every time he raced. I marveled at how my life had changed so much because of him. I dared even to wonder what would have happened to him if I had not come along, if just one thing had been different. So many things had come together at exactly the right time. I still couldn't believe how everything had just fit into place like it had been "meant to be"! Whatever forces had been at work, I would not have traded these past years for anything. I had been swept up into a whole new world, and that will always be with me. I could not have asked for more from that little gray pony from the Pawnee grasslands. He had given me more than I could have ever have foreseen or imagined. Our journey had been a dream come true.

As I turned Smoky loose to enjoy his new home, I reveled in the joy it brought to my heart to know he would live the rest of his life the way he deserved and the way he loved. He could run and frolic as Indian ponies had once done, perhaps even on this very land.

Enjoy, Smoky! This is yours! You have earned every square inch of this, your new home.

Smoky enjoying his retirement

29 years of age

with buddies..Aurzel, Special Deliverie and Shotgun Willie

INDEX

A

A-Bar Ranch 222, 237, 271
Adams County Fairgrounds 7, 8, 52, 60, 66, 174
AHA (Arabian HorseAssociation) 278
AJC (Arabian Jockey Club) 71, 155, 156, 260
Allred, Doc 139, 140, 237, 308, 310
Anderson, Steve 231, 235
Antoine 249, 250, 251, 252, 253, 254, 268, 271, 277, 278, 285, 309
ARA (Arabian Racing Adventures) 9, 16, 45, 51, 53, 54, 63, 65, 271
Arabian Horse World Open Handicap 124, 129
Arabians vii, 2, 3, 6, 7, 8, 9, 10, 17, 18, 54, 64, 65, 66, 67, 68, 70, 71, 76, 77, 82, 84, 86, 90, 91, 92, 93, 103, 104, 105, 109, 110, 111, 112, 114, 122, 123, 124, 129, 132, 140, 142, 147, 150, 154, 155, 157, 158, 159, 167, 168, 170, 178, 179, 203, 209, 212, 216, 221, 223, 225, 226, 228, 229, 238, 240, 241, 242, 243, 253, 260, 278, 279, 280, 286, 287, 295, 297, 298, 300, 301, 302, 308, 310
ARAC (Arabian Racing Association of California) 159, 177, 178, 218, 229, 230, 270, 279, 280, 289, 290, 308
ARC (Arabian Racing Cup) 76, 77, 91, 154, 157, 274

Arisya (KA Arisya) 106, 107, 108, 113, 114, 122, 123, 128, 173, 174, 175
Augustine, Rick 280
Aura Maria 94, 285
Aurzel 94, 95, 96, 97, 98, 99, 100, 102, 103, 104, 105, 106, 107, 108, 109, 114, 142, 143, 144, 151, 153, 222, 230, 249, 255, 270, 272, 276, 278, 285, 293, 296, 308, 313

B

Barbaros 277
Barnett, Marj 136
Bay Meadows 175, 177, 230
Berg, Lisa 45, 46, 47, 49, 50, 51
BJ 250, 251, 252, 253, 254, 255, 270, 272, 274, 276, 300, 310
Braithwaite, Bryan ix, 76, 77, 84, 85, 86, 87, 88, 90, 91, 93, 94, 103, 106, 113, 118, 119, 120, 121, 122, 123, 124, 125, 127, 128, 129, 130, 131, 135, 136, 139, 140, 141, 142, 143, 144, 145, 146, 147, 148, 149, 150, 151, 152, 155, 156, 157, 158, 159, 161, 162, 163, 164, 165, 166, 168, 169, 170, 171, 172, 173, 174, 175, 179, 181, 182, 183, 184, 186, 187, 188, 189, 196, 197, 198, 203, 204, 205, 209, 210, 211, 212, 213, 216, 218, 222, 226, 227, 228, 237, 238, 239, 240, 241, 242, 243, 244, 248, 249, 250, 251, 253, 255,

266, 268, 271, 272, 274, 275, 276, 277, 278, 280, 281, 287, 288, 289, 293, 294, 297, 299, 301, 309, 311, 312, 313
Brent, Lea 93, 109, 170
Bright Fortune 70
Broyuri 89, 159, 203, 204, 222, 225, 255
Brusally Orlen 147, 299
Brusally Orselar 94, 144, 186
Burghart, Ed "Eddie" 125, 126, 127, 134, 135, 136, 203, 204, 205, 224, 225, 248, 267, 285, 287, 288, 297, 305, 306, 309
BW Rasputin 68, 71

C

California Derby 132, 308, 309
California Heritage Stakes Race 271
Carter, Yancy 221, 228, 243
Cash on the Spot 213, 287, 297
Cat, (Catcando) 99
Charles O. Pollard Stakes Race 248
Charlie Valentine 124, 125, 126, 127
Chaser 294
Chino Veterinary Clinic 189
Church, Ronnie 123, 130
CJ Steed 216, 276
Clark, Mary 8
Creator LTD 174
CSU (Colorado State University) 45, 96, 97, 223
Cyroga 2, 4, 5, 18, 76, 84, 88, 127

D

Dae Gaa Zhay 278
Darley Arabian 82
Darley Awards 91, 154, 155, 157, 158, 229, 279, 290, 310
Delaware Park 142, 147, 150, 151, 250, 313
Deste Onismus 249
Dr. Carr (Dr. Bridgette Carr) 21, 22, 23, 24, 25, 36, 37, 39, 41, 42, 96

Dr. Goodberry 133, 135, 187
Dr. Larry 42
Dr. Liskey 189, 190, 191
Dr. Moak(Robert) 135, 200, 201, 202, 205, 210, 219, 223, 224, 260, 287, 309
Dr. Naugle 38, 39
Dr. Stashak 97, 98, 99, 223
Dr. Vachon 189, 190, 192

E

Eden Rabi 109, 110, 112, 172
Energy Downs, WY 67
Etiw 88
Evans, Dick 1, 2, 5, 6, 7, 8, 9, 10, 14, 15, 17, 18, 22, 23, 24, 26, 27, 32, 33, 34, 39, 41, 43, 44, 45, 46, 49, 52, 57, 60, 64, 66, 67, 70, 76, 77, 78, 79, 80, 85, 90, 91, 92, 93, 94, 95, 96, 97, 99, 100, 102, 103, 104, 108, 119, 124, 142, 144, 151, 152, 153, 173, 218, 230

F

Flores, Rico 272
Francis, TJ 69
FS Orion 177, 213
Fuentes, Jose 260, 266, 267

G

Gault, Denise 136
Georgia (Bryan's ex-wife) 171
Gibson, Peg and Ed 213
Glaze, Melvin 117
Guerrieri, Paul 100, 103, 104, 105, 106, 107, 108

H

Hafeli, Ed 52
Harbor Lites 124, 126, 127
Hardmoney Basque 255
Harrison, Sam 91, 147, 154, 242

Hawkinson, Bruce 139
Heidi(Heidi Sommer (ARA) 51, 54, 57, 65
Holly, CO. 92
Hollywood Park 215, 216, 243, 244
Hood, John 54, 58, 114, 174
Hood, Robin 109, 112
Hussein, Kevin and Mona 64
Hyannis Cattle Co. 17, 18

I

IAHA (International Arabian Horse Association) 68, 69
Ibn Bint Hilyuri 63, 77, 88, 120, 129, 147, 159
Impressive 2, 42, 124, 204, 239, 295
Indy (Independence Dai) 17, 25, 43, 44, 46, 49, 50, 51, 54, 66, 79, 81, 85, 86, 90, 99, 112, 113, 122, 123, 128, 145, 146, 147, 148, 149, 150, 151, 152, 153, 169, 199, 202, 212

J

Jubb, Mike 115

K

KA Czubuthan 203, 204, 205, 210, 223, 224
Kaleidoscope 182, 237
Kentucky Derby 64, 82, 132
Kiarctic 142
Kimorf 135, 136
Kingman Fairgrounds, AZ 179
Kit Chamanet 51, 63
Knight, Robert 210, 223, 224
Korbel Performance Arabian Cup Stakes Race 64
Koshada Star 213, 272, 276, 308

L

Lambert, Jerry 243, 244, 254, 255, 279, 287, 288, 295, 309

Lang, Roger 88, 89, 179, 242, 281, 293, 305, 308
Li'l Smok 89, 285, 293, 294
Llightning Road 293, 300
LL Manteeya, (Manteeya) 16, 17, 26, 44, 50, 54, 56, 58, 59, 60, 63, 64, 65, 66, 67, 68, 69, 70, 71, 72, 79, 80, 81, 83, 86, 87, 90, 91, 99, 108, 113, 122, 123, 128, 176, 199, 293, 308
Los Alamitos Racing Program 260, 299, 302
Los Al (LosAlamitos Race Course, LARC) ix, 103, 116, 120, 127, 128, 133, 139, 143, 151, 154, 155, 157, 164, 167, 168, 177, 179, 187, 196, 199, 210, 212, 213, 215, 216, 221, 222, 224, 225, 226, 230, 237, 240, 241, 242, 243, 244, 248, 249, 261, 266, 271, 273, 278, 279, 280, 286, 290, 293, 294, 295, 299, 300, 304, 308, 309
Louise (ARA) 9, 16, 45, 51, 53, 54, 57, 63, 65, 271
LP Conquest 89, 293

M

Magna Terra Smoky (Smoky, Colorado Invader, One Eyed Wonder) vii, 3, 10, 37, 84, 88, 122, 126, 127, 135, 136, 142, 151, 157, 158, 204, 205, 225, 238, 260, 267, 280, 287, 288, 293, 294, 300, 301, 302, 305, 306
Magnifica MA 293
Martinez, Severiano 177, 221
Mays, Sheila 123
McAlaster, Garland 174, 243
MCA Maariya 69
Milewski, Crystal 57, 103
Minos 221, 238

Mom and Dad 29, 64, 75, 99, 103, 104, 106, 107, 108, 114
Monarch AH 151, 260
Montoya, Daryl 297
Murphy(Ona Natural High) 169, 192, 222, 276

N

Native Diver 243, 244
NATRC (North American Trail Ride Conference) 18
Neivens, Guy 238, 298
News Release 129, 142, 229, 240, 241, 249, 255, 261, 270, 271
Ninatchka 51, 63, 64, 65
Norton, Rick 176

O

Orzel 40, 84, 85, 94, 144, 203, 204, 299

P

Paducah, Kentucky 76
Painter, Janine 295, 297
Parenti, Jerry 223
Pauline, Ralph 122, 123, 134, 168
Payne, Felix 109, 112, 131
Petti, John 225, 257, 271, 279, 294
Pfau, Richard 226, 228, 241, 286, 295
Pollard, Chuck (Charles Pollard) 177, 178, 255
Pollock, Alice 1, 2, 3, 4, 5, 10, 11, 12, 13, 14, 16, 18, 37, 39, 40, 60, 75, 76, 77, 84, 88, 90, 94, 151, 152, 202, 222, 230

Q

Quesada, Frank 168, 193, 202, 211, 220, 222, 223

R

Ravalli County Fair 71, 75
RDZell 299, 300, 301
Reese, Ed 134
Refrigerator 261, 302
Rey Romer 214
Richardson, Duane and Pat 67
Rinker, Frankie 103, 162
Rio Hondo 109, 161, 162, 163, 164, 166, 167, 168, 172, 173, 174, 177, 226, 243
Rollie 295, 296
Ross, Emmett 293
Roylance, Pam 68
Rudolph, Bob 162, 224, 255
Rutten, Judy 129, 241

S

Saafari 86, 87
Sahibers Diamond 54, 57, 58
Sam's Fix Cup 111, 113
Sanchez, Polo 253, 254
Scottsdale Cup 168, 240, 274, 276, 278, 293
Seufer, Darrell 109, 114
SGR Orzel 203, 204
Shakil Rakkad 155, 168
Sierra Knights Stakes Race 222
Silver sp Carter 64, 66, 71, 87, 109, 110, 113, 163
Slender, George 134, 269
Soaring Big Red 241, 271
Soaring Fastneasy 89, 271, 272, 285, 287, 293, 296, 297, 298
Soaring Michael 109, 110, 111, 112, 113
Sparks, Deanna 308
Spring Fling 17, 26, 44, 71, 79, 98
Starting Gate 121, 123, 126, 135, 161, 164, 165, 176, 203, 204, 211, 214, 266
Stonewall Springs 49, 51, 54, 60, 61, 94, 95, 287
Strauss, Robert 135, 200, 260, 309

Strawberry Fields 271, 278, 280, 293
Styxx 241, 242, 248, 249, 255, 278, 280, 281, 288
SW David 17, 76, 84, 85, 88, 89, 127, 159, 222, 242, 271, 272, 285, 293

T

Tahnoon Bin Zayed 221, 238, 298
TC Tomtyr 223, 228, 229, 238, 243, 270, 271, 276, 279
Teutsch, Jane 8, 54, 57, 92, 109, 157, 241, 271, 280
Teutsch, Ray 293
Thunder (German shepherd) 24, 39, 44, 68, 104, 106, 108, 114, 118, 120, 121, 122, 123, 143, 145, 148, 164, 165, 166, 171, 172, 192, 204, 220

Tiki Banderlera 305, 306
Tiyuri 293
Tolbert, Chuck 251
Turf Paradise 167, 168, 179, 193, 230, 240, 271, 272, 293, 299
Twei Lian 301
Twilight 29, 30, 31, 32, 33, 34, 125

V

Vals Bl Stryker 266
Vals Starburst 166, 177

W

Wagner, James 130

Z

Zachzell 313
Ziegfried 87, 120, 128

Printed and bound by PG in the USA